How A Pro Se Won Justice

How A Pro Se Won Justice

AN INSIDE LOOK AT AN EDUCATOR'S
STUNNING CIVIL RIGHTS-
EMPLOYMENT VICTORY AGAINST THE
CHICAGO BOARD OF EDUCATION
IN THE US COURT OF APPEALS
FOR THE SEVENTH CIRCUIT

Joyce Hutchens, NBCT

© 2017 Joyce Hutchens, NBCT
All rights reserved.

ISBN-13: 9781530021543
ISBN-10: 1530021545

Keynote or Elevator Pitch

THIS TRUE "DAVID V. GOLIATH" story chronicles a courageous black woman's hard fought and disturbing eight years of legal proceedings and stunning victory over the Chicago Board of Education in the US Court of Appeals for the Seventh Circuit, after her character was assassinated, her livelihood was seized, and her civil and constitutional rights were violated.

This book is dedicated to hardworking, committed educators, *pro se* and other litigants, and beleaguered employees everywhere who are seeking justice.

Contents

Keynote or Elevator Pitch ·v
Introduction · xi

Chapter 1	Starting a Teaching Career ·	1
Chapter 2	The New Teacher ·	5
Chapter 3	The Entrepreneur ·	9
Chapter 4	The Jail Teacher in the Jail School—Division 10 · · · · · · · ·	14
Chapter 5	The Jail Teacher in the Jail School—Division 4 · · · · · · · ·	22
Chapter 6	The Jail Teacher in the Jail School—Divisions 3 and 8 · · · ·	24
Chapter 7	The Unwarranted Persecution of an "Excellent" Teacher · · ·	45
Chapter 8	The Team Leader ·	71
Chapter 9	The Curriculum Facilitator ·	78
Chapter 10	The Pre-litigation Process ·	86
Chapter 11	09 C 7931 — Year One ·	90
Chapter 12	09 C 7931 — Year Two ·	121
Chapter 13	09 C 7931—Year Three ·	140
Chapter 14	09 C 7931—Year Four ·	161
Chapter 15	13 C 6447 and 13-3648 Proceeding *pro se* in the District and Appellate Courts · · · · ·	184

Chapter 16	An Oral Argument, an Appellate Court's Decision, and a Victory!........................255
Chapter 17	The Aftermath........................299
Chapter 18	The Final Chapter........................305
	Works Cited........................315

Introduction

It's inconceivable that lies can sully the names, character, and reputations of people, destroy the careers they spent a lifetime planning and building and ultimately ruin their lives. But that's precisely what happened and resulted in eight consecutive years of legal proceedings between my former employer, the Chicago Board of Education, (the Board) and me. What began as lies from the mouth of a mentally disturbed Cook County Jail inmate, snowballed into multiple legal proceedings, including a union grievance and state and federal complaints against my former principal, a lawsuit against a correctional officer and two lawsuits against the Chicago Board of Education. During the latter, deposition testimony by the defendant and her witnesses was fabricated almost in its entirety.

Although *Hutchens v. Chicago Board of Education* did not include a last-minute stay of execution for a death row inmate, the impact and outcome of my federal appeal were the same. With God, US Court of Appeals for the Seventh Circuit Judges Richard Allen Posner, John Daniel Tinder, and Michael Stephen Kanne saved me from my own death row. They literally saved my life. I thank each of them for carefully examining the evidence I presented to the court, allowing my voice to be heard, shunning Chicago's infamous politics, fairly applying the law, reversing the decision of US Northern District of Illinois Court Judge Edmond E. Chang, and rendering their opinion expeditiously. Although the entire litigation process was the most stressful and excruciatingly painful period of my life, it showed me how strong, how determined, how resourceful, how resilient, and how fearless I am.

My friends, family, and other supporters repeatedly said to me during those eight horrific years, "Tell the world what happened to you; tell the world what they did to you." Initially, I refused even to consider telling my story, for I did not want to put pen to paper and relive this unbelievable and unimaginable nightmare. However, the trauma of those eight years was so real, and the pain, so raw and unfathomable, I *had* to tell the world what happened to me, because I do not want another person to endure the injustices I did—ever!

Taxpayers deserve to know the *entire* story behind my eight-year legal ordeal against those whose salaries they pay, and not simply what was published in the March 24, 2015 opinion of the US Court of Appeals for the Seventh Circuit.

CHAPTER 1

Starting a Teaching Career

July–August 1994

The Saturday morning exam was scheduled for 7:00 a.m. My former professor had cautioned the eight of us who were enrolled in her Methods of Teaching Secondary English course at Roosevelt University that the certification test for high school English Language Arts teachers was very difficult. She told us many of her former students who previously had taken the exam, had to retake it a second or even a third time before they passed it. "Before applying for a teaching position, allow yourselves enough time to retake the test in case you don't pass it the first time," she said. Given her warning, I was nervous as I exited my South Loop residence at 6:00 a.m. and headed for 23rd Street and King Drive on Chicago's Near South Side.

When I arrived, thousands of aspiring teachers already had gathered at the McCormick Place Convention Center to take one or more of the dozens of Illinois teacher licensure subject-matter exams being administered that day. After completing our respective teacher education programs at colleges and universities throughout the country, which included a semester each of field experiences and student teaching, we were required to pass the basic skills and appropriate subject-matter knowledge test(s) to fulfill the Illinois Certification Testing System requirement. Otherwise, we would not be allowed to teach.

I already had passed the basic skills exam, so this—the subject matter exam—was the only requirement standing in the way of me teaching high school English. I walked slowly along the convention center's lower level until I saw the room in which my specific exam was to be held. I entered and found a seat toward the back of the room. The exam was scheduled to start shortly.

After listening to instructions and receiving my exam from the proctor, I quickly perused the test booklet to determine the exam's breakdown. It was just as I figured it would be: 60 percent was related to literature, and the remaining 40 percent was a mixture of writing and grammar exercises. I did not kid myself; I knew I would need almost a perfect score on the composition and grammar, because literature, especially British lit, was far more challenging for me than composition and grammar. This was evidenced by my undergraduate and graduate degrees in journalism and the significant coursework I had completed in English at that time.

We were allowed six hours to complete the 125 test questions, many of which required a good deal of writing. The stress and pressure quickly set in and increased as I slowly completed the literature section. I never had flunked a test I absolutely had to pass. However, that did not stop me from wishing I was anywhere other than where I was and doing anything other than what I was doing on that hot, muggy July morning. Unsurprisingly, it took me almost three hours to complete the literature section. I felt insecure when I was done. The stress and pressure continued to mount, and I looked out of the window at the cars passing along King Drive, wishing I was in one of them and driving far away from McCormick Place.

Composition was next, and the pressure subsided. Regardless of the requirement, I knew this would not be problematic because I had been a strong writer since elementary school. I moved through this section effortlessly. After I completed it, I knew I had done very well, and my confidence soared. The grammar section also presented no problems for me. Like composition, I always had loved and excelled in it.

I took my time completing the exam. I repeatedly reviewed the questions and my answers even when I knew for sure they were correct. Although initially there were hundreds of teacher wannabes who were taking the same exam, most had filtered out of the room by the time I completed mine which was shortly before the scheduled stop time. I reviewed my answers one final time before handing my exam to the proctor. Although I was confident I had done an excellent job on composition and grammar, the literature section worried me. I was confident about what I knew, but the test items on which I had to guess the answers stressed me out.

When I arrived home after completing the exam, I immediately began checking my study materials for answers to as many of the test questions as I could remember. This proved to be a bad idea, as some of the answers clearly were different from what I had recorded on my exam response sheet. After a few days of torturing myself, I stopped doing this and decided to wait for my test scores. The Illinois State Board of Education (ISBE) had informed the test takers we would receive our scores in about six weeks, and waiting for the results was agonizing.

In early August 1994, I received phone calls from the principals of Hyde Park Career Academy and Lincoln Park High Schools. In response to résumés I had submitted to them, the principals invited me to interview for English teacher positions at their schools. Both high schools, especially Lincoln Park, had reputations for academic excellence.

The interviews were held one day apart, with the first at Hyde Park Career Academy. The following day, I interviewed at Lincoln Park High School and had a voicemail message waiting for me when I arrived home. The principal had offered me a position as an English and business education teacher. The principal of Hyde Park Career Academy called the following day and also offered me a position as an English teacher. Both were aware I had not received my certification exam scores, and both were clearly unfazed by this fact. Apparently, they were convinced I had passed.

I asked them to give me a day or two to ponder my decision, and after an agonizing twenty-four hour wait, I accepted the position at Lincoln Park High School. The principal was elated I was joining her staff, and the principal at Hyde Park Career Academy was disappointed I was not joining his. I hoped I had made the right decision.

Prior to the job offers I received from both principals, I was approached by the superintendent of an elite suburban North Shore school district who had been referred to me by the district's attorney for whom I previously had worked as a legal assistant. The school district was out of compliance with staffing minority teachers, and the superintendent wanted to hire me to help meet state and/or federal hiring requirements in that regard. Although the pay was far more than I ultimately would earn as a teacher for the Chicago Public Schools (CPS), I thanked the superintendent and refused his offer. My allegiance was to the community in which I had been born and raised, and that was not the wealthy North Shore.

I received my test exam score report in the mail on August 19, 1994. I was shocked, for this was less than one month after I had taken my exam, and the scores had arrived two weeks earlier than I had anticipated. Now, I had a new form of stress—the anticipatory kind. I was terrified to open the thin, perforated envelope, for I knew the information it contained—good or bad—would alter my life forever.

For several hours, I refused to open it. Instead, I called one friend and family member after another and told them I had received my scores. Each person asked me if I had passed. "I don't know; I'm scared to open it," I responded. Everyone was shocked that I actually could hold the envelope in my hands and after waiting nearly one month to receive my scores, I had not rushed to open it the second it arrived. With every minute and hour, I sat holding the envelope, my stress soared.

Finally, after six hours of pure agony, I held my breath, closed my eyes, and slowly tore open the envelope. When I opened my eyes, I screamed so loudly my neighbors *had* to have heard it. I had passed! After many years of service in the private business sector, my lifelong dream had become a reality. I was a *real* teacher, I had a *real* job teaching *real* students in a *real* high school!

CHAPTER 2

The New Teacher

SEPTEMBER 1994–OCTOBER 1999

WHEN ASSESSING THE CREDENTIALS OF teacher candidates for certification in a specific subject, ISBE reviews their successfully completed coursework to determine if it meets a certain standard for that subject. According to ISBE (at least when I received my teaching certification), in subjects for which there were no established standards, teacher candidates were required to have earned 32 semester hours in a subject to be endorsed. An endorsement is a statement appearing on a teaching license which identifies the specific subjects or grade level the license holder is authorized to teach.

While pursuing my bachelor's degree in journalism at Columbia College, a downtown Chicago private liberal arts college, my initial plans were to teach business education, and my coursework reflected those plans. Based on ISBE's requirements, I completed more than enough courses to receive an endorsement in business, marketing, and management. Therefore, after passing my teacher's certification exam, I was licensed to teach high school English and journalism, and under ISBE's endorsement requirements, my license also allowed me to teach middle school language arts, business, marketing, and management.

At my request, my new principal assigned me to teach a "split program." That is, I taught both English and business education courses at Lincoln Park High School. Known for its famed International Baccalaureate (IB) and double honors/honors high school programs, the school is located in

Chicago's upscale Lincoln Park neighborhood, a largely white-populated area on Chicago's North Side. In 1981, the school became one of the first within the district to offer the IB program. I was proud to have been offered a teaching assignment as a rookie teacher at this elite Chicago high school and even prouder to have been chosen to teach within School District 299, which is where I received my elementary and high school education at the now-closed Birney elementary, Emerson Upper Grade Center, and Fenger High School, (currently Fenger Academy High School). Fenger gained international attention in 2009 when a video captured honors student, Derrion Albert, being beaten to death on his way home from school after accidentally walking into the middle of a fight between teenagers from two neighborhoods. Several teens were charged with his death and ultimately received lengthy prison sentences.

At Lincoln Park High School, I was assigned to teach senior English, a core subject requirement. Although each year I had the occasional group of students who decided they were going to cut my first period World Literature class (senior level English) regardless of what I said, if they were serious about graduating, they usually knew long before the end of the school year not to push their luck with me. Although I loved *all* of my students, I would be less than truthful if I did not admit that my students who resided in the Cabrini-Green housing projects had a very special place in my heart.

I also had been raised in one of Chicago's housing projects, so I understood how inferior the Cabrini-Green students might have felt attending school with wealthy white children. What I loved most about Lincoln Park High School was its racially, culturally, and academically diverse student population. Whether or not it is true, I believe that during my five-year teaching tenure at the school, I taught nearly every racial group the world has to offer.

I was known as a "strict teacher," a title I well deserved. My students *had* to attend my class, they *had* to arrive on time, and they *had* to complete their work. This was non-negotiable. I asked for nothing more or less. Those were my rules, and I aggressively enforced them. The same students who thought I was the "meanest teacher in the world" have told me on numerous occasions to this day when our paths have crossed that now they "understand" and "appreciate" my tough love. I had a very successful five-year stint at Lincoln Park High School where I received "Superior" performance evaluations every year, including my rookie year of teaching.

In September 1997, I returned to Roosevelt University and completed the three courses I needed to acquire a second master's degree. I had received my first master's degree in journalism, also from Roosevelt University, in 1987. In May 1998, I invited my students to attend my graduation ceremony which was held on a Sunday evening at Roosevelt University's Auditorium Theatre. Several of my students attended and cheered loudly as I received my master of arts degree in secondary education which, despite teaching full-time and attending college at night, I earned while attaining a 4.0/4.0 grade point average.

Many of my students, particularly those who resided in the Cabrini-Green housing projects, had never attended a college graduation, and I wanted them to have this experience. They told me afterward the ceremony inspired them to work hard so they could earn their own college degrees. When our paths cross, as it frequently does, I am proud when I learn they are college graduates who are enjoying successful careers of their own.

Shortly after the 1999-2000 school year began, I knew I could not make it through another year of teaching. There were two reasons I came to this conclusion—heartbreak and burnout. I desperately missed my first homeroom class—all of whom had graduated the previous year, in June 1998. My Division 098 students had begun high school in 1994, the same year I began my teaching career, and they remained with me for the daily brief homeroom period until 1998. I cried every day as their high school graduation approached, I cried even more during their graduation ceremony, and I continued to cry long after they had graduated. The school simply was not the same after they left, and I could not get over it. To be honest, nearly two decades later, I still miss and think of them quite often.

I also was suffering from what research repeatedly has shown happens to many new teachers after serving in the profession for the first three to five years—burnout. I was tired of grading papers, I was tired of teenagers, and I was tired of teaching. The thought of creating another lesson plan, putting up another bulletin board and listening to another student explain to me why he or she had cut my class, turned me completely off, so I quit.

After giving my principal the required notice, on a warm October day in 1999, I walked away from the profession of which I had dreamt since childhood. I was very happy. I had begun putting into place plans to start my own business. Because of my extensive training, administrative, communications, and business background in the private and media sectors, as well as my teaching experience, I was interested in launching a training and consulting business. Earlier that year, I had reached out to the Women's Business Development Center of Chicago (WBDC) for assistance, and completed a series of small business start-up workshops the organization offered.

The WBDC is a nonprofit organization which strives to fuel the economy through entrepreneurship and offer programs designed to help women in every phase of business development and growth. It supports and accelerates women's business ownership, including Women's Business Enterprise (WBE) Certification, which can be a powerful marketing tool for expanding a company's visibility with corporate and government procurement decision-makers. I was excited about my future.

CHAPTER 3

The Entrepreneur

NOVEMBER 1999–APRIL 2002

AFTER RESIGNING FROM MY TEACHING position at Lincoln Park High School, I moved forward with my plans to start a new professional development and media/business communications firm which I named JDH Training & Communications Group. As good students generally do, I immediately began applying the knowledge I had acquired while attending the enormously informative small business start-up workshops I had taken at the WBDC.

I decided on a sole proprietorship as my business structure with the idea that if my business was successful, I would incorporate it within two years. Sole proprietorship is the most basic type of business structure. After applying for and receiving my Assumed Name Certificate, I began writing my business plan. I again sought and received help from the WBDC which also assisted me with obtaining financial support from a local bank in conjunction with the US Small Business Association.

Next, I hired a web designer and wrote the content while my website was being created. In the meantime, I attended as many local and national training and consulting workshops as I could in order to get a better idea of how to operate and manage this type of company. I learned a lot from those experiences.

I decided I would offer workshops related to business and life skills. With this in mind, I began developing a catalog of course descriptions. By the time I finished, I had created forty workshops including those which focused on customer service; business etiquette and image management; diversity;

presentation skills; job readiness; educator's staff development; new employee orientation; workforce development; office politics; personal and professional empowerment; administrative support skills; teambuilding; interpersonal skills; organization and time management.

I also created several writing and editing workshops, a train-the-trainer workshop for individuals who were interested in starting a training and consulting business similar to mine and entrepreneurial readiness training for those who wanted to start their own small business of any kind. You will learn more about the latter two workshops later in this chapter.

JDH Training & Communications Group offered to businesses of all sizes and employees of all levels personnel training on issues which affected life experiences and the evolving workplace. I tailored programs to meet company objectives, time constraints, and the exclusive developmental needs of employees, from support staff to senior executives. The workshops were led by industry leaders and educators I hired as consultants who provided practical and proven instruction to meet work-related and personal challenges.

My company's mission was to provide services for the *entire* business of living, not just to meet the rigorous demands of 9 to 5. My aim was to develop employee potential and improve performance for large, small, public and private organizations. My focus was to ensure my clients achieved the greatest possible personal and professional success by creating a workplace which was productive, clearly directed, and left no room for disorganization and confusion.

JDH Training & Communications Group was profitable. Almost immediately after I began marketing my services and advertising them on my website, I received requests for my workshops and individualized writing coaching services from private businesses, government agencies, and individuals.

Although the writing, customer service, and administrative support workshops I offered were very popular, I received so many requests for the train-the-trainer and entrepreneurial readiness workshops, I created a two-day program offering both at a downtown Chicago hotel.

I began advertising the workshop locally, and occasionally, I travelled to other cities to conduct it. I presented the train-the-trainer workshop on Saturdays and the entrepreneurial readiness on Sundays. As part of their fee, attendees received a different training manual each day for each course. They were loaded with information I had written and compiled from other sources, and the weekend program generally took seven to eight hours both days. This became my best seller.

As word quickly spread of my highly informative two-day program, I began to advertise it nationally. This was a great period in my life, and because of the almost instantaneous success of JDH Training & Communications Group, people who did not know me assumed that becoming an entrepreneur was relatively easy. However, those who knew me were aware of how much time and energy I had put into establishing and making my small business successful.

I received national contracts for my company's basic training courses from large and small organizations and requests from individuals for my personal writing coaching sessions. As my business flourished, to create sustainable, profitable relationships between my business and major buying organizations, I registered the firm to become certified with the Minority Business Development Council of Chicago.

Soon thereafter, I applied to become an 8(a) business owner with the US Small Business Administration. The 8(a) Small Business Development Program (SBA) is a business assistance program which helps small, disadvantaged businesses compete in the marketplace. The program assists firms that are owned and controlled at least 51 percent by socially and economically disadvantaged individuals. As a small business start-up, JDH Training & Communications Group certainly fit into this category. According to the SBA, program participants can receive sole-source contracts up to $4 million for goods and services and $6.5 million for manufacturing. Such firms are able to form joint ventures and teams to bid on contracts.

I also applied with the US General Services Administration to become a vendor on the GSA Schedule. The Schedule is a contracting vehicle for customers and vendors which provides access to millions of commercial products and services at volume discount pricing. My application was accepted, and I began offering my workshops on the GSA Schedule. Many businesses have been successful with their 8(a) Certification and GSA Schedule affiliations. For unknown reasons, despite my aggressive advertising and marketing efforts, I had very limited success with both programs.

In addition to my website, I advertised the workshop in a few magazines, including *Black Enterprise*. The response was excellent. I held the sessions once each month, and attendees came from throughout the country. I was particularly successful with East Coast clients, and the workshops provided excellent opportunities for aspiring entrepreneurs and those who already had established their businesses to meet, learn, network, and share information and ideas.

The train-the-trainer/entrepreneurial readiness workshops were very instrumental in the recognition I quickly received from the WBDC which had helped me to jumpstart and grow my business. In the fall of 2000 and only 11 months after my resignation from Lincoln Park High School, the WBDC announced that because of the perseverance, commitment, creativity, and unequaled strength I had demonstrated in expanding my business and helping others succeed, along with two other women, I would receive the organization's Entrepreneurial Woman of the Year Award and would be inducted into its Hall of Fame during an upcoming ceremony. The *Chicago Sun-Times*, *Chicago Tribune*, and *Chicago Defender* published articles about my company, the Hall of Fame ceremony and the honorees.

We received our awards in September 2000 during an induction ceremony held at Chicago's Navy Pier. More than five-thousand people, including the governor and mayor, attended. After I posted news of my award on my website along with the beautiful glass plaque I received, my business grew even more. Everybody loves a winner, and as it related to the success of JDH Training & Communications Group, other businesses and individuals wanted a winner to provide training services for them.

Like businesses of all sizes across the country, things quickly changed for my company after September 11, 2001. My company had been successful because of the two-day train-the-trainer/entrepreneurial readiness workshop which attracted people who travelled to my sessions from across the country. Following the "9/11 Attack on America," many people were afraid to travel by airplanes. The economy also took a major nosedive, and businesses and individuals simply were unable or unwilling to spend money on travelling, training, or both. As business owners who experienced the financial aftermath of 9/11 know, this lasted for quite some time.

Almost immediately, my company began to suffer mightily. Many firms cancelled their contracts with my business, and only a handful of people continued to register for my weekend train-the-trainer/entrepreneurial workshop. Eventually, it was not worth it for me to continue to pay the expenses associated with renting a hotel room for my two-day train-the-trainer/entrepreneurial readiness sessions, so after a few months, I discontinued them for what I hoped at that time would be temporarily. However, as time passed and the economy failed to improve in the wake of this unforeseen and unprecedented tragedy, it became increasingly clear my company was headed for financial despair.

JDH Training & Communications Group was my livelihood, and I was not earning enough to pay my business expenses and survive. Therefore, I took temporary administrative jobs to supplement my income. I also had begun to miss my students and teaching, so after realizing I had to make a move fast, nine months after the 9/11 attack, I returned to the classroom. Although I did not dissolve my company, I discontinued doing business with other organizations. In 2016, I reopened a restructured JDH Training & Communications Group. (visit jdhtraining.com)

CHAPTER 4

The Jail Teacher in the Jail School—Division 10

May–September 2002

I KEPT MY TEACHING LICENSE current after I resigned from Lincoln Park High School. Therefore, when I decided to return to teaching, the first thing I did was peruse the Chicago Board of Education's Job Bulletin to determine if any English teaching vacancies existed. There were several; however, because of my interest in working with at-risk and incarcerated students, I applied for a job at Consuella B. York Alternative High School (York Alternative High School and York), which is located on the grounds of the Cook County Jail. I received a response to my résumé within twenty-four hours after submitting it to the principal. Forty-eight hours later, I interviewed with her and the two assistant principals for the job. I was hired the following day.

At that time, York Alternative High School was the only public high school nationwide accredited by the North Central Association which operated within a jail. The staff held the same teaching licenses and other credentials as those who served in other District 299 schools, and many staff members held doctorate and multiple master's degrees. Most had previous experience in education. When I was hired, York's staff was comprised of slightly more than one hundred employees, including administrators, teachers, and social workers.

Unlike most Chicago public schools which typically operated on a 38.6-week schedule, York Alternative High School operated on a 46.6-week schedule. Therefore, we earned substantially more annually than other teachers and staff members who had the same credentials within our school district.

The school's monthly enrollment usually hovered around 650-700 students. Although some student inmates were enrolled for as little as one day, a few days, or a few weeks, others remained for years as they proceeded through the legal system awaiting the court's ruling on their criminal charges which included anything from marijuana possession to carjacking and murder.

Even today, sometimes people erroneously believe York is a high school for juvenile detainees. Although we as nurturing staff members thought of our students as kids, they were not considered juveniles. Comprised of both male and female jail detainees, our students were aged seventeen to twenty-one. Inmates incarcerated at the nearby Cook County Juvenile Detention Center were transferred to the Cook County Jail on their seventeenth birthday and could immediately enroll in classes at York. Although detainees were required to attend school at the Cook County Juvenile Detention Center, once they were transferred to the Cook County Jail, because they were seventeen years old, enrollment at York Alternative High School was entirely voluntary.

York had traditional classrooms with desks, chairs, and blackboards, and the students changed classes just as they did in any other high school. The teachers supplied pencils to the students and collected them at the end of the day, as they were not allowed to have them in their jail cells. The concern of the Cook County Department of Corrections (CCDOC) was the pencils could be used as weapons, and that concern was not meritless. Teachers always had to be mindful and watchful of pencils and other classroom items students could take from the school and use in their cells as shanks or other weapons. We also could not provide ink pens to our students because they were considered even more dangerous than pencils.

Students who remained at the jail long enough to graduate received a *real* high school diploma, as this was not a General Education Development (GED) program. To avoid disclosing a student's incarcerated status, the name of the last high school the student attended before they were incarcerated, was printed on their diploma. I had applied for and was offered a position at York in 1995 while teaching at Lincoln Park High School. I chose to remain at Lincoln Park High School because I had become much too attached to my students, and they meant far more to me than the higher salary I would have received at York.

My first teaching assignment at York was in Division 10, one of the jail's male maximum security divisions. My students were being detained allegedly for committing very serious crimes. Although many of them were only seventeen and eighteen years old, they were facing life sentences if convicted. Three other teachers who taught core subjects—math, science and history—also were assigned to Division 10, as well as a special education teacher. A school social worker and physical education teacher provided services to the students on assigned days. This generally was the entire school's setup in the eight school divisions established throughout the jail compound at that time. It was not unusual for me to watch the nightly news of the arrest of a young man for his alleged crime, only to see him staring at me the following day as he enrolled in our school division.

Although correctional officers were stationed nearby and were very protective of us, they did not sit in our classrooms, and there were no closed-circuit cameras monitoring activity while school was in session. But we weren't worried; fights and other commotion in our classrooms were rare. The students knew if there were, they could be assigned to the "hole," which is solitary confinement, or they could be locked down, during which time, they would be unable to attend school for several days or possibly weeks at a time. They certainly did not want that to happen. School was their only opportunity to escape from their cells for extended periods each day, have fun with their "homies" or "dawgs," and with the CCDOC's permission, receive treats from their teachers during holiday parties and special events.

I immediately bonded with my students. Although most were hardened by lives of criminal activity, drugs, domestic abuse, and other social ills, with few exceptions, I had no problem getting most of them to do their work. Because I was a veteran teacher, I knew that sometimes boys were more cooperative with their female teachers than girls. This was especially true at the jail, because with the exception of female CCDOC and court personnel and visits they were allowed from family and friends, York's students were deprived of interacting with females.

My students were distracted with issues such as opposing gangs, being assaulted while incarcerated, court hearings, convictions, and possible lengthy sentences. Therefore, I worked hard to make my English class as much fun and as appealing as I possibly could. It worked. They spoke constantly of how much they looked forward to attending my class each day and how sad they were on weekends when there was no school. On Fridays, I frequently rewarded good work and behavior with popular magazines and music, as the students seldom had a chance to enjoy those genres. Given a magazine, they went straight for any section which contained perfume samples so they could enjoy the "scent of females." Even when I threatened profusely they would face serious consequences if they tore *anything* from my magazines, when I collected them at the end of the class period, the perfume samples would be missing every time. Apparently, enduring my wrath was worth the "scent of females."

There were, of course, many downsides to teaching in the jail, one of which was being searched. Anyone who entered the facility at any time, including CCDOC staff, was searched by other CCDOC personnel. Although this was annoying, eventually I became accustomed to it. Another downside was our inability to bring newspapers, which are considered contraband, into the jail. As an English and journalism teacher, newspapers always had been a critical part of my curriculum. Now, I had to settle for bringing specific, clipped newspaper articles into the jail, but still only after receiving prior approval from the CCDOC.

Because the Cook County Sheriff and the jail's executive staff were concerned about inmates contacting members of their gangs via email, we also were not allowed to have Internet access on our classroom computers. Research was a critical part of lesson planning and curriculum writing for me. Therefore, being unable to access the Internet severely hindered my productivity during school hours, and I was forced to create most of my lesson plans and other important projects at home.

The biggest downside of teaching at the jail was the pain of watching my students, who primarily were black and Hispanic, locked up like animals. These were troubled kids who had come from troubled homes and had led troubled lives. Nothing saddened me more than knowing that if convicted of their alleged crimes, many of them would spend the rest of or most of their remaining lives in prison. On weekends and holidays, I thought of my students constantly. I did not condone what they had done and I believed if they had committed their alleged crimes they should be held accountable for them. But it still saddened me that they could not enjoy things we all take for granted, such as a meal at McDonald's, a family holiday gathering, or their senior prom.

It was a daily ritual for them to return to their cells and watch me from their windows as I headed to my car at the end of the school day. They would bang on the windows, hoping I would turn around and wave good-bye to them. Sometimes I would, and sometimes I would not, because I did not want them to see me crying. On those occasions when I did not turn around and wave to them, surprisingly, they knew why. The following day, they would ask me, "Ms. Hutchens, why were you crying when you were on your way home yesterday?" I would deny I had been crying, but I never could fool them.

We were strictly prohibited from giving the student inmates *anything* unrelated to school without the CCDOC's permission. It was difficult for me to see them clothed in jail garb, wearing raggedy gym shoes, and watching the sad looks on their faces when other student inmates discussed the money they had received for commissary which allowed them to buy treats, new gym shoes and other items. On Monday mornings when many of my students would discuss their weekend visits from friends and relatives, several would remain quiet. Over time, I learned from the troubled looks on their faces that they had not received visits from friends and family—sometimes ever. It also saddened me tremendously to see them shackled or handcuffed when they travelled to court for hearings or prison after they had been sentenced for their crimes.

It was not uncommon for the CCDOC to interrupt a teacher's class, bring the students into the hall, line them up against a wall, have them undress, and search them. Sometimes we were told not to exit our classrooms until further notice. This usually meant an inmate under protective custody was being brought into the building, and for security purposes, the CCDOC did not want the teachers to see the inmate. If there was an escape attempt or if a serious security-related issue occurred while school was in session, our students were quickly ushered out of our classrooms and back into their cells. If the

CCDOC ultimately placed the jail on lockdown, we were not allowed to leave our classrooms or go home until the lockdown was lifted. Perhaps this sounds like a "no way could I have been bothered with working in an environment like this" situation. However, most of us loved working at the jail, and we loved our students, so we considered these types of incidents just another day on the job.

My students were tough; there was no question about it. Even though they had not been convicted—at least of these particular alleged crimes—there was a reason they were being detained in the jail's maximum-security division. "I don't gangbang; I bang gangs," one of my students said to me when I warned the class one day while discussing Chicago's senseless violence that gangbanging would lead to further incarceration or death. As I write this, that detainee is now thirty-four-years old and a twenty-nine-year "Guest of the State of Illinois." In other words, he is incarcerated at the Illinois Pontiac Correctional Center, where he is serving a twenty-nine-year sentence for being an "armed habitual criminal," and because he "bangs gangs."

Although nearly all of my students were members of one of Chicago's numerous street gangs, in my classroom they had no choice but to participate in group cooperative learning activities and show respect for each other. They realized soon after I became their teacher there was only one gang in my classroom—the education gang—and I was the leader. There never were fights or even the threat of a fight in my classroom during the entire period I taught in Division 10. I mentioned this once during a private conversation I had with a student. "We get along in your classroom. But when we get *out* of your classroom and back on the deck, it's an entirely different story," he said. My students frequently told me, "Ms. Hutchens, if I had had a teacher or a mother like you, I *never* would have ended up in this place." Most likely, that was true, for many of their mothers *and* fathers also were incarcerated—sometimes within the same jail division.

I grew up in the Henry Horner Homes, one of Chicago's tough housing projects which were located on Chicago's West Side near the United Center (home of our beloved Chicago Bulls and Blackhawks). Therefore, very little scares me. However, one day, an older non-student inmate somehow made his way to my classroom, stood in the doorway, and exposed his penis to me. My students had returned to their cells for lunch, the other teachers had gone downstairs to a break area, and I was the only teacher in the "school wing" of the jail, which was slightly segregated from other areas of the floor. The inmate did not say a word. As if proudly displaying a trophy or waving an American flag, he just showed me his penis.

I knew if I showed fear, he might take advantage of the situation. He had blocked the doorway and easily could have entered my classroom and shut the door. But nothing scares a black man like a black woman, so although I was terrified, I gave him my most effective Angry Black Woman look and said quietly but firmly, "Get your ass away from my door!" He backed out of my classroom and quietly walked away. I immediately reported the incident to the CCDOC and continued to do my work. Thereafter, I avoided being alone in my classroom unless the other teachers were in theirs.

I have told this story to many women over the years, and they emphatically have remarked that I was crazy to have continued working at the jail, especially in Division 10 after such an incident. But I was unfazed. I remained at the jail, I continued to teach in Division 10, and I never gave the incident much thought afterward.

October 2002

My principal frequently made changes to the teaching staff within school divisions when she thought there was a need to do so. After I had worked for several months in Division 10, she transferred me to Division 4, one of the two all-female divisions. I said tearful good-byes to my Division 10 students and made them promise to stay out of trouble, to continue to work hard in school, and to never again return to jail after they were released.

Since my 2002 transfer from Division 10, I have learned from others or read in the newspapers of the murders of several of my former Division 10 students. All had been released from jail or prison when they were killed. I attended the December 2010 funeral of one of those students who was seventeen years old and the youngest in my class when I taught in Division 10. He had served his jail and prison sentences and was twenty-five years old when he was murdered execution-style in an alley behind his girlfriend's house after dropping off medicine he had purchased for their ill one-year-old daughter. I learned of his murder while reading a local newspaper.

The most recent murder of one of my former Division 10 students (of which I am aware), was July 26, 2015. When he was enrolled in my class, that student was nineteen years old. He was thirty-two years old when he and another man were gunned down as he drove on Chicago's Northwest Side. Television reports and an Internet video which went viral the next day, discussed how a riot nearly ensued afterward as the police removed his car with the body of one of the men hanging from the window.

My former student had been released from prison just one month before he was murdered and was the father of two young children. According to the Illinois Department of Corrections' website, on which his mug still appeared months after he was killed, his offender status was "absconder," which meant he had stopped reporting to his parole officer, and the Illinois Department of Corrections did not know his whereabouts.

When I learned of his death, I thought of the words contained in his autobiography which I had assigned the class to write. "I'm not into gangbanging; all I wanna do is sell drugs," he wrote, explaining the reason for his incarceration. That very crime caused his repeated recidivism during his entire adult life and ultimately is what caused his death. Many of my students promised me they would do better when they were released from jail. He made no such promise to me. They still make me cry.

CHAPTER 5

The Jail Teacher in the Jail School—Division 4

ALTHOUGH I HAD BECOME ATTACHED to my Division 10 students and missed them terribly, I loved working in Division 4. It was a much smaller division on the opposite side of the jail compound from Division 10. Because this was not a maximum-security division, teachers and inmates had more freedom to move about, and as they had been in Division 10, the correctional officers were very protective of York's staff. More students were enrolled in the Division 4 school than in the Division 10 school, and because the student inmates were females, the curriculum included fashion design.

NOVEMBER 2002–APRIL 2003

Shortly after I began teaching in Division 4 during the fall of 2002, I learned of a federal grant opportunity that could increase the funding for our afterschool programs. With my principal's approval, I wrote a proposal for one of the grants. I worked for several months on the proposal, and the final product included letters from my Division 4 students about the impact such a program would have on the school and on them personally. I was unsuccessful though; President George W. Bush's administration awarded the grants to jails and prisons in fourteen states, and Illinois was not one of them. I was despondent for weeks, but I refused to allow my disappointment to get me down or deter me from pursuing other grant opportunities.

Our school desperately needed new computers and other supplies, so I began to seek funding from private businesses. Although I had a heart for the incarcerated, I quickly learned not everyone felt the same way. Although each of the businesses to which I submitted grant proposals indicated that education was a priority when it came to charitable donations, with the exception of a major office supplies retailer which provided my school a $1,000 gift card to purchase office supplies from its store, we received not a cent from any other business. They made clear they had no interest in helping detainees, even those who were attempting to acquire an education while incarcerated.

Most of my female Division 4 students were being detained basically for the same alleged crimes as those of my Division 10 male students. During the spring of 2003, we held report card-pickup at another school, as we were not allowed to do so at the jail. I was happy so many of my students' parents attended, and several of them brought along the children of my students. The following day, I discussed with my class the physical and emotional toll their incarceration was taking on their families, especially their children, for many of my Division 4 students were mothers. Several of them hung their heads, many of them cried, and all of them listened quietly. "I'm not coming back to this place when I leave here," a few of them told me.

After I had taught for about six months in Division 4, my principal announced that two new school divisions would be opening in the near future. She asked for volunteer staff members to move from our current divisions to the new school divisions, which would be located in Divisions 3 and 8, the jail's Residential Treatment Units. I sent her a note indicating I might be interested in teaching both English and computer science in the new divisions. "I need a strong, veteran teacher for the girls," she told me, as Division 3 was the jail's other female division. Shortly thereafter, she transferred me. I was excited to help launch the new educational program in the jail's new school division.

CHAPTER 6

The Jail Teacher in the Jail School—Divisions 3 and 8

May 2003–June 2006

I BEGAN TEACHING IN THE divisions 3 and 8 schools during the spring of the 2003-2004 school year. Like the CCDOC staff, teachers assigned to Division 3 also were assigned to Division 8. Division 3 was a female jail division and Division 8 was comprised of males. Inmates housed in both divisions generally had medical issues, and quite often, the issues required the services of a psychologist or social worker. Many of my students received some form of daily medication, and they frequently were under the influence of that medication when they attended school. Several of my Division 3 students were pregnant or had recently given birth. Once the babies were born, if possible, they were released to the families of the inmates. Otherwise, they were placed into the custody of the Illinois Department of Children & Family Services.

The Divisions 3 and 8 classes were much smaller than the classes in Divisions 10 and 4 because the inmate populations were smaller than those in other divisions. From 8:00 a.m. until 11:30 a.m., I taught in Division 3, and from noon until 1:30 p.m., I taught in Division 8, which was one block away.

Shortly after I began my new assignment, I considered creating a two-divisional school newsletter. After discussing the idea with my students, we named the newsletter *3 & 8 Voices*. The plan was for students in both school divisions to write news items each month related to their respective divisions. My students were excited, and I never had seen such pride as I did when we "published" our first edition on the school's computers.

When the school day ended, my students would return to their cells and allow the correctional officers to read the monthly newsletter. They also sent copies home to their families. As we gradually published more newsletters, the CCDOC staff and other inmates who were not enrolled in school would ask me when the next newsletter would be published. They always looked forward to reading it.

During the beginning of the 2003-2004 school year, my principal asked me to become a Golden Teacher mentor to three teachers. Golden Teacher was a teacher induction program which provided new teachers with mentoring and information related to their craft. It was designed to maximize the effectiveness of their teaching performance, raise student achievement levels, and increase the retention of high-quality teachers. I ultimately served as a Golden Teacher mentor and coach during the 2003-2004, 2004-2005, and 2005-2006 school years.

Nearly one year after the publication of our first newsletter, my principal informed me she had learned of a two-week journalism fellowship being offered for English and journalism teachers by a professional journalism and newspaper editors' organization. The program was an aggressive, comprehensive effort to strengthen and energize scholastic journalism. One hundred forty-nine teachers from forty-one states and the District of Columbia were to be chosen and assigned to one of the four participating universities across the country for a two-week fellowship. My principal strongly encouraged me to apply for the fellowship, and I did.

I was selected and assigned to complete my program at an Ohio university which was participating in the program. Along with thirty-four other teachers from across the country, I attended the Ohio-based journalism fellowship in July 2005. Newspaper and scholastic journalism leaders partnered with the university, and we attended numerous workshops and learned new journalistic skills. Another key component of the fellowship was teachers could apply for and receive a $5,000 grant for computer hardware and software if they could convince a local newspaper to partner with their school and either launch a new school newspaper or improve their school's existing one.

I wrote a letter to the *Chicago Tribune* asking reporters to partner with my students and me to enhance *3 & 8 Voices*. As I nervously awaited their response, I learned other Illinois high school teachers had made the same request over the years, but no *Tribune* reporter had ever agreed to partner with any other school. However, a well-known reporter contacted me, agreed to work with us during the 2006-2007 school year to improve *3 & 8 Voices*, and told me several of his colleagues also were interested in participating. My students and I were thrilled!

Initially, convincing the CCDOC to allow news reporters into the jail to help us improve our newsletter was quite a challenge. However, after my principal and I met with CCDOC executives and assured them the reporters would be entering the jail for no reason other than to guide us in improving *3 & 8 Voices*, we eventually received their approval to move forward with the program. Throughout the 2006-2007 school year, several *Chicago Tribune* reporters taught journalism to my male and female divisional students once each week. They transformed *3 & 8 Voices* into a beautiful, magazine-styled publication which featured columns and articles the students and I wrote, and it became the pride and joy of Consuella B. York Alternative High School.

July 2006–February 2007

Because most of my students previously had been convicted of crimes or ultimately would be convicted of the crimes for which they were being detained, I knew it would be nearly impossible for them to find jobs if and when they completed their sentences and were released from custody. Therefore, during the summer of 2006, I incorporated into my curriculum the entrepreneurial readiness program I had created for my company, and began teaching it as a six-week lesson during which my students learned the skills necessary to start their own business. The students received free of charge the same program aspiring entrepreneurs had paid me several hundred dollars each month to attend. They were required to create a fictitious business, and at the end of the summer, they presented it to the principal, the assistant principals, the rest of the class, and me.

My students showcased their talents and creativity. The fictional businesses they "established" included, but were not limited to an interior design shop, a nail salon, a CD store, a barbershop, a beauty salon, and a daycare center. After their presentations, with the permission of the CCDOC, we had a huge party to celebrate our very successful summer program, and entrepreneurial readiness became a permanent part of my curriculum each year.

Reflective of my commitment to excellence in teaching, during the fall of the 2006-2007 school year, I began pursuing National Board Certification (NBC), which is recognized as the nation's highest teaching credential and the gold standard in teacher certification. This rigorous professional development program requires both intense self-analysis of one's teaching practice and demonstration of the teacher's content expertise. CPS teachers pursuing NBC could be placed in cohort groups, which were led by a National Board Certified Teacher (NBCT) who was state certified in the same or similar content area. The NBCT who led my cohort group held a library science certification, and she was an excellent mentor and leader.

Teacher candidates were required to complete a portfolio comprised of four written entries which were 60 percent of their score. The candidates also were required to videotape themselves while teaching their students. This was problematic for me because initially, the CCDOC refused to allow me to videotape my student inmates. However, after numerous requests from my principal, the CCDOC finally agreed with the stipulation the principal and both assistant principals would be present at all times during the videotaping, and CCDOC officers would do the videotaping. I was allowed to videotape the Division 8 students only. To provide my Division 3 students with an equal opportunity to participate, I asked them to help me assemble my portfolio. Each student pitched in, and it was an entire two-divisional team effort.

NBC teacher candidates also were required to complete six assessment center exercises which comprised the remaining 40 percent of their score. Each candidate had to earn a minimum score of 275 out of 400 points, and they could "bank" their individual portfolio entries and assessment center exercise scores. Banking allowed candidates to attempt certification for up to twenty-four months from the date shown on the candidate's initial score report. During that period, candidates who did not achieve NBC during their initial attempt were allowed to retake any combination of portfolio entries and assessment center exercises on which they did not meet the required performance standard.

The students who had consented to being videotaped entered my classroom that morning. "Only for you, Ms. Hutchens," one of them said wearily as he wiped "sleep" from his eyes and flopped wearily down at his desk in my tiny, windowless classroom. During the videotaping, in addition to my principal and two assistant principals, one correctional officer stood inside my classroom and two others sat outside in the hallway near the door. The students were patient during the videotaping which lasted at least two hours. Afterward, with the CCDOC's permission, I treated them to pizza.

Portfolios were due by March 31 of the school year the teacher candidate pursued NBC, and the assessment center exercises had to be completed later that spring. Despite my extremely late enrollment into my cohort group, I met all requirements on time. It took me hundreds of hours to complete my portfolio, and to this day, it was more rigorous, stressful, and challenging than anything in the educational arena I ever have pursued.

I received my scores in November 2007. I had achieved NBC on my first attempt. According to a January 2009 article published by the Illinois Association of School Boards, only one-half of NBC teacher candidates had been successful on their first attempt as of the date of the article. (https://www.iasb.com/journal/j010209_05.cfm). Although I do not recall the relevant data, I believe during the 2006-2007 school year, which is the year I engaged in the process, the percentage was even lower than that.

It was one of the two videos featuring my York Alternative High School students on which I received the highest of the 10 scores the National Board for Professional Teaching Standards used to assess the other candidates and me during the NBC scoring process. Had it not been for the perfect score I received on that specific video, I absolutely would *not* have achieved NBC on my first attempt.

People frequently equate crime and incarceration with lack of intelligence, but nothing is farther from the truth. Many of my York Alternative High

School students were equally as talented, capable, and smart as my former Lincoln Park High School students. I was enormously proud of them as they discussed *Brown v. Board of Education* and Ruby Bridges' impact on the Civil Rights Movement during the videotaping. Even the correctional officers were impressed with how knowledgeable and articulate my students were and how well they performed.

MARCH–MAY 2007

In early 2007, my principal asked students in each school division to select a teacher candidate for the Unilever Performance Plus Award competition. Previously named the Suave Performance Plus Award, this recognition was created by Suave® in 1997 and honored the school district's selected high school teachers who went to "extraordinary lengths to make a difference in their students' lives."

According to Unilever, it was the only program of its kind to enlist students to both nominate and select winning teachers. Students from the more than one hundred CPS high schools were invited each year to nominate a high school teacher who they believed went "above and beyond their job requirements inside and outside the classroom to make a difference in their students' lives."

Because I was busy with my after-school journalism program and pursuing NBC, initially, I was not interested in participating in the Unilever competition. In a solid block, my students nominated me anyway and urged me to compete; I finally did. The district was comprised of five high school Areas: 19, 21, 23, 24, and 25. Based on essays our students wrote and information the teachers submitted, a group of students assembled from throughout the district selected a nominee from each school, and later, five finalists from each Area. I was selected first as the York Alternative High School nominee and afterward as one of five finalists from Area 23.

In April 2007, I was chosen as the Area 23 Unilever Performance Plus Award Winner. Former Chicago Mayor Richard M. Daley, and [then] CPS CEO and former US Secretary of Education, Arne Duncan, presented the award to the other four Area winners and me during a special ceremony held in May 2007 at the Harold Washington Library (named after Chicago's first black mayor), in downtown Chicago. My principal and both assistant principals attended the event. While announcing I was the Area 23 winner, the emcee read the following from the program:

> Joyce Hutchens, an English Language Arts teacher at Consuella B. York Alternative High School has established a strong partnership with the *Chicago Tribune* so reporters can mentor her students in their quest to create a quality student newspaper within the confines of the Cook County Jail. Since her students are incarcerated, she frequently arranges for members of community organizations and churches to visit them and to provide spiritual and emotional guidance. She also provides a six-week entrepreneurial training program that gives students the skills to start their own business. Additionally, she steps outside the classroom to help her students acquire employment after graduation and keep them motivated even when they are no longer her students.

Each winner received from Unilever $3,000 and a crystal apple. Our respective schools received $1,500 and a plaque. We also received congratulatory letters from President George W. Bush and Illinois House Speaker Michael Madigan. On July 19, 2007, Mayor Daley and the city council honored us at city hall. We also were saluted in a May 9, 2007 *Chicago Sun-Times* article entitled "High School Kids Pick Top Teachers," and a May 15, 2007 editorial in the same newspaper entitled "These Educators Have Something to Teach Us All."

Later that summer, I was nominated by my lead teacher and principal to represent York Alternative High School in the DRIVE (Delivering Results through Innovative and Visionary Education) teacher award competition. The award was given each year to high school teachers within the school district who had gone "above and beyond" their classroom duties, supported other teachers in their school, demonstrated creativity and innovation, made progress and gains in student achievement, and improved their school as a whole. I was named a finalist in the competition later that year.

During the same school year, I received Elite Finalist recognition from the MetLife Ambassador in Education Award competition. This award recognized teachers who connected their schools to the community through creative partnerships and communication. My school received $250 and a plaque as a result of my recognition, and I received a crystal apple. Thus, 2007 was, by far, the most successful year of my teaching career.

June–October 2007

My principal retired on June 30, 2007, and I was extremely sad to see her leave. She had been a wonderful principal who always had appreciated my work and supported me from day one. While principal, she frequently said to me, "You know I think you're a fantastic teacher, don't you?"

On July 1, 2007, one of the two assistant principals, Brenetta Glass, became the new principal. She immediately made several personnel changes, including firing her former colleague who also had been assistant principal, and transferring teachers to other school divisions. She promoted to assistant principals the Division 4 lead teacher, Dr. Sharnette Sims, and the Division 6 computer teacher, James Jones. She also switched the Divisions 3 and 8 lead teacher, a white male, with the Division 11 lead teacher, a black female. I had had an excellent relationship with my previous lead teacher during the entire five-year period we had worked together, but I did not know the new Divisions 3 and 8 lead teacher, Karen Weed, very well.

Within three weeks of the change in divisional lead teachers, two Division 8 students told me on separate occasions Assistant Principal Dr. Sims and my new lead teacher, Karen Weed, had made disparaging remarks about me in the students' presence. I was unconcerned about the disparaging remarks they allegedly had made about me. I did, however, take umbrage at disparaging remarks being made about me by educators who did so in the presence of our students.

On October 29, 2007, my Division 3 students, including Student A, arrived more than thirty minutes late for school. A twenty-year-old detainee,

Student A had excellent attendance and generally came to school on time each day. Therefore, although she was tardy and I reminded her and the rest of the students I expected them to arrive on time each day, I scolded more harshly the others who had a history of being late. Sometimes, tardiness was unavoidable because the students were unable to leave their cells until the correctional officers allowed them to do so. However, I had noticed Student A socializing in her cell area (which was visible from the hallway) that morning when she already was fifteen minutes late for school.

Student A ignored me and began singing Aretha Franklin's hit, *Day Dreaming and I'm Thinking of You,* and talking loudly to herself while watering plants which were her science class project. I asked her if she wanted her science teacher to give her a grade for her English class, and she became combative and walked out of my classroom. Since she was a detainee, this was considered a serious violation of the CCDOC's policy, as walking out of my classroom without permission could have been considered an escape or an attempted escape. Fortunately, a CCDOC correctional officer saw her leave and intervened.

Student A already was angry with me because the previous week she had asked me to bring food, which was contraband, into the jail for her and I refused. This was not an isolated incident. Our students frequently asked us to bring food, cigarettes, and other items to them. I cannot speak to what other teachers did or did not do when their students requested contraband, but I always ignored them.

Student A had been incarcerated and enrolled in the Division 3 school since January 2006. We basically had a good relationship except when she did not get her way. Then, she had temper tantrums. I usually ignored the tantrums because they did not last very long. She always completed her assigned work and enjoyed my class, particularly the after-school journalism program. Several times she told me, "You're a good teacher; you know your stuff." She took medication for psychotic-related issues and was under the care of a psychologist. She had been diagnosed by the school's social worker as Profoundly Emotionally Behaviorally Disturbed. Students diagnosed with schizophrenia generally are included in this classification.

Student A had very low self-esteem and constantly claimed everyone disliked her, including her mother. During a private conversation with me one day, she said she became delusional and "snapped out" if she did not take her prescribed medication, and one day, she asked the correctional officers to lock her in protective custody because she felt as if she was "gonna hurt somebody." She said even her jail-based psychiatrist frequently ran from her because of the way she "snapped out." According to CCDOC officers, during a fight in her cell area earlier that year, she was sent to the "hole" for several weeks for fighting and getting the best of three other female detainees simultaneously.

Overall though, she, the other student inmates in both divisions, and I had many good times in class. We sang and danced together on the days I allowed them to listen to music while or after they completed their assignments. Despite being locked up, somehow, they kept up with the latest dance crazes, and they made sure I knew how to do those dances. When I showed my ineptness with certain dances, they would demonstrate the proper moves and tell me, "No, Ms. Hutchens. You do it like *this*!" Those were fun, memorable times. I loved my students.

The same day Student A walked out of my classroom, as I used the telephone in lead teacher Weed's Division 8 office later that afternoon, I noticed a statement Student A had written sitting on the left-hand corner of Weed's desk, as if she had allowed someone else to read it. The letter began, "I [Student A]..." After reading only a few lines, I noticed my name in the statement. (Somehow Student A had gotten the letter from Division 3 to Weed in Division 8.) I stopped reading and asked Weed to explain to me why she had a letter from Student A which contained my name in it. She replied, "Student A thinks you don't like her because she's ugly and bald-headed. I told her to vent—to get it out of her system. This is not something I'm going to give to [Principal] Glass or to [Assistant Principal] Sims, so let it go! And don't say *anything else* to them about being late!" I was stunned.

On October 31, 2007, I was absent from work due to illness. The day before, I had locked in a Division 3 cabinet small bags of Halloween candy I planned to distribute to the Division 8 students. My intent was to bring candy for the Division 3 students—the girls—the following day, Halloween, as I already had received permission from the CCDOC. Without fail, I requested permission from the CCDOC to bring treats for my students whenever I could because many of them did not receive money from their families to purchase commissary items, and those who did still could not buy the types of treats the teachers brought them, because the jail's commissary only sold certain items.

NOVEMBER 2007

On November 1, all of my Division 3 students arrived at school on time. Although I had brought candy bags for them, I did not want them eating in the other divisional teachers' classrooms while their classes were in session. Therefore, I asked the students to stop by my classroom as they headed to their cells for lunch so they could receive their candy bags from me.

Student A had left school early as did another Division 3 student. The other students returned to my classroom and retrieved their candy from me. Student A came to my classroom after I had packed my belongings and headed for my afternoon shift in Division 8. She told me she needed "extra help" with her English assignments and again asked me to bring food for her into the jail. I refused again. Because I was displeased with her request and I already had locked away the bag containing her candy, I decided to wait until the following morning to give her the candy bag I had prepared for her.

As I sat in my Division 8 classroom later that afternoon, Principal Glass entered. It was nearly 1:30 p.m., so my students were preparing for dismissal, and I was packing my bags to return to Division 3 for my after-school journalism class, which took place between 2:00 and 4:00 p.m. Glass immediately stated, "I need to talk to you about the girls. Why aren't they coming to school?" I was puzzled, and responded that they were, in fact, coming to school. I also told her I would send her my attendance sheets, since I was the girls' homeroom teacher. She added, "You know all of them [the students] have lawyers, and I received a call from downtown about your behavior toward the girls."

When I asked her for further information about the alleged phone call, she said, "I've received two calls from downtown regarding issues with students, and one of them involves you." I inferred from her message that "downtown" meant the Board's district office. Although I repeatedly asked her for the basis of the call and to provide me the name of the person to whom she allegedly had spoken, she refused to give me additional details about the phone call she purportedly had received from "downtown" concerning me.

Glass also told me we needed to increase enrollment in Division 3, so she wanted me to "appease" the students to ensure they continued to attend school since it was voluntary. She did not mention the letter I had seen on Weed's desk a few days earlier. She further claimed that "more than one of the girls" had complained I "talked down" to them, they were "intimidated" by me and "feared me."

I almost laughed out loud when Glass said my incarcerated students, most of whom were serving time allegedly for committing violent crimes against other people, "feared" or were "intimidated" by me. They feared nothing and no one, including me. However, each of them knew where to draw the line when it came to disrupting my class. As much as I loved them, I did not tolerate inappropriate behavior, foul language and foolishness in my classroom—period. I told Glass in the four years I had taught in Division 3, I had never heard anything like this. I also told her that as their teacher, I demanded respect and would continue to demand respect from each of my students, or they would "take over my classroom" if I allowed them to engage in misconduct in my classroom.

In addition to prostitution, Student A was being detained allegedly for committing two violent crimes, including one against her customer after he refused to pay her for the services she had rendered. During class one day, loudly enough for me to hear, she described how her customers would pay her to "pee on them," and she attempted to share with us graphic details about her other services. I quickly put a stop to her lewd remarks. She also spoke frequently of her pimp and how certain she was he eventually would "put a ring" on her finger. During light classroom banter one day, when I told the class I had not slept well the night before because someone dialing the wrong number had called my home repeatedly, she replied, "Sounds like a booty call to me!"

I discussed these and other issues with Glass, including the strained relationship which apparently had developed between lead teacher Weed and me, and asked to be moved to another division in the future if she thought it was best. Citing the "good little journalism program" I had in Divisions 3 and 8 and stating she needed me to work in those divisions, she denied my request. I also asked her if any of the Division 8 students had complained about me. She smiled and shook her head, indicating they had not. Months earlier, I had formed a partnership with a nonprofit foundation, and in October 2007, it provided our school a $10,000 grant to sustain *3 & 8 Voices*. Our school newsletter received national recognition, and I was invited to speak at numerous local events regarding high school journalism issues.

On November 9, 2007, I learned I was 1 of 208 CPS teachers, 1 of 511 teachers in the state, and 1 of approximately 8,500 teachers nationwide who had achieved NBC. At that time, less than one percent of CPS teachers and less than one-half percent of the teachers in Illinois had achieved this prestigious teaching credential. According to reliable information I received, it appeared I also was the first core subject teacher in the nation to achieve NBC while teaching in a jail.

From Monday, November 5, through Wednesday, November 7, 2007, I attended required civilian CCDOC in-service training at a local college. November 8, 2007 was report card pick-up day for CPS, which our school always held at another location instead of at York Alternative High School. The staff was not at the jail the entire day. I also was not at York on November 9 because I was taking a personal business day to attend a seminar. November 10 and 11 were weekend days, and November 12 was Veteran's Day, a national holiday. Therefore, I was away from the jail compound after Friday, November 2, until Tuesday, November 13, 2007.

I was excited about sharing with Principal Glass the good news I had achieved NBC. When I arrived at work on November 13, I saw her on the first floor of Old Cermak, the building in which her office was located. I generally used this building as a shortcut to reach Division 3. Because I had not seen her since learning on November 9, I had achieved NBC, I approached her, told her the news, and attempted to hand her the form displaying my scores. She stared coldly at me, refused to look at it, and walked away.

Most principals would have been ecstatic I had achieved NBC, for having even one NBCT in a CPS school was an achievement about which most principals boasted. It also was the standard at York Alternative High School for the principal to congratulate teachers on their accomplishments. But Glass did not acknowledge my achievement and did not mention it to the staff then or ever.

Later that morning, Student B, a nineteen-year-old Division 3 student inmate who was being detained for allegedly committing several serious crimes, arrived at school unusually early—before the other Division 3 students that morning. She immediately said to me, "Ms. Hutchens, I need to tell you something." She appeared to be extremely upset. I asked her to what it was related. "It's about you. It's some junk, and it made me *mad*," she said as she scowled.

By that time, I had concluded from Glass' behavior toward me, the letter Student A had written about me which I had seen on Weed's desk, and the allegations of my two male Division 8 students regarding the disparaging remarks Dr. Sims and lead teacher Weed allegedly had made about me, something negative was going on concerning me. Although I believed I needed to know what she had to say, I told Student B I did not want to hear what she was trying to tell me. She continued to try to share with me what was troubling her, but I insisted she begin working on her class assignment. Although she complied without saying anything else, it was clear that whatever she wanted to tell me, bothered her enormously.

At approximately 1:15 p.m. that afternoon, Glass interrupted me again as I taught my Division 8 class and asked me to step outside of my classroom and into the hallway. Clearly, she was unhappy about something. She told me she had received a "report" I had unplugged a computer I had purchased with grant funds and would not allow the other divisional teachers to use it. I reminded her this was my first day back at work since November 2, which was eleven days earlier, and I had no idea to what she was referring. I asked that we return to my classroom and offered to prove to her I had not unplugged the computer. I also reminded her I had purchased one particular computer to use exclusively to create my school newsletter.

All of the divisional teachers and Glass were aware of this, because she was the assistant principal when I received grant funds for the computers, and she handled the distribution of the funds. We also had several other computers in the classroom, including another one I had purchased with grant funds, which was available for everyone to use. Our discussion lasted nearly one hour and cut drastically into my Division 3 after-school journalism class time. Therefore, I informed Glass that because it was late, I would not be holding the class for the Division 3 students. After a few minutes, she left my classroom.

When I arrived home later that afternoon, to my total embarrassment, I had received an email from a staff member of the nonprofit newspaper foundation which had provided my journalism program a $10,000 grant earlier that year. She informed me Glass had called and asked her to explain the purpose of the grant funds for the computers. However, this was not the organization that had given our school the grant funds for the computers.

As I previously indicated, the professional journalism and newspaper editors' organization had provided my program a $5,000 grant which I used to purchase computers for my Divisions 3 and 8 classes. Therefore, the newspaper foundation knew nothing about the computers I had purchased. Foundation officials had provided us a $10,000 grant one year later to "improve *3 & 8 Voices* and I was using the money for printing supplies and other newsletter necessities. Yet, even after Glass received firsthand proof the allegation I had unplugged the computer was false, she added further insult to injury by surreptitiously contacting a third party to question my veracity.

The staff member of the nonprofit organization emailed me on November 13, 2007, at 3:22 p.m. During subsequent legal proceedings which I discuss later in this chapter, my attorney noticed that November 13, 2007, at 4:11 p.m. was the fax running-head date and time contained on the statement Student A wrote on October 29, 2007. Thus, the same day I proved to Glass my divisional colleagues were making false allegations about me and less than one hour after she secretly contacted the nonprofit newspaper foundation to question my truthfulness in an attempt to gather evidence in support of discipline she was planning for me, Glass faxed, or received in a fax from Dr. Sims, Student A's written statement about me.

Also, in the presence of my Division 8 students, Glass had demanded I exit my classroom in a manner which signaled I was in trouble. Since her visit was near the end of the school day and continued after the students were dismissed, the other divisional teachers and several correctional officers also saw the two of us talking in the hallway. "We all saw it, and we all knew why she was doing it," the social studies teacher said to me when we discussed the incident later. "Is everything okay, Teacher Hutchens? It looked to us like your principal was talking to you about something that was not nice," one of the correctional officers said to me as I headed home that day.

Briefly moving ahead, during the discovery phase of litigation I brought against the Chicago Board of Education in 2009, which I discuss in chapter 11, I found a memorandum Assistant Principal Jones drafted and sent to Glass the day after I spoke with her in Division 8. Prior to the litigation, I neither had heard of nor had I seen the memorandum, which was written exactly as follows:

> To: Ms. Brenetta Glass, Principal
> From: James Jones, Asst. Principal
> Date: 11/13/07
> Subject: Failure to Report After School Absence Incident Report
> Date of Incident: Tuesday, November 13, 2007
> Location of Incident: Division III
> Description of Incident: Joyce Hutchens failed to notify the administrator about her decision to forgo her after school club. When confronted by Assistant Principal Sims, she claimed to have spoken to Assistant Principal Jones and told Ms. Sims that she informed him of her absence. Ms. Hutchens telephoned Mr. Jones the following day, November 14, 2007, and informed him that she did not have her after school club the previous day. This behavior was an attempt to cover up a lie that was told to Ms. Sims the previous day.

Jones' Incident Report describes a fantasy. Almost every word he wrote in it is false. First, Jones' memo is dated "11/13/07." For instance, he claimed I telephoned him on November 14, 2007 to inform him I did not conduct my after-school program. Unless Jones somehow was able to move forward in time or is a psychic, it was impossible for him to have written a memo about an alleged incident twenty-four-hours before it occurred. Jones also wrote the alleged incident occurred in "Division III." I was assigned to work in Division 3 mornings and Division 8 afternoons. Therefore, I ended my workday in Division 8 and did not return to Division 3 afterward. If I had a reason to be in Division 3 at the end of the day when the alleged incident supposedly occurred, it would have been to conduct my after-school journalism class, and the basis of Jones' memo was I did not do so. Therefore, his allegation in this regard made absolutely no sense.

Remember, I did not hold after-school journalism for the Division 3 students that day because the amount of time I met with Glass cut into the time I would have had to conduct the class. Moreover, Dr. Sims never "confronted" me at any time or for any reason during the entire period I worked at York Alternative High School. I also never claimed to have spoken with Jones, and I did not discuss anything related to November 13, 2007 with Dr. Sims.

I never even saw Dr. Sims on the afternoon of November 13, 2007. She and I worked in different buildings on opposite sides of the jail compound, and when my meeting ended with Glass on November 13, 2007, I left Division 8, headed home, and at no time did my path cross hers as I left. I also did not telephone Jones the following day, November 14, 2007 and inform him I did not hold my after-school journalism class. That would have been unnecessary because I had informed Glass at the conclusion of our meeting I was going home, I would not be holding after-school journalism, and she wrote "No Journalism Meeting" on her calendar.

What Jones also failed to tell his boss, Principal Glass, was I had discussed with him that although the girls frequently did not attend school because they wanted to sleep late, they still wanted to attend after-school journalism. He responded, "After-school journalism is a privilege. If the Division 3 students don't show up for regular school, it's fine with me if you double up with the

Division 8 students' journalism classes on the days the Division 3 students do not attend school."

This was nothing new. My previous lead teacher had established a rule that when students did not attend school during the day, unless they had a good excuse, such as a scheduled court appearance or a CCDOC-related matter, they could not attend after-school programs. Glass was using a rule which had long been established to build a case against me for following that rule and also for doing what Assistant Principal Jones had given me permission to do.

Finally, teaching after-school programs was strictly voluntary. There was no requirement that I or any other teacher participated in an after-school program. Therefore, Principal Glass also was attempting to build a case against me by alleging I was "playing favoritism" with the Division 8 students by not holding after-school journalism classes for the Division 3 students.

I visited Glass' office before school began on the morning of November 14, 2007, because I was concerned I was being targeted by members of my divisional cluster team since it was obvious that at least one of the teachers had reported to Glass I was unplugging my classroom computers. Glass was aware Donna Craig, the Divisions 3 and 8 math teacher, and I had had our differences in the past. I erroneously assumed those old issues were behind us. After I discussed the computer allegation with her, Glass responded, "I'll stop this craziness, even if I have to shut down your journalism program and send the [non-profit] Foundation their money back!" I left her office troubled.

Several of my students in both divisions had been enrolled in York the previous school year when I was pursuing NBC. I shared with them the good news on November 14 when all of the students were present. I told them that without their hard work and support, I would not have achieved NBC. They jumped out of their seats, gave each other high fives, and cheered loudly, obviously proud that they had contributed to this important team effort. With the CCDOC's permission, I bought treats for them the following day, and we celebrated our great victory.

Although Glass refused to acknowledge my NBC achievement, throughout November 2007, I received letters of congratulations from the Illinois

State Board of Education, the Chicago Public Education Fund, and my congressman, the Honorable Danny K. Davis.

December 2007

On December 11, 2007, Student B and I were alone in the classroom during the entire class period because the other Division 3 students had either gone to court hearings or were absent for other reasons. Shortly after class began, in a very emotional tone of voice, Student B again asked if she could tell me what had been bothering her for more than one month. "Ms. Hutchens, please let me tell you because this shit has been bothering me so badly," she said. My students knew better than to use curse words in my classroom, and they definitely knew not to use them in my presence. Although they were accustomed to street life and the language they used often reflected that life, they almost never swore when they knew I could hear them. On the rare occasions they did, it almost always was a slip of the tongue for which they immediately apologized profusely. I felt in my bones I should listen to what Student B had to say this time, so I did.

She told me that on November 1, 2007, the same day Glass first visited my Division 8 classroom and harassed me, Donna Craig, the math teacher, assigned the entire Division 3 class to write an essay about me during their math period. Student B also told me Craig specifically asked the class to describe in their essay "what goes on in Ms. Hutchens' class," and to write about "any problems you have had with Ms. Hutchens." Also, according to Student B, Craig told the students that I told her I had given them food and said it was okay for them to write about it during their math class.

At no time did I have any such discussion with Craig. In fact, she and I had not discussed any student at any time. Moreover, as I previously mentioned, giving food to detainees without the CCDOC's permission was strictly prohibited. Therefore, if Craig was attempting to have the students write an "essay" stating that I had given them food, clearly it was to cause trouble for me with Glass *and* the CCDOC.

Student B said she immediately knew "something was wrong" when Craig gave the students the assignment, so she refused to comply with her request. She also told me that during the same class period, Glass entered the math classroom and questioned the students—particularly Student A, who had written the letter about me and asked me to bring contraband into the jail. According to Student B, the lead, math and science teachers were present when Glass entered the room, as the math and science teachers shared a classroom in Division 3 during the afternoon while I instructed English in Division 8, one block away. The lead teacher, Karen Weed, whose office was in Division 8. apparently was visiting the other teachers at that time. Student B said Glass asked the students if they had any complaints about me, and Student A was the only student who said that she did.

Afterward, Student B told me, "I'm so glad you let me tell you, cuz this has really been on my mind so much, I've told other people about it, including my sister when she visited me. I can't believe what Ms. Glass and those other teachers are doing to you. Student A set this up cuz she thinks you favor me over her. She said she's gonna get your ass in trouble cuz she can't stand you."

The following day, at the request of Student B, two other Division 3 students verbally corroborated her statements regarding Craig's instructions for them to write an essay about me, Glass' visit during their math class, her request for information regarding me, and Student A's threat to "get Ms. Hutchens' ass in trouble."

That afternoon while I was teaching in Division 8, I asked my male students if Craig or Glass had made the same requests of them, and they said neither had. I quickly summed up the situation: Glass and the math teacher knew it was far easier to manipulate the girls, particularly Student A, than it was the boys, who solidly had my back and would have told me in a heartbeat if *anybody* had asked them questions about me or instructed them to write anything about me.

Dr. Sims visited my Division 3 classroom on December 12, 2007, to discuss the results of an observation she had conducted of me one week earlier while I instructed my Division 3 students. She had rated me as "Weak" in the categories of "Practices Fairness in Teacher-Pupil Relations" and "Exhibits an Understanding and Respect for Students as Individuals." Absolutely nothing had happened during her observation which justified her giving me negative ratings in either of those categories.

When I asked Dr. Sims the reason for the negative evaluation, she told me, "We've been getting complaint letters from the girls, and a couple of the boys also have complained about you." This contradicted what Glass had told me when she visited my classroom one month earlier and alleged she had "received a call from downtown" about me and my behavior toward the girls. Remember, when I asked her if any of the boys ever had complained about me, she said they had not. Although Dr. Sims had not previously discussed with me any such alleged complaints or letters before she evaluated me, she had based her observation of me solely on what students supposedly had told her, rather than what she specifically observed as I instructed my class.

I held a party at my home on Saturday, December 15, 2007, to celebrate my NBC achievement. Along with family and friends, I invited more than a dozen coworkers and their guests. Despite a major snowstorm that night which dumped more than a foot of snow on Chicago, with the exception of one co-worker who had to travel to California for his sister's funeral, each coworker I invited attended my celebration.

CHAPTER 7

The Unwarranted Persecution of an "Excellent" Teacher

WHEN I ARRIVED AT WORK on Monday morning, December 17, 2007, which was two days after my celebration, there was a note in my mailbox from Glass. This is exactly what she had written: "I would like request your present in my office at Old Cermak for a meeting on Tuesday, December 18, 2007, at 7:30 a.m." Presumably, Glass meant to include the word "to" and also to spell the word *presence* instead of *present*. A sick feeling formed in the pit of my stomach; I knew trouble was on the horizon.

Glass and I met in her office the following morning. She smiled pleasantly when I arrived and invited me to have a seat. We chitchatted for several minutes about trivial matters. Then, with a peculiar smile on her face, she pushed in front of me a sheet of paper that had been lying face down on her desk. It was a memorandum written on CCDOC letterhead by correctional officer Captain Katie Harrison. She alleged that on November 7, 2007, in her office, I had used language so vulgar, so vile and so repulsive to describe my female students, I will not repeat it. Harrison described it as "vulgar profanity." She also wrote that I "terrorized daily in class" students "who were not considered favorites" of mine. Harrison further wrote that she had conducted an investigation and Student A "advised" her that she (Student A) had written "several pages to the principal of York Alternative High School" because of my "vulgar verbal abuse, harassment, intimidation, and unprofessionalism for a long period of time daily during classroom session."

Initially, I thought Glass was joking, so I waited for the punchline. But she was not joking, and although there was nothing funny about what she was telling me, as far as I was concerned, she might as well have been joking. I always have taken pride in the fact that when I make statements about people, I do so in their face, and I tell them off without using scabrous speech or borrowing language from the gutter. I have used a lot of different words to describe a lot of different people, but never have I used such language either inside or outside the classroom to describe a student.

At that time, I had taught in Divisions 3 and 8 for 4½ years. Several correctional officers sat in a security station within five feet of my classroom each day and could hear everything that happened in my classroom, including anything I said. During those 4½ years, no correctional officer ever had complained about me or written me up for even a modicum of inappropriate language or behavior involving students or anyone else. I also had never received one complaint—verbal or written—from a CCDOC staff member, including Harrison, during that period. Harrison had served as superintendent when I taught in Division 4, the other women's jail division, and never had she accused me of misconduct of any kind. In fact, it was in Division 4 where I met Harrison, and we established a good professional relationship.

I began working in Divisions 3 and 8 in 2003, and Glass' malicious attack against me began in October 2007, just a few months after the previous principal retired. During the entire four-year-period I had taught in the two divisions, numerous correctional officers, including Harrison, frequently visited my classroom and told my students, "Learn all you can from Ms. Hutchens; she's an excellent teacher who can help you when you finish high school and leave this place."

You might recall the emcee announced during the Unilever Performance Plus Award ceremony that "Hutchens steps outside the classroom to help her students acquire employment after graduation and keeps them motivated even when they no longer are her students." But only five months after receiving that award, I was being charged with "terrorizing" the very students who had selected me to receive it.

Ironically, citing the "fine job" I had done with the Divisions 3 and 8 students, Harrison had given me a beautiful leather briefcase when I won the Unilever Performance Plus Award and said in the presence of other correctional officers, "You are the finest teacher on this [jail] compound." Moreover, although

Harrison alleged I was "terrorizing" students, she neither asked Glass to transfer me from Division 3, nor did she request that the CCDOC ban me from working at the jail, which they would have done immediately if I had engaged in inappropriate conduct of any kind, especially toward my student inmates.

On every staff member's first day of work at Consuella B. York Alternative High School, the principal ensured we understood that the CCDOC could and would strip us of our ID badges, walk us out of the building, and refuse to allow us to work there at any time if we violated their rules. This had happened several times to other teachers before I worked at York. Yet, allegedly I was "terrorizing" student inmates, but not a single CCDOC official had said a word about banning me from teaching at the jail.

When I questioned other correctional officers about the matter later, none had heard of any such allegation about me. In fact, one officer said to me, "If we had *ever* heard of or seen you terrorize a student, it would have gone a lot farther than Harrison in bringing you down." Translation: My ass would have been grass, and the Cook County Department of Corrections would have been the lawn mower.

Although Harrison's supervisor was copied on the memorandum, the supervisor, who was the Divisions 3 and 8 superintendent, had known me for several years and never had she accused me of improper behavior or misconduct at any time when I worked in those school divisions. In fact, her office was just a few feet away from my Division 3 classroom, and she frequently stopped in to say hello or wave. She also occasionally attended parties and other special events I held for my students with her permission.

During my December 18, 2007 meeting with Glass, in addition to Harrison's memorandum, Glass also handed me the letter I had seen on Weed's desk which Student A had written about me on October 29—the letter Weed had claimed was "not something I'm giving to Ms. Glass or Dr. Sims." Additionally, Glass handed me a new letter dated November 1, 2007, in which Student A falsely claimed I had "teased the class with hot dogs and rib tips." She alleged that I had told the entire class, "Look at what I'm having for lunch. I'm going to share this. No, I want to eat this myself." I did no such thing. Ever. Although Student A claimed this incident occurred in the presence of her classmates, Glass did not solicit a statement from any other student to confirm or refute Student A's allegations. In a letter which I discuss later, Student B, who along with three other students was present in my classroom that day, denied every allegation contained in Student A's letter.

In other related notes I later found which Principal Glass had created regarding the incident, she wrote: "11/1/07– [Student B] was very upset because Teacher Hutchens had candy, waving it around." In her letter I just mentioned, Student B emphatically denied that I was "waving candy around" or exhibited any type of egregious or unprofessional behavior toward students that day or at any time.

Glass also inexplicably wrote the following in one of her notes which she appeared to have created as she gathered evidence to use against me: "When I was entering the building, I walked into Ms. Weed who was taking hot dogs back to her car." Karen Weed, the person to whom Glass was referring, was the lead teacher, but I was the one who was being accused of teasing the students with hot dogs. Therefore, I cannot explain why Glass wrote this particular note.

Contrary to what a principal acting in good faith would have done regarding such serious accusations, at no time did Glass ask me if Student A's allegations were true. She also did not allow me to tell her my side of the story. Not once. There are and never have been any documents anywhere containing a statement from me regarding any accusation Student A, Assistant Principal Sims or Captain Harrison made about me.

Prior to my December 18, 2007 meeting with Glass, she did not mention a single word to me about Student A's allegations, nor did she question me about the highly defamatory allegations contained in Harrison's memorandum. Instead, just five months after being promoted to principal and after waiting nearly two months after these incidents supposedly had occurred, without any warning, justification, or evidence to support any of the allegations, Glass brought the following five entirely bogus misconduct charges against me:

1) using verbally abusive language on school or Board property, but not in front of students (This contradicted a statement Captain Harrison had written about me in which she said I verbally abused students daily in my classroom.)
2) inattention to duty

3) insubordination such as failure to carry out a rule, order, or directive
4) violating or failing to perform any duty required by the Board's Code of Ethics
5) violating school rules, Board rules, policies, or procedures that result in behaviors that disrupt the orderly educational process in the classroom, in the school, and may occur on or off the school grounds or assigned work location

Glass' Suggestions for Improvement were as follows:

1) Mrs. Hutchens is to treat all of her students with respect.
2) Mrs. Hutchens is not to refer to her students or any other student in a derogatory manner.
3) Mrs. Hutchens is to conduct her after-school program on their assigned dates.
4) Mrs. Hutchens is not to discuss what she is having for lunch with her students.
5) Mrs. Hutchens is not to give or pretend to share her lunch with her students.
6) Mrs. Hutchens is not to deny any after-school programs to students because they are late to class.

At the end of our private meeting, Glass handed me a Notice of Pre-Discipline Hearing which was scheduled in January 2008, and asked me to contact my union rep who would speak on my behalf during the hearing. Because of the seriousness of her charges, I preferred having an attorney to represent me. Therefore, as soon as I arrived home that afternoon, I called my attorney and told him what had happened. He asked me to bring the letter to his office immediately, and I took it to him that day. After reviewing the information contained in the letter, my attorney referred me to his colleague, an employment lawyer, whom I later retained to represent me during the Pre-Discipline Hearing.

Initially, it did not occur to me that I had not even worked at Consuella B. York Alternative High School on November 7, 2007. Remember, I was away from York beginning November 5, and I did not return to work until

Tuesday, November 13, 2007. Harrison's memorandum was dated Thursday, November 8, 2007, and she alleged I had engaged in "vulgar profanity" and other misconduct on November 7, 2007, just one day earlier. Harrison had not seen me since November 2, 2007, something she obviously did not consider when she wrote the memorandum on November 8, 2007.

On December 19, 2007, I informed Glass that an attorney would represent me during the Pre-Discipline Hearing. Although I did not want to get students further involved in this mess, my new attorney requested that I ask Student B to provide me with a written statement of exactly what she had told me on December 11, 2007, when the two of us were alone in my classroom. She complied with my request, and in nearly five pages, Student B wrote precisely what she had said to me during our private conversation one week earlier. She also wrote that when Craig directed the students to "write an essay" about me as she instructed her math class, she refused to write it. She further wrote that Craig then told her not to worry because "No one will find out what you are writing on paper," and "They need it from more than one student." Student B did not clarify who Craig meant by "They."

Later that day, I asked my Divisions 3 and 8 students to write a letter to me as an English class assignment and describe what they liked or disliked about my class, how they viewed my discipline, if they believed I showed favoritism to certain students, what they had learned, and what, if anything, would be helpful to them if I changed or corrected the way I conducted my English class. The response was overwhelmingly positive. Almost every student wrote that although I was "strict," I was "fair." I did not receive a negative response from a single student. Student A, who had written the two letters about me which ended up in Glass' possession, also wrote a letter describing how much she liked my after-school journalism class. She wrote nothing else.

I discovered that somehow students in both divisions had learned that trouble had visited me, and together (I don't know how, since the Divisions 3 and 8 students were in two separate buildings), they united and took extra care when writing the letters for me. My students were very upset that other teachers were working against me and I was in trouble with Glass.

Student A and I were alone in the classroom on the morning of December 21, 2007. The other Division 3 students were attending scheduled court hearings. As I sat with her and watched her complete an assignment on the computer, she initiated a conversation about the two letters she had written about me. "I know I got you in trouble, and I did it because you don't like me," she said defiantly and without remorse. "I think you just like light-skinned girls with long hair like [Student B.]"

The strong suggestion by Student A was that because I am a light-skinned black and she is a dark-skinned black, I preferred Student B, a light-skinned Hispanic, to her. Colorism, a shameful prejudice or discrimination against individuals with a dark skin tone, typically among people of the same ethnic or racial group, is what it is called and what Student A was implying. Colorism purportedly disadvantages dark-skinned people while privileging those with lighter skin, and has been the cause of countless numbers of emotional and psychological battles in the black community for a long, long time. As a "light skinned," "high yellow," and "redbone" black person, I know it all too well and have had to combat the stereotypical beliefs associated with it my entire life.

I denied Student A's claim, and she began to cry. "I don't know why I always hurt people," she said. "I always hurt people who care about me. But you don't like me, and [the social studies teacher] don't like me either. He only likes [Student B] too." Although Student A claimed the social studies teacher also did not like her, I was the only teacher Weed had reported to Glass and I was the only teacher Glass was disciplining. There were only six teachers in our school division, including the lead teacher, so we all knew what was going on with each other. Therefore, I knew the social studies teacher was not being targeted by Glass for anything related to Student A. She was too busy disciplining him for other purported misconduct.

"Why do you think [the social studies teacher] does not like you?" I asked Student A. "Because he always brings [Student B] special books to read and not me," she said. I felt badly for Student A. Despite the problems she had caused me, I did not blame her. I blamed the adults who had used and taken advantage of this mentally disturbed young lady to blemish my reputation and stellar employment record for no reason other than their personal dislike of me.

Also around this time, although both had attended my party on December 15, 2007, two female staff members with whom I frequently socialized during non-work hours began to distance themselves from me. One simply stopped calling and returning my calls, but the other did far more. I learned she was relaying to Dr. Sims information I had discussed with her about my problems with Glass. (Employees everywhere: Please, please, please keep your business to yourself.)

"I gotta work here for the next two years," my colleague said, explaining her obvious betrayal of trust when I questioned her after she inadvertently revealed to me her two-facedness. Although she was repeating to Dr. Sims and perhaps others, discussions I had had with her about what was happening to me, she also frequently repeated to me what Dr. Sims allegedly said to her about me. Dr. Sims would be utterly shocked to know that her now-retired friend told me on numerous occasions the unflattering remarks she allegedly made about me. I immediately stopped communicating with her and the other colleague, both of whom served in special education-related capacities at York. When our paths cross in the neighborhood in which the three of us still live, neither can look me in the eye.

January 2008

January 7, 2008 was our first day back at work following a two-week Christmas break. As I entered my second-floor classroom that morning, I waved to Former Student C, who I saw standing in line with other inmates as they prepared to leave the building and head to court for their scheduled hearings. She avoided looking at me and waved back as if it was something she really did not want to do. This was uncharacteristic of her, and I immediately knew something was wrong. I quickly found out what it was.

After I informed Glass an attorney would represent me at the Pre-Discipline Hearing, she obtained three additional statements which she ultimately presented during the hearing. The first statement was from Former Student C, who was being detained on charges which had resulted in the loss of life to a minor and a serious injury to the minor's sister. The crimes were detailed in Chicago's local newspapers.

While enrolled in my class, loudly enough for me to hear, Former Student C frequently volunteered information about her alleged crimes to other student inmates, and although she admitted she had committed the crimes, she showed absolutely no remorse. Former Student C had been my student for eight months prior to her graduation, and we had an excellent relationship during the entire period she was enrolled in my class. I allowed her to write her own monthly column for *3 & 8 Voices*. She was one of my biggest supporters, she spearheaded the effort for me to receive the Unilever Performance Plus Award, and she wrote the most compelling essay of any of my students in relation to my receiving the award. She was an outstanding student and was named valedictorian of York's graduating class that school year.

In response to questions she was required to complete for the graduation program, although she indicated she did not have a favorite class because she loved them all, Former Student C wrote: "Ms. Hutchens is a wonderful person and has taught me a lot since I have been here. She has taught us the skills necessary to become successful journalists and has taught us business skills so we can succeed in our careers once we are released from jail. She has also taught us entrepreneurial skills so we can start our own business. I call her my guardian angel because she has guided me through this jungle of jail."

With the CCDOC's permission, I frequently allowed Former Student C to attend class with my Division 3 students after she graduated so she would not be confined all day to her cell. One day, after I allowed her to do so, she stole colored pencils (jail contraband) from my classroom, and I immediately notified the correctional officers on duty. Before I did, I questioned her about the missing pencils and she lied to me about taking them.

Captain Harrison, who had given Glass the memorandum in which she accused me of "terrorizing students" and using "vulgar profanity" was aware of the incident involving the colored pencils, for she was the officer who had confiscated them from the jail cell of Former Student C. When Harrison returned the pencils to me, she said, "I told you, you can't trust these inmates!" Later, Harrison discovered several additional boxes of stolen colored pencils from the cells of both Student A and Former Student C. I had not realized the pencils were missing, and when she returned them to me, Harrison again said to me, "You can't trust them!"

Student A had implicated Former Student C when I initially learned my colored pencils were missing. However, after conducting a follow-up sweep a week later, Harrison found boxes of the pencils in the cells of both inmates. Former Student C sent me a letter of apology which Student A hand-delivered to me. I accepted her apology, and despite her thievery and subsequent lies, I asked for and received permission from the CCDOC for her to join the Division 3 students and staff for our Christmas luncheon in December 2007.

In a brief statement Glass produced and submitted to the Board's labor relations director, Cheryl Colston, prior to my Pre-Discipline Hearing, Former Student C wrote in part, "Ms. Hutchens is an excellent teacher, but her attitude needs to let up." Then, as if someone had asked her to provide an example of something I had done which showed that my attitude needed to "let up," she wrote underneath her signature, "If I took too many pieces of paper (she gave permission to) she would yell 'Put that back.'"

When Glass obtained the statement from Former Student C, because she had graduated the previous school year and this was not one of the occasions I had allowed her to visit my classroom after her graduation, she was not present during either of the alleged incidents Student A had described in her letters. Glass also was aware that Former Student C previously had stolen color pencils from my classroom after she graduated from York; however, because she needed as much ammunition as she could get to use in her quest to discipline me, she obtained a statement from Former Student C, another obviously troubled inmate. Thus, Glass used statements from two mentally disturbed student inmates—Student A and Former Student C, both whom had stolen contraband from me, to set up and ultimately discipline her own teacher.

Glass also enlisted Dr. Sims, (who as of this writing is principal of Consuella B. York Alternative High School), to provide her with a statement which she also presented during the Pre-Discipline Hearing. In a document dated January 4, 2008, Sims first discussed events which allegedly had occurred six years prior when I had worked in Division 10. She claimed the retired former principal had transferred me from Division 10 to Division 4 because of a personality conflict I allegedly had had with other teachers. However, on January

21, 2008, two of my former Division 10 colleagues, specifically the math and science teachers, wrote and asked that I present at my Pre-Discipline Hearing, their following joint statement, which strongly refuted Sims' allegations:

> To whom it may concern:
> We worked with our dear friend and colleague, Ms. Joyce Hutchens, in 2002 in Division 10 of York Alternative High School, which is located within the Cook County Jail. We found her to be one of the most professional teachers we have ever met. During the period she served in Division 10, she developed a very positive professional relationship with the Division 10 students and staff and performed her duties in a most excellent way. Although we retired in 2004, both of us continue to maintain very strong professional ties with her. We are outraged at this assault upon her character.
> Sincerely,
> [Former Division 10 Science Teacher]
> [Former Division 10 Math Teacher]

Dr. Sims also wrote that shortly after I arrived in Division 4, she noticed that I "interacted positively with certain groups of students" and "ostracized" others. She claimed she observed the following: "Ms. Hutchens intentionally demoralized students in the presence of others (by talking about their low academic levels and/or the criminal cases that students were being detained for) and being verbally aggressive toward students in a capacity in which students were not allowed to reciprocate that aggression (yelling and screaming)." Sims ended her written statement by claiming "despite having multiple meetings addressing issues of fairness and professional decorum," with me, the problems continued, and she finally sought assistance from the principal who transferred me to Divisions 3 and 8. Dr. Sims neither saw me exhibit this type of behavior toward my students nor did she have a single meeting with me to "address issues of fairness and professional decorum" as she claimed. She also never had a meeting with me to address *any* type of inappropriate behavior which I purportedly had exhibited toward a student.

My former principal, who supposedly had transferred me to Divisions 3 and 8 because I allegedly had not gotten along with teachers and students, assessed me as "Excellent" in my performance evaluation during the school year which was the subject of Dr. Sims' statement. Specifically, my performance evaluation, which covered June 2, 2002, through August 19, 2003, the period I served in both Divisions 10 and 4, and included assessments of my relationship with students and my ability to work well with other teachers and supervisors, reflected the following: "Harmonious Relationships with Other Teachers" – "Excellent;" and "Motivates Students to Achieve Success" – "Superior." She cited no performance weakness in any category. In fact, during the entire five-year period I served as classroom teacher under the former principal's leadership, she never identified a single weakness in any area in which she evaluated my performance. Because Glass was assistant principal at that time, she was aware of and had copies of my evaluations.

You also might recall that during the summer of 2007, my previous lead teacher, (a white male), and my former principal, had nominated me to receive the DRIVE (Delivering Results through Innovative and Visionary Education) teacher award because I had "gone above and beyond my classroom duties" and had "supported other teachers in my school." Moreover, my school personnel file contained a Building/Subject Preference form, dated April 24, 2003, and a memo dated May 21, 2003, which showed that I personally requested to be transferred from Division 4 to Divisions 3 and 8, but not because of alleged conflicts with teachers. I made the request because as I previously indicated, I was interested in teaching computer technology in addition to English, and I also was excited to help launch the new education program in the jail's new school division. As I also previously indicated, the former principal assigned me three rookie teachers to mentor and coach in the Golden Teacher Program during the 2003-2004, 2004-2005, and 2005-2006 school years, which was *after* my supposed personality conflicts with other teachers.

Also, immediately after I transferred from Division 4 to Divisions 3 and 8, I returned frequently to visit and conducted an after-school reading program twice each week for the Division 4 students. Several students whom I purportedly had "demoralized," voluntarily enrolled in my after-school program. Had my former principal transferred me to Divisions 3 and 8 for exhibiting *any* type of egregious behavior toward those students, *never* would she have allowed me to return to teach in Division 4 at any time. In fact, she never would have allowed me to continue to teach at Consuella B. York Alternative High school, as she had zero tolerance for such behavior. Dr. Sims' claims about me were outright lies, and she knew they were lies.

The fourth document Glass obtained after I informed her an attorney would represent me during the January 2008 Pre-Discipline Hearing was a statement she had written apparently after having a discussion with Student A. Glass solicited and obtained the statement after meeting with Student A on December 30, 2007, during our staff's two-week Christmas break. Thus, in her zeal to gather evidence to use to build a case and ultimately discipline me, on a non-school day, Glass gained access to this severely emotionally disturbed student inmate, who was housed in the psychiatric division of the Cook County Jail, and continued to compel that student to manufacture statements she could use in conjunction with my upcoming Pre-Discipline Hearing. Thereafter, the document was placed into a file which contained my name, presumably in the Board's Labor Relations Department, and Glass ultimately used it during my Pre-Discipline Hearing.

Like many other documents, I only became aware of it during the discovery phase of litigation I initiated against the Board in 2009. The document contained the following contradictory statement of Student A, which was written by Glass precisely as follows: "She [Ms. Hutchens] is a nice teacher; she is real good. I know she doesn't like me because of the way she treats me." That Student A would describe me as a "nice teacher" and then claim she knew I did not like her because of the way I treated her, shows how deeply troubled she was. I began applying for other teaching and administrative jobs throughout CPS. My friends, family, and other supporters constantly decried my "persecution" at the hands of Glass and her "posse."

On January 7, 2008, a male substitute teacher threw an eraser and hit another student inmate, Student D, causing a red bruise on her arm. This happened during the morning hours when both he and I taught in Division 3. Student D left his classroom, came into mine, and showed me the bruise. I reported the incident to lead teacher Weed who informed Principal Glass. She and Dr. Sims visited the substitute teacher's class and presumably spoke with him about the incident. Although Student D clearly had a visible red mark on her arm, according to Student D, Glass and Dr. Sims did not ask her if she was okay.

The following day, the substitute teacher returned, and yet another student, Student E, left his classroom, entered mine, and informed me he had told her she had a "sexy walk," and she was "uncomfortable" being in his presence. I also reported this to Weed, and the substitute teacher was then transferred to an all-male school division.

During the January 22, 2008 Pre-Discipline Hearing, which was held in Glass' office, my attorney provided her documentary evidence which proved what she already knew—I was not present at the jail at any time on November 7, 2007, and in fact, I had not been at work from November 5 until November 13, 2007. Therefore, Harrison's statement was false. During my attorney's independent probe into Harrison's claim she had "conducted an investigation," she discovered Harrison had obtained no documents during the course of her so-called investigation and there was no investigative file.

Despite my attorney's repeated assertions Harrison's statements were false, despite Harrison's failure to produce one shred of evidence she had conducted an "investigation," as she had alleged, despite knowing I was not at work during the entire week of November 5, 2007, Glass found the misconduct charges "substantiated." Neither she nor Harrison provided any other date on which I could have engaged in this misconduct, and Harrison's so-called witness refused to corroborate Harrison's allegations I supposedly had used "vulgar profanity" in Harrison's office.

Glass also made it abundantly clear during the Pre-Discipline Hearing the only reason she was not firing me was because I was a tenured teacher, and there was a long, drawn out legal process she would have had to go through to accomplish this. (She realized a long, drawn-out legal process would have revealed the truth, and the truth was the last thing she wanted exposed.) However, she knew regardless of what she did to or said about her teachers, the Board's Law and Labor Relations Departments had her back, even when there was no evidence to support her allegations.

Also during the Pre-Discipline Hearing, at my attorney's insistence, Glass acknowledged at least one of my Divisions 3 and 8 colleagues had made negative allegations about me, but she refused to identify the teacher or disclose what had been said about me. My attorney told Glass during the hearing Student B had informed me Craig had instructed the Division 3 students to "write an essay" about me during her class period, and Glass responded, "Ms. Craig has nothing to do with this Pre-Discipline Hearing!" Glass also claimed another person, who was not a Board employee, but an employee of a CCDOC vendor, provided her an additional statement to use against me during my Pre-Discipline Hearing. That surprised me, as I frequently had invited the person she identified to parties I held for my students, and each time, she almost ate herself into oblivion.

Although every Division 3 student except Student A corroborated the statement of Student B that Craig had instructed them to write "essays" about me, and three of them complied with her request, during my Pre-Discipline Hearing, Glass did not produce a single "essay" from a student. There was a very good reason she did not use their "essays." The other Division 3 students' "essays" contained positive information about their interactions with me and what occurred in my classroom. Therefore, their "essays" were of no value to Glass in her quest to portray me as a teacher who mistreated my students.

Glass recommended to the Board's Department of Labor and Employee Relations and [then] CPS CEO, Arne Duncan, I receive five days' suspension without pay and a Warning Resolution, which is a public rebuke that would (a) state I had "exhibited conduct unbecoming to a CPS employee," (b) warn me that my conduct may result in my dismissal if not immediately corrected, and (c) contain directives for improvement. The official documents Glass provided me stated the disciplinary action I received as a result of my "actions" could be a (1) Written Reprimand, (2) Suspension Without Pay, or (3) Recommendation of Termination.

Despite having no evidence to support any of the charges she had brought against me, Glass accused me of "acts too egregious against a student at York

Alternative High School" to be considered for progressive discipline, a system of discipline where the penalties increase upon repeated occurrences. Yet, she did not consider it "egregious" the substitute teacher had thrown an eraser at Student D and caused a visible bruise on her arm. In fact, she allowed him to continue working at York Alternative High School for at least as long as I remained at the school.

Glass observed me on January 26, 2008, as I instructed my Division 3 students. She told me I was a "fantastic" and "exemplary teacher." She also told my students, "You are blessed to have Ms. Hutchens as your teacher." I couldn't believe what she had said to me. At 7:30 a.m. on January 29, 2008, she returned to my classroom as I was preparing to receive my Division 3 students for the start of school, and reviewed with me what she had written during her observation three days earlier. She had rated me as "Weak" in "Complies with the Policies, Rules, and Regulations of the School System and of the Building," "Exhibits an Understanding and Respect for Students as Individuals," and "Uses Sound and Professional Judgment," the very categories in which she had rated me as having "Strengths" for each of the previous five years she had served as York's assistant principal.

In fact, Glass never had rated me as "Weak" in *any* category when she was assistant principal. However, just five months after becoming principal, according to her, my performance in those critical areas had deteriorated significantly. Before she left my classroom, she said, "Joyce, I'll be glad to change [those weaknesses] if your attorney can prove you are innocent of what the captain said. I had to do this because of what the captain said," she stated, obviously referring to the CCDOC's Captain Harrison.

FEBRUARY 2008

It was the Board's policy to provide an employee a review hearing if, "where appropriate," the principal had not followed progressive discipline. Therefore, I appealed Glass' ruling, for I never had been disciplined and never had received even a cautionary notice during my entire eleven-year CPS career. I was shocked and dismayed there had been no progressive discipline, particularly when there was no supporting evidence to corroborate any of the charges Glass had brought against me. More important, the undisputed facts proved I was not at work on the date Harrison accused me of misconduct, and no one had (and to this day no one has) determined when I supposedly stood in her office and used multiple highly inappropriate terms to describe my female students.

For these reasons and because of the glaring lack of evidence which supported her charges against me, I was confident the appeal hearing officer would determine I had done nothing wrong. Meanwhile, I applied for other teaching and administrative positions throughout CPS, and in mid-February 2008, I interviewed with the manager and two team leaders in the National Board Resources Department for a position as team leader.

Later that month, the Divisions 3 and 8 special education teacher, John Bell, told me either or both Donna Craig and Karen Weed had asked him and the other divisional teachers to pitch in and buy a birthday cake for me, as my birthday was the following day. By this time, the entire divisional teachers cluster knew an attorney had represented me during my Pre-Discipline Hearing, and I strongly suspected Glass or Dr. Sims had informed Craig her name had surfaced during the hearing. I already had scheduled to take my birthday off and use one of my three personal business days to tend to business regarding my teaching certification endorsements. I was happy I had made that decision because I had no interest in receiving *anything* from Craig and Weed.

When I returned to work the next day, both teachers feigned disappointment I had missed my birthday cake the previous day. During an all-teachers professional development session later that morning, Craig handed me a birthday card which she and the other Divisions 3 and 8 teachers had signed. Later that day, Bell told me Craig wanted me to have the cake so badly, she had asked him to bring it to my home when I did not show up at work on my birthday, but he refused. I never asked him and never found out what became of the cake, or if it was filled with my favorite—fresh strawberries.

On February 28, 2008, at approximately 7:20 a.m., as Bell and I were talking in Weed's office, he received a phone call. Later that morning, he told me the call had been from Glass who instructed him to write a note regarding a past conflict he allegedly had had with me. Bell also told me he responded that he did not consider the incident to which she was referring a conflict. Glass, who was mentoring a principal-in-training, allegedly told him she was developing the mentee principal's conflict resolution skills, and wanted to show the mentee how to handle conflicts. Bell further told me that after he insisted there had been no conflict with me, Glass responded, "If there is no longer a conflict between you and Ms. Hutchens, then write the note anyway, and state in it there is no longer a conflict." She also asked him to have Craig contact her when she arrived at work, which he did.

Bell, who was very much afraid of Glass, said to me, "Joyce, I don't want to write anything that will hurt you. Please write the note for me yourself. Write whatever you want." I did as he asked and wrote the following memo:

    To: Ms. Brenetta Glass, Principal
    From: John Bell, LBS [Learning Behavioral Specialist]
    Re: Teacher Conflicts
    Date: February 28, 2008

    In our conversation on February 28, 2008, you indicated that you and your mentor want to resolve any conflict situations between teachers, and you indicated that you wanted me to describe a potentially conflicting situation between Joyce Hutchens and me.

    About two years ago, when you were Assistant Principal, I was called into your office in Division 6. You mentioned that Joyce Hutchens had complained to you about my coughing and nose blowing. It was said to make her ill. I asked you what should I do about the situation and you suggested that I leave the room for heavy coughing and nose blowing. Since that time, there have been no additional complaints regarding this or any other matter. The situation was resolved at that time and Ms. Hutchens and I have had no further conflicts since that time whatsoever.

I had not, in fact, complained about Bell. I merely had asked Glass when she was assistant principal how I should handle a habit he had which made me ill and also caused the students to complain it was making them ill. I had spoken with him about it first, but nothing changed. When I discussed the matter with Glass, she frowned as if it disgusted her. Two years later, she wanted Bell to use that incident to help her work against me, but he wanted no parts of it.

Bell gave the memo I had written to Glass. I kept a copy and gave another to my attorney and told her I believed Glass was directing any teacher who had had any type of disagreement with me, regardless of how minor or insignificant it had been, to write a memo she could use against me in my upcoming appeal hearing. Like numerous other documents, the memo I wrote for Bell surfaced two years later during the discovery phase of litigation I initiated against the Board and had been stamped "**CONFIDENTIAL.**" I had, of course, maintained a copy of the memo, which had no such stamp.

In another document I later found, of which I also was unaware before I initiated litigation against the Board, Glass had written: "Mr. Bell/Conflict Resolution New Principal." In yet another document, she simply had written the names of Donna Craig and John Bell. I also found a memo Donna Craig had written. It was dated February 29, 2008, which was the day after Glass instructed Bell to write the memo and asked him to have Craig call her. Like Bell's memo, Craig's memo was stamped "**CONFIDENTIAL**." It was addressed to Glass and Dr. Sims, and the subject was "Reflections: Resolution of a Problem."

In the three-paragraph document, Craig "thanked" Glass for "resolving the cacophonous situation which made the executions of my daily duties as a teacher and Math Department Chairperson extremely stressful and nearly impossible." She used numerous scathing adjectives and adverbs to describe me, and as if to show she had initiated the correspondence instead of receiving directives from Glass to write it, she concluded as follows: "I just feel compelled to write you concerning the positive change, after you resolved the situation by pairing me with another teacher. One cannot imagine that the resolution to this problem was as simple as changing my school division movement teacher from Ms. Joyce Hutchens to [the science teacher]. Your speedy amelioration shows your concern for the smooth and efficient operation of our school."

It always has been my understanding that information placed in an employee's personnel file or any file containing the employee's name must be factual, and staff opinions; random notes; gossip; unfounded rumors; reports; or tattletale allegations from other employees that are unexplored, not pursued or investigated; and non-factual information and commentary, must be excluded from an employee's personnel file. However, apparently, the memos of Bell and Craig were placed into a file containing my name in the Labor Relations Department after Craig wrote it on February 29, 2008, and I discovered both two years later during litigation I ultimately filed against the Board.

The ceremony honoring the school district's new NBCTs was held at a downtown location in March 2008. Although the event organizers sent Glass an invitation, she neither mentioned it to me, nor did she attend. When the 208 new NBCTs from School District 299 were asked to stand with their principals during the ceremony to be saluted, I appeared to be the only teacher in attendance who stood without a principal or a principal representative.

March 2008

I truly believed the appeal hearing I requested would clear my name of the phony misconduct charges Glass had brought against me, but I was sadly mistaken. According to Page 16, Paragraph 4 of the Chicago Public Schools Policy Manual, (EMPLOYEE DISCIPLINE AND DUE PROCESS POLICY FOR SCHOOL–BASED UNION EMPLOYEES (EXCEPT CTU) Section: 500A.1 Board Report: 13-0828-PO1 Date Adopted: August 28, 2013), "The rules of evidence do not apply."

Alan Grossman, a hearing officer who worked for and was paid by the Board, conducted the March 26, 2008 appeal hearing, during which he accused me of committing perjury. Both he and Glass asked me, "Why would Harrison lie on you?" Glass never questioned why her own teacher, who never had given her any trouble when she served as assistant principal and at that time as principal, would lie to her. Her statements during the appeal hearing also significantly contradicted those she had written and attached to the initial Pre-Discipline Hearing form. Grossman repeatedly sighed loudly when my attorney attempted to present my side of the story, and he told her, "Hurry up, so I can go to lunch!" My attorney and I immediately requested and received an audiotape of the hearing which remains in my possession.

Apparently, either someone who worked in the Board's Labor Relations Department or Glass determined Harrison had, in fact, lied about me. Remember, Harrison had written in her memorandum that while "investigating" me, she learned, supposedly from my students, I had engaged in "vulgar verbal abuse, harassment, intimidation, and unprofessionalism for long periods of time daily" while my classes were in session. However, the first "Act of Misconduct" Glass brought against me was I had "used verbally abusive language on school or Board property, *but not in front of students.*

Although Student A and Former Student C had submitted to Glass or worked with her to create four written statements which she produced during the Pre-Discipline and Appeal Hearings, neither of those statements contained a single word about me using verbally abusive language in or out of the classroom at any time. Therefore, Glass and the hearing officer both knew Harrison had lied about me, and her entire written statement lacked credibility. Nonetheless, Grossman, affirmed each of Glass' "substantiated charges." My attorney and I were stunned beyond belief.

April 2008

Assistant Principal Jones visited my Division 3 classroom on April 24, 2008, and handed me a copy of a Classroom Teacher Visitation Form on which he had evaluated my performance one week earlier. He rated me as having "Strength" in each of the six major categories and also in each of the thirty-three combined subcategories on the form. He did not rate me as "Weak" in any category.

As he handed me the evaluation form, he said, "Ms. Hutchens, I don't know what the problem is; I don't have a problem with you. You do everything I ask you to do." Then, he walked out of my classroom. Although I was unaware of it at that time, this was the same Assistant Principal Jones who only five months earlier had written a memorandum to Glass in which he falsely claimed Dr. Sims had confronted me, and to "cover up a lie," I had told her I contacted him the following morning about not holding my after-school journalism class.

In late April 2008, I was hired after a second interview with the manager of the National Board Resource Center and the director of the Professional Development Unit, Amanda Rivera. My new position was team leader, and I was assigned to the National Board Resource Center; however, I could not begin my new job until the required paperwork was completed, which I was told would take a few weeks. That was fine with me, for I believed I was facing a suspension, and I wanted to complete it before starting my new job. I informed Glass by letter I would be transferring to a new administrative position, and she did not respond.

May 2008

Cheryl Colston, the Board's labor relations director, wrote in a May 5, 2008 memo which she sent to Glass and a copy to me affirming Glass' decision to suspend me for five days without pay, "The imposition of a suspension of five days without pay was entirely reasonable." Also, in a letter which was dated May 9, 2008, Colston, a black woman and attorney, informed me that as a result of the March 26, 2008 hearing, my "appeal of school-based discipline proposed by the principal of York Alternative High School is denied." My five-day suspension was scheduled to begin on June 2, 2008, and end on June 6, 2008.

The letter was hand-delivered to my high-rise residence. I had given my building's door staff permission to sign for packages and letters I received. Instead of using a separate form or placing the letter in an envelope, without any regard for my privacy, the person who delivered the letter had my doorman affix his signature directly on the letter, thereby allowing him to read it. Apparently, that was the Board's copy. I received another copy that day from my doorman who placed it inside an envelope. It did not contain his signature. I also received the same copy by certified mail.

I still worked at York Alternative High School at that time, but for unknown reasons, I was not given the letter while at work. Thus, confidentiality to which I was entitled regarding a private matter between my employer and me was severely breached. Obviously to avoid embarrassing me, my doorman never mentioned to me he had seen and signed a copy of the letter, and I found the Board's copy containing his signature three years later during the discovery phase of the 2009 lawsuit I filed against the Board. I never knew it existed before then.

I also received a Warning Resolution, signed by Arne Duncan and which was approved "as to legal form" by the Board's general counsel, Patrick Rocks, Jr., and contained the following "Directives for Improvement:"

- Do not make offensive or inappropriate comments to or in the presence of any Chicago Public Schools' students, parents, staff members or others.
- Do not provide food or candy to York students under any circumstances without the express permission of the York school administration and the administration of the Cook County Department of Corrections.
- Follow all York school policies and procedures when engaging in conversations with York students, their parents, staff members and others.
- Follow all Cook County Department of Corrections, rules, policies and procedures when interacting with York students, Cook County Department of Corrections employees and others.
- Conduct yourself in an appropriate fashion such that you present yourself as a role model to your students.

The directives also warned me my dismissal would be requested if I failed to comply with the above-referenced directives for improvement. The Warning Resolution was placed on the Board's website for the entire world to see via any search engine. Although it was rescinded in September 2015 for reasons I discuss later, my personal and professional name was forever sullied for absolutely no reason, and it has caused me tremendous despair and public humiliation.

I was devastated that false allegations which had been made by emotionally disturbed students whom I tried so hard to help, false statements by both assistant principals and my colleagues, defamatory statements by an individual who was not a CPS employee, and bogus misconduct charges by my principal, who should have treated *all* of her staff members fairly and equally, were used to bring entirely unwarranted charges against me. Given my superb work record and the seriousness of the misconduct charges leveled against me, at a very minimum, the Board should have investigated those charges. Incredibly, neither Glass nor the Board ever conducted a probe into a single misconduct charge Glass, Sims, Harrison and Student A made about me.

Former Student C did not accuse me of doing anything wrong. She simply stated in her letter I was an "excellent teacher," but my "attitude needs to let up," whatever that meant. Instead of conducting a complete investigation of Glass' allegations, the Board used its archaic, unjust, and dysfunctional disciplinary process against me when there was no evidence whatsoever which warranted discipline. When I repeatedly questioned the Board's attorneys about it years later during unrelated litigation, they objected to the questions and sidestepped the matter altogether.

On May 15, 2008, a CCDOC correctional officer supervisor, (a "white shirt" is what the inmates call them), stopped in my Division 8 classroom while my students were having lunch in their cells. She told me that several weeks earlier, in the presence of lead teacher Karen Weed, Glass had attempted to persuade the officer to provide her a negative written statement about me. According to the officer, when she refused, Glass showed her the document either Student A or Harrison had written about me, then handed her a business card and asked her to contact her if she decided later to provide a statement.

"I have *never* seen hatred like this from so many people," the officer said to me. When I asked her to identify the people to whom she was referring, she simply said, "*All* of them. There were a lot of them, including the one in the office next door with *that weave in her head*," she said, referring to lead teacher Weed. She also said, "I'm hurt and I'm offended by what I'm seeing them do to you! I'm hurt to see all of these black women going after another black woman, and I'm offended your principal is trying to get me to go after one of her own teachers. *You're* the one who works for her—*not me!*"

Indeed, every person involved in this vicious attack against me was black, including Student A and Former Student C. Students B and D were Hispanic, and they were one hundred percent in my corner. Student A and Former Student C were kids, and troubled, psychologically challenged kids, so their behavior was understandable. With the exception of Dr. Sims, every person involved, including a school social worker who also contributed behind the scenes to the attack on me, was close to retirement age.

I told the officer I would be leaving the jail soon to begin a new job within the school district. "As much as we hate to see you go, Teacher Hutchens, it's time. You gotta get outta here," she said. I began to hate my job and dreaded coming to work each day, but the support of my students, Bell, and the social studies teacher was enormously helpful.

May 30, 2008, was my last day of work at Consuella B. York Alternative High School. That morning, Glass summoned me to her office and issued me an "Unsatisfactory" performance evaluation for the 2007-2008 school year. Her reason was "Inability to perform her job duties in a manner that promotes the best interest of CPS." She also had written on the Teacher Evaluation Review form every criticism Assistant Principal Sims had made during her December 2007 evaluation of me but omitted everything Assistant Principal Jones had written about me just one month pearlier in April 2008, when he evaluated me as demonstrating "Strength" in every category. I refused to sign the evaluation form and walked out of her office. She ultimately placed it in my personnel file.

I waited until close to the end of the class period that day to tell my students in both divisions I was leaving. After many hugs and good-byes, they promised me they would continue their education, obtain their high school diplomas, and lead a crime-free life after they were released from jail or prison. At the end of the school day, Bell and the social studies teacher helped me carry my belongings to my car. They knew it was my last day, but we vowed to keep in touch with each other. Although they were the only two Divisions 3 and 8 teachers I had informed I was leaving the school, I suspected the other teachers were aware it was my final day.

After placing my bags into my car, I drove to Division 6, which was on the opposite side of the jail compound from Divisions 3 and 8. I entered the office of Assistant Principal Jones, thanked him for "treating me like a human being," handed him my school identification card, and left. I was thrilled to be away from that place. I felt liberated, unleashed, and free! It was not until three years later I discovered the memo Jones had written about me to Glass, in which he claimed I was "attempting to cover up a lie" regarding my failure to hold my after-school journalism class. Had I known about it beforehand, I certainly would not have praised him for his behavior toward me.

People frequently ask me why I wanted to work in the Cook County Jail where I was surrounded by "tough, hardened criminals" after returning to CPS in 2002 when I could have taught at any of the other CPS high schools or for other Illinois school districts. First and foremost, I wanted to do what I could to help alleviate the recidivism rate of the highly at-risk children I served and to ensure they had an equal opportunity to learn. My other reason was deeply personal; I wanted to teach at the jail because my older brother was incarcerated within the same jail for much of his life, and I watched the pain it caused my mother year after year. I believe it ultimately contributed to her untimely death when I was only thirteen years old and she was age forty-five. Even after she died, my brother remained a lawbreaker and spent a significant part of his life in the Cook County Jail and Illinois prisons. I hoped if I used education to help keep children out of jail, their mothers would not have to endure what my mother did.

Glass' phony misconduct charges cost me nearly $15,000 in legal fees and indescribable pain and stress. Worse, the charges set the stage for a grievance the Chicago Teachers Union filed on my behalf against Glass, a lawsuit I filed against the CCDOC and two lawsuits I ultimately filed against the Chicago Board of Education which took six years to resolve. As you will see, several of the same Board attorneys who helped Glass persecute me—particularly, but not limited to Ciesel, Rocks and Colston—were involved in my two lawsuits against the Board. Their names also surfaced during my lawsuit against Captain Harrison and the CCDOC, which you will learn more about in the following chapter.

Although several of my York Alternative High School students were sentenced to Illinois prisons, and some remain incarcerated as I write this, we still keep in touch.

CHAPTER 8

The Team Leader

JUNE 2008

I SERVED MY SUSPENSION FROM Monday, June 2 through Friday, June 6, 2007. I knew my discipline was unjust, but I was happy to have time to de-stress before beginning my new job. A few months later, I learned from my former colleague, the Divisions 3 and 8 social studies teacher, that Student A was convicted of her crimes and sentenced to several years in prison. My former colleague also told me a few weeks later that Former Student C asked him if he had heard from me, and she wanted to know how I was doing. She and Student B also were convicted and sentenced to prison for their crimes later that year.

I began my new job on June 9, 2008, and joined the National Board Certification Department where I served as team leader. The department was a subunit of the Professional Development Unit (PDU), which was a subunit of the Board's Human Resources Department. The National Board Certification Department was charged with preparing teachers to achieve National Board Certification, and the PDU supported several other district initiatives, including the Golden Teacher program. The National Board Certification departmental staff was comprised of the manager, two other team leaders, and two administrative employees.

I joined the PDU, in part, to recruit and support black teachers who were interested in assuming the challenges and rigors of NBC because I felt strongly about its positive impact on teaching and learning. I also realized the critical need for more black teachers in CPS and throughout the nation to become nationally certified. During my first interview, I had discussed with the departmental manager and the other two team leaders who also participated in the interview I hoped the position would afford me an opportunity to establish more equity and diversity within the NBC program. I was aware of the low number of black National Board Certified Teachers (NBCTs) in CPS and nationwide, and I wanted to help the school district increase that number.

In mid-June 2008, I filed a grievance with the Chicago Teachers Union against Principal Glass for her violations of "Articles 3, 39, the Preamble, the Employee Discipline & Due Process Policy, the 2007-2008 Teacher Evaluation Plan and Handbook of Procedures as stated in the Agreement between the Chicago School Reform Board of Trustees and the Union." The Handbook outlined a very specific remediation plan for "poorly performing tenured teachers," which Glass had not followed.

I also complained in my grievance that because of personal vendettas, Glass and Dr. Sims had repeatedly subjected me to harassment, had solicited other teachers to write negative letters about me, and Glass also had given me a five-day suspension based entirely on unsubstantiated allegations and misconduct. For reasons I do not recall, I did not mention Glass also had solicited mentally disturbed students to write letters about me which she ultimately used to discipline me.

Two weeks after I began my new job, the manager who had hired me transferred from the department and accepted a position as an elementary school teacher. Lily McDonagh, the PDU's manager of operations who worked closely with Rivera and "assisted her overall," temporarily assumed the resource center's managerial role. I loved my new job and working with the other two team leaders. We sometimes joked that we had created a "rainbow," comprised of one black, one white, and one Latina team leader. I frequently told my colleagues they were the best group of people with whom I ever had worked, and I meant every word. We were a good team.

July 2008

Soon after I joined the NBC staff, I began what ultimately became a record of volunteering, collaborating, teacher candidate recruitment, and "selling" the program. Although I certainly wanted more black teachers to become national board certified, I began working to increase the number of NBCTs overall—not just the number of black NBCTs. Between June and October

2008, my activities and efforts in this regard included, but were not limited to the following:

- volunteering to assist with the "Shout Out" event, in which thirty thousand CPS students gathered at Soldier Field (Chicago Bears stadium) and issued a call to action to their schools, communities, and government to do more to invest in their schools and make their neighborhoods safer;
- collaborating with the National Board for Professional Teaching Standards (NBPTS) to increase awareness and recruit teachers locally and nationally about NBC during the American Federation of Teachers' Annual Conference. The NBPTS oversees the NBC program and is an independent, nonprofit organization working to advance accomplished teaching for all students;
- traveling throughout the school district to conduct NBC informational sessions;
- creating brochures and other marketing material to encourage teachers to enroll in a component of the NBC program, *Take One!*;
- drafting letters for CPS administrators and teachers to encourage candidate participation in the NBC program;
- advertising the NBC program at local colleges and universities; and
- collaborating with my colleagues, mentors, and lead mentors to conduct the NBC Summer Institute.

Also, because of my strong writing skills, McDonagh and the rest of the staff usually designated me to write the talking points for CEO Duncan, Rivera, and other CPS officials during NBC-related special events and programs.

In July 2008, The Hispanic team leader and I also asked PDU Director, Amanda Rivera, to allow us to attempt to increase the enrollment of minority teacher NBC candidates. Although she did not tell us to move forward with the project, she also did not direct us to refrain from proceeding with it. Because she also was Hispanic, it never occurred to us she would not think it was a good idea. Therefore, we drafted a proposal which addressed how we would recruit more African-American, Hispanic, Asian, and American-Indian NBC candidates district-wide. After we finished the proposal and were ready to implement it, Rivera would not allow us to move forward with our plans. Her numerous reasons for not permitting us to launch the program have forever remained unclear to me.

Also in July, contending there had been a "violation of the Board-Union Agreement involving a work situation complaint and a misapplication of and a deviation from past practice and policy as stipulated in Article 3 of the Agreement," the Chicago Teachers Union filed a formal grievance on my behalf against the Board. The grievant notice from the Chicago Teacher's Union president, Marilyn Stewart, was addressed to Cheryl Colston, the Board's director of Labor/Employee Relations, and stated, in part: "In order to resolve this matter, the Chicago Teachers Union requests that Ms. Glass rescind the efficiency rating and that she issue Ms. Hutchens a 'No Rating' for the 2007-2008 school year. We also request that the Board immediately instruct Ms. Glass to strictly adhere to the Board-Union Agreement for Teacher Evaluations and follow the Teacher Evaluation Plan and Handbook of Procedures. Finally, we request that the Board instruct Ms. Glass to cease and desist from using the Employee Discipline and Due Process Policy for personal vendettas." A "No Rating" would have reverted my performance evaluation to "Superior," which was what it had been before Glass issued me the "Unsatisfactory" rating.

August 2008

Alleging Libel/Slander, on August 15, 2008, I filed Lawsuit 2008-L-009042, *Hutchens v. Harrison, et al.*, in the Circuit Court of Cook County against the CCDOC's correctional officer, Captain Katie Harrison. At the advice of my attorney, I also named CCDOC officials as defendants. The following day, the *Chicago Sun-times* published an article regarding the lawsuit entitled *Teacher Sues Jail Guard*. I was extremely unhappy about the article because I did not want my new bosses and colleagues to find out about the problems I had had at the jail. Although Glass and the Board had disciplined me, as much as I wanted to sue both, I chose not to because I did not believe in suing the entity on which my livelihood depended.

Later that month, Colston denied the Chicago Teachers Union's requests to (a) rescind my "Unsatisfactory" performance rating, (b) direct Glass to comply with the contract and Teacher Evaluation Plan Handbook, and (c) direct Glass to cease improper use of the Board's Employee Discipline Policy. Colston wrote in her responsive letter to the Chicago Teachers Union Glass denied she (a) had a personal vendetta against me, (b) had engaged in harassing conduct toward me, (c) had issued disciplinary action against me based on unsubstantiated allegations of misconduct, and (d) had solicited teachers to write negative letters about me. Colston knew full well Glass' denial that she had solicited teachers to write negative letters about me was false, because by that time, Glass had sent Bell's and Craig's memos to Colston's department, and they had been placed in a file containing my name.

In mid-August, the entire PDU staff was notified a reorganization was imminent, and each of us had to reapply for our jobs. I was disenchanted because had I known of the reorganization beforehand, most likely, I would not have accepted the position with the National Board Resource Center. I had been offered a position as a mentor teacher at another high school at nearly the same time I was offered the job with the Center. Had I accepted it, I would have earned far more than I earned at the National Board Resource Center, and I would have remained a member of the Chicago Teachers Union which would have provided me more job security.

My only interest was in performing duties related to NBC, and my colleagues felt the same way. We had numerous discussions about the reorganization. All of us were unhappy, and we began to look for other jobs within the school district. One member of our support staff already had left CPS a few weeks earlier, so by that time, there were only the three team leaders and our administrative assistant supporting the NBC program.

The other two team leaders and I continued to travel throughout the district conducting NBC informational sessions and engaging in other activities to help recruit teachers for our program. We also learned we would begin facilitating a new teacher evaluation system which was being implemented district-wide. In addition to our already established duties, employees in each of the PDU's departments were trained on the new program and then travelled throughout the district to train administrators and teachers. Also, citing "failure to resolve this problem at the lower level," the Chicago Teachers Union filed a grievance appeal on my behalf in response to Colston's denial of the Union's requests regarding the issues I had had with Glass.

Although I had an extremely busy schedule, I continued to keep in touch with Student B and three of my male former York Alternative High School students, all of whom had been convicted of their crimes and sentenced to Illinois prisons by this time. Eventually, Student B and one of my former male students were released from prison, and we lost contact with each other. Two of my former male students remain imprisoned to this day, and we still communicate.

SEPTEMBER 2008

The Hispanic team leader and the administrative assistant found new positions within the school district. Therefore, only the white team leader, Tabita Sherfinski, and I were left to support the work of the NBC program. I continued conducting informational sessions and performing other duties in an effort to recruit teacher candidates throughout the district. This included initiating and coordinating the Candidate Support Provider Training, a two-day professional development session for NBCT mentors and lead mentors which was conducted by outside vendors.

OCTOBER 2008

On October 22, 2008, accompanied by my former Chicago Teachers Union rep, I attended a hearing regarding the grievance the union had filed on my behalf. It was conducted by a hearing officer of the Board's Labor Relations Department. Although I no longer served in a teaching capacity since I had assumed an administrative position, because I had initiated this action while I served as a teacher, the Chicago Teachers Union still represented me. Shortly after the hearing was held, Colston again denied the requests the Chicago Teachers Union had made in relation to my grievance.

One week later, my attorney wrote a letter to CEO Duncan and the Board's president, Rufus Williams, both of whom along with the mayor had presented me with the Unilever Performance Plus Award just one year earlier. She asked the Board take the following actions to "prevent further harm" to me:

- removal from my personnel file the "Unsatisfactory" performance evaluation Glass had given me
- rescission of the Warning Resolution

- reversal of the five-day suspension and reimbursement of my salary and the $15,000 in attorney's fees I had incurred defending myself against Glass' bogus misconduct charges
- removal from my personnel file all 2007 and 2008 discipline imposed by Glass so it could not in any way be used against me in the future
- prevention of Glass, Dr. Sims, Weed, and Craig from "proceeding to further damage" my reputation, including admonishing them from making oral or written derogatory or defamatory remarks or comments, and showing, giving, or relaying to others the false statements made by Harrison and all other involved parties who had created such statements

Duncan and Williams referred the letter to the Board's Law Department. In a letter dated October 28, 2008, senior assistant general counsel, James Ciesel, wrote the following: "Ms. Hutchens has initiated much litigation against the Board and CCDOC surrounding the alleged adverse job actions taken against her during the 2007-2008 school year. Accordingly, without some type of global settlement of all litigation against the Board, it would not be in the Board's best interest to discuss Ms. Hutchens' demands." Ciesel also suggested that my attorney contact Jennifer Wu, a Board attorney who had been assigned to represent Glass, if necessary, presumably since I had obtained an attorney, filed a grievance with the Chicago Teachers Union against Glass, and I also had filed several complaints against Glass with the Equal Employment Opportunity Commission, (EEOC) which I did not pursue. When my attorney contacted Wu, she did not respond.

Later, my attorney told me Ciesel had asked her why did I "have to get an attorney" as it related to either the Glass or CCDOC matters; I am not sure to which issue he was referring. The unwarranted "Unsatisfactory" performance rating remained in my personnel file, the Warning Resolution remained on the Internet, and the Board refused to pay the $15,000 it had cost me in attorney's fees to defend myself against Glass' phony misconduct charges. That month the Chicago Teachers Union also demanded arbitration in connection with my grievance, and a date was set for a hearing.

CHAPTER 9

The Curriculum Facilitator

NOVEMBER—DECEMBER 2008

NOVEMBER WAS AN EXTREMELY BUSY month. Every Professional Development Unit (PDU) department underwent a reorganization whereby we were expected to diversify our skills and become generalists so we could support each PDU program instead of only the one to which we were assigned. The departments under the new PDU structure were Program Development, Training & School Support, Assessment & Compliance, and Operations.

Sherfinski and I were assigned to the Training & School Support Department. Although we were required to perform duties in all four departments, our major responsibilities were divided between NBC and the Golden Teacher program. Therefore, our workload increased. Immediately prior to the 2008 reorganization, Lily McDonagh, the PDU's manager of operations (who also had temporarily served as the resource center's manager) informed me there would be no team leader title when I requested that mine remain the same following the reorganization. McDonagh's statement was not true; Sherfinski's title in her new position remained team leader, but mine was changed to curriculum facilitator.

Sherfinski and I quickly settled into our new routines of the reorganized PDU. Because she was team leader, she primarily attended meetings and performed administrative tasks related to the Golden Teacher program. She did not conduct Golden Teacher workshops. In addition to NBC-related duties, my new responsibilities included travelling across the school district to conduct Golden Teacher workshops and a few minor tasks for the other PDU programs.

With the exception of the National Board Resource Center, all other PDU programs were located at 320 W. Elizabeth Street, which was about two miles away from the National Board Resource Center. Therefore, instead of working solely at the resource center each day, Sherfinski and I supported the other PDU programs at the Elizabeth Street location from 8:30 a.m. until noon, Mondays through Thursdays. Then, we headed to the resource center where we performed duties related to NBC for the remainder of the work day. On Fridays, unless there were specific reasons we needed to work at the resource center, we remained at the Elizabeth Street office the entire day. We were crushed we no longer could work the entire day at the resource center. Although our cubicles at the Elizabeth Street office were just a few feet from each other, promptly at noon each day, Sherfinski would text me with the message, "Let's go!" We would then assemble our belongings, dash out of the building, and hurry to the resource center where we would spend the rest of the day doing our beloved NBC work.

Despite management's intent for PDU employees to share responsibilities across programs, this rarely happened. Because the reorganization also required other PDU employees to serve as generalists, the staff members who worked in the other three departments were assigned to help Sherfinski and me with NBC-related duties once each week for three hours. Since they were not NBCTs, they did not have the required skills and training to do most of the work related to the program. Instead, they basically performed clerical duties such as answering phones and preparing classrooms for NBC-related cohort groups and/or other events which teachers attended after their regular work day ended.

JANUARY–MARCH 2009

Deborah Glowacki joined the Training & School Support department in early January 2009. Although her title also was curriculum facilitator, her primary responsibility was the Golden Teacher program. Like the rest of us, she was required to support the other PDU programs. Therefore, she assisted Sherfinski and me with NBC-related duties once each week for three hours at the National Board Resource Center. Because she was a NBCT, she also frequently helped us when there were special events or activities. Glowacki had served as a CPS elementary teacher for about eleven years before joining the PDU, and she and Sherfinski held Illinois elementary school teaching certifications. I was the only Training & School Support department NBCT who held an Illinois high school teaching certification.

During the first week in January, I received an email from PDU director, Amanda Rivera, in which she stated that she hoped I had had "a restful holiday season," as I had taken a few vacation days during the Christmas holiday season. She also thanked me for my "contributions to the PDU's work." She asked Sherfinski and me to attend the annual mayor's press conference announcing the new NBCTs for the 2008-2009 school year. She did not invite Glowacki to attend.

Following President Obama's appointment of Arne Duncan to the position of US Secretary of Education, Mayor Daley replaced him with Ron Huberman, a veteran public servant who also had held various other city government positions within Mayor Daley's administration.

April—May 2009

In mid-April, we began hearing rumors the Board would be undergoing a district-wide reorganization resulting in hundreds of layoffs which would include the PDU. I was concerned, but not as much as most of my other colleagues because I never had had difficulty getting a job. Moreover, I was a NBCT with an English core subject and multiple other teaching certifications. Because of its importance to education and the mayor, we all knew most likely, the NBC program would continue. Glowacki and I frequently agreed if anyone would be retained, it would and should be Sherfinski because she had the most program knowledge and experience.

On April 28, 2009, my union rep notified me the Board had decided not to move forward with arbitration and agreed to rescind the unjust "Unsatisfactory" performance evaluation Glass had given me. One of the stipulations of the agreement was the Board would immediately purge my personnel record of the "Unsatisfactory" rating and issue me a "No Rating" for my

2007-2008 school year performance evaluation. This was a huge victory for the Chicago Teachers Union and me.

JUNE 2009

During a meeting Rivera held on June 17, 2009 with all staff, she announced most of us would be laid off from our positions before the end of the month. She read from a list of names those who would be retained which included Sherfinski, but Glowacki and I were being laid off. Although Rivera also told us one person who was being laid off would be called back, she did not indicate who that person would or might be.

There was complete silence as Rivera read the names of those who were keeping their jobs. As I looked around the room, I saw panic on the faces of my co-workers when she finished. I thought of my own situation, including my bills and other obligations, and I felt stressed. I wished I had remained in a teaching position so I could exercise my seniority rights and be protected by the Chicago Teachers Union; however, like the rest of the PDU employees, I served in an administrative capacity. Therefore, I had no such rights or protection.

I returned to my desk and began submitting résumés for teaching and administrative positions within CPS, which I found in the internal job bulletin. I also contacted the Illinois Department of Unemployment Security to learn how to apply for unemployment benefits. Also after the meeting, I sent a department-wide email in which I volunteered to create résumés for my colleagues who also were being laid off. At least ten PDU employees, including Glowacki, immediately contacted me and took me up on my offer. I ultimately wrote résumés for each of them. Rivera told us to create a letter of recommendation for ourselves if we needed to, and she would "tweak" and sign it for us. I did not create a letter of recommendation for her to sign because with my employment background, education, and teaching certifications, I believed I would not need it.

On June 23, 2009, Rivera again summoned the entire PDU staff to a meeting and announced the official layoffs of staff. Although we were told to clean out our desks, gather our personal belongings, and exit the office that day, the layoffs were to become effective in mid-July. Rivera also told us until then, we would continue to receive paychecks and remain covered by the Board's health insurance. Many of my co-workers hugged each other and cried openly. Others sat in stunned silence. Although we knew the layoffs were imminent, it was still a shock to us. Although I did not shed a tear, I was scared. I was entirely self-supporting, I had never before in my life been laid off, and it was a horrible feeling.

After every PDU employee returned to their respective units, I remained in the meeting room and talked briefly with Rivera. I expressed my displeasure with the short layoff notice the district had given us, but I also told her most of us had expected this to happen. She said to me, "Joyce, don't take this layoff personally. There are many NBCTs who will be losing their jobs." I did not believe I should have been treated any differently than anyone else simply because I was a NBCT. Given that fact, I wondered why she thought it was necessary to say that to me.

Later that day, after announcing the 2009 layoffs, in response to an email I had sent Rivera earlier regarding the layoff, she sent me a return message thanking me for my "thoughtfulness and contributions to the PDU's work." She also wrote, "Let me know if there's anything I can do to help you." A short time later, our manager, Karen Cushing, gave letters of recommendation to her staff members who were being laid off in the Training & School Support Department. At no time did I ask Cushing for a letter of recommendation; it was entirely unsolicited.

I was not privy to the contents of anyone else's letter, but Cushing appeared to have created mine based on my credentials, experience, and strengths. Erroneously dated June 23, 2007, (instead of 2009), Cushing wrote the following:

> I have worked with Joyce Hutchens in the Training and School Support division of Human Resources and I strongly recommend her for employment. Joyce's responsibilities included support for National Board Certification (NBC) and Induction programs and facilitation

of professional development for Induction and the CPS Excellence in Teaching Pilot. She also wrote many of the articles publicizing the program and events.

Joyce provided support for NBC candidates and resource centers, handling the many details for support of the 3 satellite site resource centers as well as the main Resource Center at Talcott. In addition to her writing talents, she has also supported recruitment of NBC candidates by presenting information sessions around the city.

Joyce has presented trainings for lead mentors and mentors in the Golden Teachers Program as well as those for the CPS Excellence in Teaching pilot program and is well regarded as a facilitator of professional development by her audiences.

Joyce is conscientious and dependable, and willingly accepting [sic] new challenges. Her writing talents are an asset.

I would be happy to provide any additional information as needed.
Karen Cushing

Overall, approximately seventy-five percent of the PDU staff was laid off, including the director, Rivera. Of the thirty-four PDU staff members, only eight remained. The predominant race of those who were laid off was black, including every black person who served in my unit, Training & School Support, and almost everyone who was laid off was over the age of 40. Glowacki, Cushing, and another white Training & School Support employee also were laid off. Sherfinski and a white employee who had been hired in Training & School Support just a few months prior to the layoff were retained. Glowacki and I had begun communicating by phone after work hours since the layoffs were announced, and we talked later that night. We pondered what we would do and spoke of returning to teaching if we could find a position within the school district.

Exactly six days after the layoffs, Glowacki informed me by phone she had returned to CPS. I was confused and tried to understand what she was saying to me. According to Glowacki, she had received a call from McDonagh, who told her to return to work to "close out" the Golden Teacher program. I do not recall if Glowacki indicated she also would be performing NBC duties with Sherfinski, but I was 100 percent certain she would be. There was no need to "close out" Golden Teacher. All work associated with the program had been completed before we left the PDU, so I knew that excuse simply was a smokescreen to reinstate Glowacki into CPS and probably to serve the NBC program. The conversation was awkward, we hung up quickly, and we never talked by phone again.

I felt betrayed. After all of my hard work for the NBC program and overall in the PDU, and despite the very minimal amount of work Glowacki had done for the program, it was she and not I who was reinstated to work for NBC. Worse, it was clear I had not been given an equal opportunity to be considered for retention. Instead of Sherfinski and me, who were the two surviving NBC staff members following the first reorganization in 2008, now it was Sherfinski and Glowacki, both of whom are white. Combined with the fact every black Training & School Support employee also had been laid off, I believed Glowacki's reinstatement into a position in which she would be performing duties I had performed for one year, and for which I was not even considered, was racially motivated.

July 2009

On July 1, 2009, I drafted and sent a letter to Ron Huberman, the Board's chief executive officer; Michael Scott, president; Dr. Barbara Eason-Watkins, chief education officer; and Robert Runcie, chief academic officer, in which I wrote "My civil rights were violated under the guise of a layoff." The letter also included details of my credentials, which were distinctly superior to Glowacki's, and my years of CPS service, which were equal to hers.

By mid-July 2009, I had received no response from any of the Board's officials. Therefore, as required before launching a civil rights lawsuit, I filed with the US Equal Employment Opportunity Commission Charge Number 846-2009-31843 in which I alleged I had been discriminated against because of my race and age and retaliated against because of the actions I had taken against Glass, the CCDOC, and Harrison. I asked the EEOC not to waste my time or theirs determining if there was sufficient evidence for the agency to conduct an investigation, and instead, to issue me a Notice of Right to Sue, after which I would have ninety days to file a lawsuit.

On July 22, 2009, I received a letter from Cheryl Colston, director of the Board's Labor Relations Department. She was the person who repeatedly had denied my grievance requests regarding Glass the previous year and whose signature was affixed to the letter my doorman signed, informing me I had been suspended. She wrote she was responding on behalf of the four CPS officials to whom I had written on July 1, 2009. She also wrote the Board was referring my letter to its Equal Employment Compliance Officer, and a representative from that office would be in contact with me.

CHAPTER 10

The Pre-litigation Process

AFTER THE BOARD REHIRED GLOWACKI and did not provide me an equal opportunity to be rehired, and did not even consider me for rehiring, I made up my mind that this time I was going to sue the school district. I was not interested in retaining the same attorney who had represented me during my legal proceedings against Glass and the CCDOC, so in late July 2009, I reached out again to my longtime attorney for a referral. He recommended attorney James R. Fennerty of Fennerty & Associates LLC, whom I hired to represent me in my lawsuit against the Board. Although I paid Fennerty a retainer's fee, he represented me on a contingency basis because he believed I had a very strong case against the Board. My lawsuit against my former employer, the Chicago Board of Education, was on!

Not long after I was laid off, I discussed my plan to sue Rivera and McDonagh with a former PDU colleague who had retired just one week after the June 2009 layoff. The former colleague is black, and although she, like everyone else, had observed nearly every PDU employee who had been laid off was black, she called me at home late one night and tried to convince me not to name Rivera as a defendant in my lawsuit. However, she definitely wanted me to sue McDonagh. She was convinced Rivera had nothing to do with blacks being laid off and McDonagh had everything to do with it. It was the strangest phone call I ever have had. Hour after hour passed, and she did all she could to convince me not to sue Rivera. She wasted her time; I named both Rivera *and* McDonagh as defendants in my lawsuit. She and most of the other black laid-off PDU employees disliked McDonagh, so they were extremely pleased I was suing her. I was suing neither Rivera nor McDonagh because

I liked or disliked them. I was suing them because my civil rights had been violated, and I believed both had something to do with it.

Those of us who had been laid off received paychecks until the end of July. I awoke early on the first Friday we stopped receiving our paychecks and accessed my bank account online. My heart pounded as I looked at it, hoping desperately my layoff had been a bad dream and somehow, some way, my paycheck had been direct deposited into my bank account the night before as usual. It had not been, of course, and my layoff became an undeniable reality for sure.

August–December 2009

In mid-August, I began receiving unemployment benefits. The $820.00 bimonthly check drastically differed from the nearly six-figure annual salary I received before my layoff, and it stung mightily. I also signed up for Consolidated Omnibus Budge Reconciliation Act (COBRA) health benefits, and because of a plan implemented by President Obama, I was required to pay a significantly reduced and affordable monthly rate for coverage.

I applied for nearly three dozen teaching and administrative positions within CPS between June and August 2009. I interviewed for two English teacher's jobs for which I was not hired, and I was not contacted to interview for a single administrative position. I frequently wondered if my problems with Glass had contributed to my layoff and unsuccessful search for other CPS jobs.

Throughout the remainder of 2009, I submitted hundreds of résumés to other Illinois school districts, universities, and organizations for positions in education, communications, training and administration, since those were fields in which I had credentials and experience. I rarely received responses, and when I did, they did not result in job opportunities for me. I became more and more suspicious the Board was retaliating against me by blackballing me because of my issues with Glass and also because I had filed a lawsuit against the CCDOC.

Although I realized the economy might be a factor, I never had had this much difficulty getting a job. I thought age also might have contributed to my continued inability to get a job, as I was over the age of 40. I also was mindful of one significant issue which I was certain factored in preventing employers from hiring me: The unjust Warning Resolution was on the Internet for the entire world to see and stated I had "engaged in conduct unbecoming to a CPS employee." I knew prospective employers who read it would have second thoughts about contacting me to interview for job openings.

I was extremely sad on the first day of the 2009-2010 school year. Although I no longer was a teacher at the time of my layoff, I was still a teacher at heart, and I believed I should at least have been given an opportunity to return to the classroom after I was laid off.

Only two months after Sherfinski retained her job, she resigned from the NBC program after acquiring a position as a classroom teacher. However, she was allowed to return to the program at night from November 2009 until June 2010 to earn extra money as a retake mentor (mentoring those who were retaking NBC portfolio or assessment entries), while I remained unemployed and deprived of an equal opportunity to earn a living, even part-time, with the Chicago Public Schools.

As a requirement of the US EEOC's standard charge handling process, in early August 2009, the Board submitted to the agency a five-page Position Statement which explained their "side of the story." The Board denied in its Position Statement it had "unlawfully discriminated or retaliated against me, the Complainant, in violation of Title VII of the Civil Rights Act of 1991." The Board touted its "non-discrimination policy," which "prohibits discrimination on the basis of an employee's race and age and prohibits retaliation." The Board claimed "budget cuts" as its reason for laying me off. Jennifer Wu signed the Position Statement. She was the Board's attorney with whom my attorney had attempted to contact to have my "Unsatisfactory" performance rating and Warning Resolution rescinded, and who would have represented Glass when I filed EEOC charges against her which I did not pursue.

The Board also submitted to the EEOC a declaration signed by Alan Anderson, acting deputy chief executive officer for human capital, who had been instructed by Huberman to implement the layoffs. A declaration is an explicit, formal announcement, either oral or written, and is signed under penalty of perjury (supposedly) by the author. Paragraphs six through ten of the ten-paragraph declaration immediately caught my attention. Combined, they declared Anderson had discussed the retention of staff with PDU director, Amanda Rivera, and based on that discussion, he had laid off certain individuals, including me. The declaration further stated Anderson had retained Sherfinski and Glowacki based solely on Anderson's discussion with Rivera. Paragraph ten of Anderson's declaration stated: "Ms. Hutchens was not supporting the National Board Certification program at the time of her layoff and was not as knowledgeable in the National Board Certification program," apparently meaning I was not as knowledgeable as Glowacki, Sherfinski, and a third employee he indicated who was neither a teacher and, therefore, certainly was not a NBCT.

At the end of 2009, I learned CPS had been named the nation's number one school district for new NBCTs for the 2008-2009 school year. During that time, Sherfinski and I had supported the NBC program for several months by ourselves or with minimal support, mostly clerical, from the PDU staff. Yet, despite contributing greatly to this effort, I was out of a job, and Glowacki, who had been hired in the PDU six months after I had been hired, and who had worked with the NBC program for only three hours one day each week between January and June 2009, was retained to support the program. I considered this extraordinarily unfair. Just six months after the election of America's first black president, I had personally experienced the worst act of employment discrimination in my life—right in his hometown.

In September 2009, I received my Notice of Right to Sue. Because the Board is a branch of local government, the US Department of Justice, rather than the EEOC, issued me the notice. In November 2009, while reviewing my personnel file in the Board's Employee Records Department, I noticed despite the Settlement Agreement seven months earlier between the Board and the Chicago Teachers Union regarding the "Unsatisfactory" performance rating Glass had given me for the 2007-2008 school year, it remained in my personnel file. The Agreement stated specifically the evaluation would be removed immediately, but it was still there. I notified my former union rep who told me she would contact the Board's Labor Relations and Law Departments and have it purged from my personnel file.

The Board advertised Sherfinski's former National Board Resource Center position in the CPS job bulletin, but I did not learn of the job opening until the final day of the advertisement when I happened to search the bulletin for available positions. Rather than rehiring me to fill Sherfinski's vacant job, in December 2009, the Board hired a less-qualified white male to fill it.

CHAPTER 11

09 C 7931 — Year One

ON DECEMBER 22, 2009, I filed a seven-count lawsuit in the US Northern District of Illinois Court and named the Board, Amanda Rivera, and Lily McDonagh (whose name I initially misspelled in the lawsuit) as defendants. Although Rivera was director of the PDU, because of information I received regarding McDonagh's role in my layoff and Glowacki's rehiring, I also named her as a defendant in my lawsuit. The counts were as follows:

Count I	42 U.S.C. § 1981 – Race Discrimination, which pertained to McDonagh and Rivera.
Count II	Section 1983, Equal Protection Clause, Race Discrimination, which pertained to McDonagh and Rivera
Count III	Race Discrimination, Title VII, which pertained solely to the Board
Count IV	Age Discrimination, which pertained solely to the Board
Count V	Retaliation, Title VII, which pertained solely to the Board
Count VI	Intentional Infliction of Emotional Distress, which pertained to McDonagh and Rivera

Count VII   Interference with Contract, which pertained to McDonagh and Rivera

To prevail on a Title VII race discrimination claim, I was required to prove Deborah Glowacki and I performed work substantially equal to each other, we were subject to the same work policies and performance standards, and we had the same supervisor; but she, who was not in a protected class, was treated more favorably than me. Thus, Glowacki was my similarly-situated comparator.

My lawsuit was assigned Case Number 09 C 7931, and US District Judge, Rebecca R. Pallmayer, assumed jurisdiction over the case. Immediately after I filed it, several of my former PDU colleagues with whom I occasionally had spoken by phone, stopped calling and talking to me. Some of them wanted to return to work for the Board, and because of my lawsuit, in their eyes I was tainted. Moreover, like the former colleague with whom I had spoken by phone for hours, they were displeased I had sued Rivera because since she was Hispanic and we were black, for some nonsensical reason, they thought she had an allegiance to us and could not have been involved in our layoffs and Glowacki's rehiring. Incredibly, those same individuals also had lost their jobs, and they knew every Hispanic and most of the white employees in the PDU had maintained theirs. They actually believed (or pretended to believe) Rivera had played no role in our layoffs, even though three years earlier under Rivera's directorship during another layoff in the PDU, everyone who lost their job at that time purportedly was black.

Eventually, in addition to my friend, Juanita Jones, who had served as the Training & School Support Department's administrative assistant, only one other former PDU employee continued to communicate with me. I believe the employee was trying to get information from me regarding my lawsuit so she could relay it to others, who most likely conveyed it to Rivera. I suspect this is true because she knew quite a lot about Rivera, and she shared what she knew about her with me. That former employee, a black woman, and another black woman had served as Rivera's clerical assistants, and both were laid off with the rest of us. Rivera's Hispanic clerical assistant was not laid off.

January—May 2010

I landed short-term contracts with two local colleges in January 2010. I had inside help at one of the institutions, and because the person who hired me at the other college previously had been laid off during her career, she empathized with me. Although both contracts were for only one semester, they were lucrative. Therefore, during this period, I was able to live the lifestyle to which I had become accustomed before my layoff. Additionally, the schedule I established allowed me to work the hours necessary to fulfill my obligations to both institutions.

On February 2, 2010, Sabrina L. Haake, Jennifer Wu, Sunil Kumar, Susan Margaret O'Keefe, and Patrick J. Rocks filed attorney appearances in my lawsuit. Haake was the lead attorney and represented Rivera and McDonagh, and Wu represented the Board. O'Keefe and Kumar were Law Department supervisors, and Rocks served as the Board's general counsel who presumably filed appearances in all lawsuits against the Board. With the exception of Haake and Wu, each of the Board's attorneys who filed appearances in my lawsuit did so only for the purpose of receiving notifications regarding the case which was the standard practice in all Board lawsuits.

Haake filed affirmative defenses, answers to the complaint, and a jury demand for Rivera and McDonagh, and Wu did the same for the Board. Both denied "any violations giving rise to liability as allegedly occurred." You might recall Wu, Kumar, and Rocks' names surfaced in either or both the Glass matter at York Alternative High School and my litigation against Harrison and the CCDOC.

On February 17, 2010, a hearing was held during which Judge Pallmayer established a date in late November 2010 for the close of discovery in my case. That month I also noticed the "Unsatisfactory" performance evaluation Principal Glass had given me was still in my personnel file. I notified my former union rep again, and she assured me she would contact the Board's Law and Labor Relations Departments and request to have it removed.

From the beginning of my lawsuit, I assumed a very active role in every phase of it. I gathered nearly all of the documents Rivera and the Board requested of my attorney when they submitted their Requests for Production of Documents. I was perusing information he had received when I found the documents Assistant Principals Sims and Jones and math teacher Craig had written about me.

I also discovered a form entitled "Narrative Running Record of Observations of Classroom Activity and Interaction with Focus on Teacher," which contained notes Glass had written during her observation of what appeared to be a poorly performing English teacher. Although the teacher's name was not displayed on what clearly was a copy of an original document, I knew the students to whom she was referring were not my students and I was *not* the teacher to whom she was referring. The observation notes referenced incidents which never had occurred in any of my classes and to students who never had been enrolled in any of my classes, but were enrolled in another teacher's class.

Based on her other egregious behavior toward me, I concluded that Glass had deliberately placed the notes of another teacher's poor performance into a file containing my name in the Board's Labor Relations Department when she was gathering information to discipline me. I also believed that to make it appear I was the poorly performing teacher, she had copied the notes in a way the actual teacher's name was not displayed. She also had placed into the file another "Narrative Running Record of Observations of Classroom Activity and Interaction with Focus on Teacher" form for the same period with notes which contained my name and the correct names of my students. She accurately described her observation of my Division 3 class on the form, and because it was my class she had observed, the notes were not of a poorly performing teacher.

With the exception of my initial Request to Produce Documents, which my attorney submitted, I created each of my own requests, and my attorney also submitted them to the Board. I made dozens of requests, including the following related to my matter at York Alternative High School and Glass: (a) the fraudulent performance evaluation documents; (b) the names of students in the evaluation who were not at any time enrolled in my classes; (c) information regarding the Board's policies related to Glass' manipulation of mentally disturbed student inmates; and (d) violation of CCDOC policies in meeting with students to gather information Glass had used to discipline me.

The Board refused to provide any such information. Because my 2009 lawsuit had nothing to do with the matter concerning Glass, I knew the Board had every right not to produce the information I requested. To put the Board's attorneys on notice I was aware of what they and Glass had done to unfairly discipline me, I requested the information anyway. Although the Board's attorneys frequently complained my numerous requests were "overly broad" and "unduly burdensome," if they had the documents in their possession and they were related to my lawsuit, they usually produced them to my attorney. I visited his office at least twice each week to review the documents.

In other notes the Board produced to my attorney, Glass also had written and submitted to the Board's Labor Relations Department the following note exactly as it appears here: "Teacher Hutchens works in the RTU (Residential Treatment Unit) and these students have severe emotional problems, and they are apt to over-react at any given time, that's why we have social workers, psychologists, lead teachers with Special Education Degrees to help our students learn conflict resolution skills, learn self-control techniques and better understand actions and consequences... Our jobs as educators is to show compassion, teach skills, and hopefully, through our actions, empart [sic] ethical behaviors that will make our students better citizens."

Apparently, Glass believed influencing mentally disturbed student inmates who were receiving psychiatric therapy to write letters against their teacher was "ethical" and would make them "better citizens." Apparently, she also believed using other teachers, correctional officers, and whomever else she could find to stage bogus misconduct charges against one of her own teachers in full view of mentally disturbed students, also would make them "better citizens." Apparently, Glass believed too that it was "ethical" for Craig to instruct these emotionally disturbed students to "write an essay" about their English teacher under the deceptive guise of it being a "math assignment."

As she concluded her letter to me, which I previously mentioned, this is how Student B described the pressure she encountered by Craig allegedly compelling her to write an "essay" about me: "I am glad to have gotten this off of my chest. For a while after I found out what was going on I was trying to talk to Ms. H about it, but she told me she did not want to talk about it. I was very upset with everything that was going on, that's why I'm writing this letter." Student B's oral and written statements following what she allegedly witnessed in Craig's classroom when she asked the class to "write an essay" about me, clearly showed Student B was traumatized and psychologically injured as a result of the pressure allegedly placed upon her to "write an essay" containing negative information about me, her English teacher. This did not, by any measure, make Student B a "better citizen."

I also discovered the documents Glass had solicited from Student A, Former Student C, and numerous other documents related to my discipline which had been exchanged between Glass, the appeal review hearing officer, Grossman, and labor relations director, Colston, with copies to Rocks and senior assistant general counsel, James Ciesel. I never had seen most of those documents and was unaware they existed. In even more notes I discovered, Glass had written the following to describe how I allegedly had treated my Division 3 students: "This type of insensitive and cruel behavior is not what I want our students to experience at Consuella B. York Alternative H.S. Students have told their parents, me, and my mentor that 'teachers care.' That is the type of climate I want exhibited at York, a student-centered environment where teachers and ancillary staff care." This was the same Principal Glass who had observed me on January 26, 2008, and told my class I was a "fantastic" and "exemplary" teacher, and they were "blessed to have Ms. Hutchens as their teacher," which I discussed in chapter 7.

Glass also had written the following, presumably for labor relations director Colston to consider when preparing to discipline me: "The best interest of students is not considered when there are teachers who can't work with Ms. Hutchens because they feel as though they are working in a hostile environment. If teachers feel stressed in her presence, it's understandable students would not feel comfortable." The names of John Bell and Donna Craig appeared next to this statement.

My supposed inability to work with teachers because they felt they were in a "hostile environment" and causing them to be "stressed" were not among the initial complaints Glass had lodged against me when she began setting me up for discipline. However, like the supplemental documents she solicited from Dr. Sims and Former Student C after I informed her an attorney would represent me during the Pre-Discipline Hearing, Glass had enlisted teachers to create letters complaining about me for the same purpose.

Clearly, it was Glass who rendered the environment hostile and toxic by conspiring with members of her staff, CCDOC correctional officers, students, and other non-CPS employees to work against one of her own teachers. If students were "uncomfortable" attending my class, it made no sense Glass insisted I conduct my after-school journalism class. Glass alleged I was "punishing students by refusing to have after-school journalism." If the students felt "punished" or "uncomfortable," it was incomprehensible they repeatedly had told both Glass and me they enjoyed my class.

Even more disturbing, these student inmates were housed in cells directly across from my classroom, and they had access to me each day when passing through the halls. Glass' actions severely compromised my safety and security, for it was she who stirred hostility toward me in these emotionally disturbed and violent inmates. Although I knew my students were very fond of me, I also knew that because of their mental health issues, they could very easily be manipulated, and I became increasingly concerned her actions would cause them to turn against me, or worse.

In addition to the letter from Craig and the one I had written for Bell, in all, I discovered nearly one dozen documents Glass, Sims, Student A and Former Student C had created, and most were labeled **"CONFIDENTIAL."** Apparently, they were so confidential, even I was not aware they existed until the discovery phase of my litigation against the Board, which by this time was several years later. I frequently had exercised my right to review the contents of my personnel file during my employment and the initial stages of my lawsuit, and I never had seen any of those documents in it. Obviously, a file with my name on it was being maintained in the Board's Employee and Labor Relations Department, as all of the documents were related to the Pre-Discipline and appeal hearings initiated by Glass' false misconduct charges against me in 2007-2008, and that department oversaw those processes.

We worked in a jail, not a typical Chicago Board of Education school, of course, and according to CCDOC, our students were inmates first, and then they were students. Shortly before I left York, another correctional officer had spoken with me about the statement Glass solicited and received from Student A on December 30, 2007, a non-school day, and from Former Student C, who no longer attended York Alternative High School when all of the commotion was occurring. The officer specifically told me "Glass' actions in taking hostile statements from inmates, particularly from a non-York Alternative High School student, and using those statements against a teacher or anyone else, was strictly against the CCDOC's policies."

Meanwhile, because I was a consultant, my paychecks were not always timely, and several weeks often passed before I received any money at all. By this time, I had been laid off from my job for nearly one year, and like anyone else, I needed my pay. My bills were piling up, and I could barely afford the basic life's necessities. I pounded the steering wheel of my car in frustration one evening as I drove home from one of the colleges empty handed because my paycheck was a full month late—again. To this day, I still think of that incident, and each time I drive down the street on which the college is located, I remember how stressed I was at that time.

My lawsuit against Captain Harrison and the CCDOC was settled in early April 2010. While reviewing documents at my attorney's office one day, I discovered the CCDOC had communicated with the Board's attorney, Sunil Kumar, to retrieve my personnel file during my lawsuit against Harrison and the CCDOC. After the CCDOC investigator and attorney assigned to the case conducted their initial investigations, it appeared there was minimal communication between the CCDOC and the Board, and no depositions were held during the two-year lawsuit.

Although my attorney had advised me to include CCDOC officials, and I did not object to her advice, I had no issues with the CCDOC's other officers or the administrative and executive staffs. They treated me respectfully and were protective and supportive of me during the entire six-year period I worked at York Alternative High School. My issue was with Harrison and only with Harrison. However, because she was their "agent," my attorney determined it was necessary to include CCDOC officials in my lawsuit, which to this day, I regret I had to do.

The Board's attorneys, Sabrina Haake and Jennifer Wu, took my deposition in relation to my first lawsuit on May 21, 2010, and there was nothing remarkable about the nearly six-hours of pre-trail discovery. May also was the final month of my contract jobs with the two colleges. Initially, there was a possibility of me acquiring full-time employment with one of the colleges once my contract ended; however, the department head was unable to get the position funded. Therefore, it did not materialize.

Once again, I started receiving unemployment benefits and submitting dozens of résumés. I received very few responses. When I was fortunate enough to be called for an interview and the company, organization, or school district conducted a background investigation, once they received the results, they lost interest in me. I had no criminal background. Therefore, when this continued to happen, I became convinced the Board was blackballing me and preventing me from getting another job because of my lawsuits against the school district and CCDOC.

June 2010

In June 2010, my attorney asked the Board to provide him information describing any work performance deficiencies I had during the period I worked in the PDU. In plain and concise statements and using consecutively numbered paragraphs, the Board and Rivera were required to present their "nondiscriminatory justifications" for circumventing my rehiring and instead rehiring Glowacki. They articulated allegations which encompassed the use of all twenty-six letters in the alphabet, and they used the "kitchen sink" approach to do it. That is, they accused me of every work deficiency and act of misconduct imaginable (and unimaginable), including, but not limited to the following:

a) lack of collaboration with my peers
b) lack of borderline knowledge of the National Board Certification program
c) failure to follow-up on and follow-through with work assignments
d) deficient computer skills
e) deficient writing skills
f) deficient skills with data analysis

g) sleeping on the job
h) chronic tardiness
i) chronic absenteeism
j) lack of flexibility
k) inability to provide answers to others regarding program logistical matters, operational functions, and how things functioned
l) disengaged and withdrawn from working
m) failure to volunteer for special projects
n) failure to take professional initiative
o) inability to learn fast enough
p) inferior ability to sell the NBC program
q) inferior ability to recruit new National Board and Golden Teacher program candidates
r) inferior ability to establish and build relationships
s) inferior ability to establish rapport with internal and external constituents
t) poor communication and interpersonal skills
u) lack of program knowledge regarding other PDU programs
v) lack of willingness to learn more about the departmental programs
w) I was lethargic
x) I was aggressive
y) I was angry
z) Because I had taught at what the Board called a "Prison School," which was among the 1% of Chicago Public Schools, meaning Consuella B. York Alternative High School, and Glowacki had taught at a "regular" school, she allegedly was better qualified for the position.

By "inferior ability," the Board was alleging my skills were inferior to Glowacki's in that specific regard. Despite the Board's laundry list of complaints, I had never been written up, disciplined, or warned at any time about my so-called poor performance, behavior, or misconduct.

In relation to Rivera and the Board's purported "Prison School non-discriminatory justification," someone from the "Prison School environment would be less familiar with general Board practices regarding the PDU's programs." The Board's attorneys also claimed I "had no knowledge of any of the PDU programs except NBC." However, I had filed with my summary judgment information proof that I had served as a Golden Teacher mentor for three years while I worked at York, and Golden Teacher was, of course, a PDU program.

Rivera was aware of my experience with the Golden Teacher program because I had indicated it on my résumé which she perused before she interviewed me. We also discussed it during my job interview. Moreover, Rivera and the Board pretended it did not matter that even before I taught at York Alternative High School, I also had taught for five years at Lincoln Park High School, which is a "regular" CPS school. This fact alone ensured I knew about the PDU's other programs.

Rivera also claimed she considered Glowacki's teaching experience "more valuable" than mine because of my "Prison School" teaching history. She apparently perceived my commitment to serving a diverse student population as having less value than Glowacki's simply because the students I served during a period I taught at CPS were incarcerated. Rivera's intent was to convey to the court Glowacki was somehow superior to me because my incarcerated students were somehow inferior to Glowacki's non-incarcerated students.

As a former teacher and administrator in one of America's largest public school districts, which is charged with providing equal educational opportunities to *all* of its students, apparently, Rivera was suggesting that non-incarcerated CPS students had greater value than those who were incarcerated. That in and of itself was discriminatory, as both groups were CPS students. Moreover, because most of the inmates incarcerated in the Cook County Jail are black and Hispanic, including my former students, I suspected this added to her discriminatory rationale, even though she also is Hispanic.

My teaching experience at the "Prison School" (York Alternative High School), obviously did not trouble Rivera when she interviewed me, because she hired me immediately afterward. In fact, Rivera testified during her deposition that my high school teaching experience was "of interest" to her and the PDU when she hired me, and she never expressed any reservations about my teaching experience at York Alternative High School either before or after she hired me.

Thus, Rivera and the Board turned that positive attribute into a negative one for me, and their "non-discriminatory justification" regarding this issue was nothing but a smokescreen they were using to attempt to cover up that they had violated state and federal anti-discrimination laws by blatantly discriminating against me.

The evidence Rivera and the Board filed in court to support their claims against me? My deposition, the depositions of Anderson, Rivera, Cushing, and McDonagh, a PDU organizational chart, and Part III of the Board's Employee Discipline and Due Process Policy. That was it; they filed nothing else. They filed nothing else because they had nothing else to file, and they had nothing else to file because their allegations about me were fabricated. They made them up. All of them. During the depositions of Cushing, McDonagh, and Rivera, my attorney repeatedly requested supporting documentation to substantiate the Board's claims about me, and a combined total of 46 times, (yes, I counted them), they stated they did not have a single document to corroborate their testimony and "non-discriminatory justifications" for Rivera preventing me from being reinstated to my former position and instead, influencing Alan Anderson to reinstate Glowacki.

July 2010

Exactly 392 days after I sent my letter to Huberman, Scott, Eason-Watkins, and Runcie, in which I wrote the Board had violated my civil rights, I received a phone call from the Board's equal employment compliance officer who informed me she was following up with the letter. She asked me if I still wanted the Board to "investigate my charge of discrimination." I asked her why she was calling more than one year after I had complained to the four Board officials, and she gave me a vague answer which I do not recall. I also asked her if she realized I had filed a charge of discrimination with the US EEOC and subsequently, a lawsuit. Without admitting or denying either, she stated she still would investigate my charges if I wished, but I refused her offer.

Meanwhile, thirteen months after my layoff, I was still unemployed, and the "Unsatisfactory" performance evaluation remained in my personnel file. My savings were becoming more and more depleted, and I was becoming more and more stressed out. In July 2010, I was unable to afford the cost of travelling to Atlanta for my niece's wedding. Although friends and family members offered to pay for the trip, I refused their offers because I knew if I still had no job in the months ahead, I would need their help in order to survive. Never, ever in my wildest dreams could I even have begun to imagine that those months would turn into far too many years.

I had nothing but time on my hands, so I continued to assist my attorney with the discovery phase of my lawsuit. I also began to study the case laws relevant to my case, specifically Title VII and Section 1983. Other than a business law and journalism law class I had taken in undergraduate and graduate school respectively, I had no formal legal training. However, I had served as a legal assistant for many years prior to becoming a teacher and frequently during summer break when I taught at Lincoln Park High School. Therefore, I was somewhat familiar with the legal jargon associated with my case. I always had found law interesting and fascinating, so I spent hundreds of hours reading numerous Title VII and Section 1983 cases which were pending or had been decided in various US district courts and courts of appeals.

Eleven witnesses were deposed in my case. The Board conducted five depositions, including mine, and my attorney deposed the remaining seven deponents. I wrote the questions he asked of every person he deposed and attended most of the depositions. On July 21, 2010, the Board's attorneys deposed two of my former PDU colleagues and Tonika Terrell, founder and former director of the National Board Resource Center. Although Terrell, a black woman, had secured grant funding of more than $1 million to launch the resource center several years prior to my employment with the PDU, during the PDU's 2006 layoff, she was included in the group of those who were laid off, and Rivera was the director at that time.

Near the end of July, I stopped by the home of my good friend and former PDU colleague, Juanita Jones. She also had been laid off during the June 2009 layoffs and was replaced in her position with a white female who had been hired in the PDU near the time Glowacki was hired. Anderson had claimed in his declaration the person who replaced Jones had more knowledge about NBC than me, even though she was not a teacher. I noticed how unhappy Juanita looked, and I asked her what was wrong. "Depressed," she said. "I can't hang on any longer; I'm going to have to move back home to Springfield." Jones had served as the Training and School Support Department's administrative assistant, and we had bonded and supported each other after we were laid off. As much as I hated to hear she was leaving Chicago, I knew she had made the right decision, for she also had been unable to find another job.

August 2010

One day in early August while reviewing documents my attorney had received during discovery, I came across Glowacki's Salary Information Form. I was shocked that her annual salary in the PDU had exceeded mine by almost seven thousand dollars, even though both of us were curriculum facilitators and had been employed by CPS for the same length of time. Up until that point, I thought one of the Board's defenses in my case would be Glowacki's salary had been less than mine, and because the stated reason for the PDU's 2009 layoffs was budget cuts, laying me off instead of her would have made good business sense. Illogically, however, Glowacki assumed my former position earning far more than I had, and she continued earning the same higher salary once she was reinstated. Consequently, the Board had no defense at all in this regard.

    I also noticed something else regarding the Salary Information Form. Although Glowacki and I were hired as curriculum facilitators at a salary band (pay scale) of 06, the Salary Recommendation Form which had Rivera's signature, but contained the initials *"LM"* next to it, showed Glowacki's title as "teacher training specialist" with a Salary Band of 07, which was a higher salary band than the curriculum facilitator's. All accompanying paperwork showed the correct title of Glowacki's position. Someone in the PDU had submitted Glowacki's Salary Recommendation Form to the Board's Salary Administration Department for approval at the higher salary band. Once the position was staffed at the higher salary, all additional paperwork reflected her correct job title as curriculum facilitator.

Thus, in a school district which was struggling mightily and thousands of employees were losing their jobs, someone had hired Glowacki under the salary band guise of teacher training specialist. Therefore, the entire time she was staffed in that position, she received a higher salary than the position for which she was hired, curriculum facilitator, allowed. At no time when I worked in the PDU had the Board advertised a teacher training specialist position. In fact, there was no such position in the PDU at all during the period I worked there.

Later that month, at my insistence, my lawyer brought this matter to the attention of the Board's two attorneys who were assigned to the case. In a Request for Production of Documents which I created, the attorneys were asked to submit evidence that a teacher training specialist position had been posted and Glowacki had applied for it as required by the Board's Human Resources Department. The attorneys objected to the request, denied such a position ever existed or Glowacki had applied for it, and they did not produce a single related document to my attorney because, of course, no relevant documentation existed.

Also in August, I asked my attorney to request my email correspondence for the entire one-year period I had worked in the PDU. I told him I believed the emails would be helpful to us. That was an understatement. I couldn't believe how many emails I had sent and/or received between June 2008 and June 2009. It took me several hours each day for nearly one week to print what ultimately ended up being thousands of emails I had exchanged with my PDU colleagues and internal and external constituents. I had attached work documents to most of the emails, and I break down the categories and explain in chapter 12 the very critical role they ultimately played in proving the Board's "non-discriminatory" justifications for laying me off and re-hiring Glowacki instead of me was pretext for discrimination. In other words, they were outright lies.

September—October 2010

My attorney deposed former CPS Human Capital chief, Alan Anderson, on September 1, 2010. Although other PDU employees were laid off, one position remained unfilled following the layoffs. (You might recall when Rivera held the June 17, 2009 meeting to announce the layoffs, without identifying who the person would or might be, she told the staff one person would be reinstated after the layoff.) Details which emerged during Anderson's deposition revealed the unfilled position was with the National Board Resource Center, so the person retained would have been either Glowacki or me.

Since I had been employed in the PDU longer than Glowacki, and my credentials were distinctly superior to hers, one might have expected Glowacki to be laid off rather than me unless evidence showed Glowacki was the better performer. But it was Glowacki who was called to return to work. Thus, Sherfinski and Glowacki were retained, and I was not even considered for retention of a job in which I already had served for one year.

During his deposition, Anderson, who is black, discussed his written declaration to the EEOC which I mentioned in chapter 10, wherein he stated he retained Glowacki because she had "previously supported" and was "knowledgeable in the National Board Certification program," whereas I "was not supporting" and "was not as knowledgeable in the National Board Certification program." Actually, I had been hired in the PDU seven months before Glowacki and achieved National Board Certification one year before she did.

Anderson had been misled. He testified he had discussed layoffs with Rivera, and he "specifically asked her for the names of those who supported National Board Certification" so he could make an informed decision about whom he should reinstate following the layoffs. Rivera did not tell him I also had supported the program. In fact, she did not tell him I existed. Instead, without mentioning anything about me or my credentials, Rivera gave Anderson only Glowacki's name. Thereafter, he reinstated Glowacki based solely on the information Rivera had provided him.

Anderson also testified he had never met me and knew nothing about me until the day of his deposition. He made clear that had he known I existed and had achieved NBC a full year before Glowacki, "it would have been useful information" in determining who would have been rehired. He stated that had he known I had in my possession hundreds of emails which showed I was supporting the work of NBC at the time of my layoff, he "absolutely" would have considered that information in determining who he would have laid off. Anderson said that such information would have come from [then] PDU director, Amanda Rivera. He also conceded the declaration submitted to the EEOC had been prepared by the Board's counsel, Jennifer Wu. Although he stated and signed under penalty of perjury that he had personal knowledge of what was written in the declaration, in truth, it was based not on his knowledge, but on information Rivera provided.

Anderson, who no longer worked for the Board at the time of his deposition, had been used as a tool of Rivera's deception. A "cat's paw" is what the court system calls it. Anderson based his decision to rehire Glowacki rather than me despite my greater seniority and superior credentials solely on what Rivera told him. Because Rivera did not mention me when he asked for the names of those who had supported NBC, he had no one other than Glowacki to consider for retention, which automatically prevented me from being rehired.

One might surmise that because both Anderson and I are black, Rivera assumed that had he known about me, he would have rehired me rather than Glowacki. In truth, there was no good reason for Anderson not to rehire me since I was performing the duties related to NBC and Glowacki was primarily performing work related to the Golden Teacher program at the time of our layoffs. Moreover, Rivera had absolutely no evidence which proved I was not performing my job and/or Glowacki was performing the work of NBC better than I was.

Immediately after Anderson's specific testimony in this regard, my attorney called for a break. I was sitting next to him, and he somehow sensed this new information had knocked the wind out of me. It certainly had; I couldn't believe Rivera had used such deceit to prevent Anderson from rehiring me and even to ensure he did not know I existed. My attorney and I walked out of the deposition room, proceeded down the hallway, and entered his office. He shut the door, motioned for me to sit in a chair, and without saying one word, he leaned down until we were facing each other.

He stared wide-eyed at me as if to say, "Can you believe what Anderson just said?" I was ecstatic, for I thought this critical information certainly would end the lawsuit which had proceeded for nine months by that time. "Nope. Not a chance. Now, they'll just try to dig up something else negative about you; just watch," my attorney responded when I asked him if he thought Anderson's testimony would cause the Board to settle my lawsuit. You will see he was absolutely correct.

My attorney deposed Rivera, my former managers, Lily McDonagh and Karen Cushing, and my former colleague Glowacki in September 2010. He took Sherfinski's in October 2010. I was present during the depositions of Rivera, McDonagh, Sherfinski, and Glowacki. I did not attend Cushing's deposition. Because of my previous experience working in the legal arena, I was aware of the seriousness of lying under oath, particularly during depositions, so I was stunned and listened in amazement at the testimonies of Rivera and Sherfinski. Throughout their depositions, each continuously provided false, inconsistent, incoherent, and implausible statements. They became so caught up in their perjured testimony and there was so much perjury, they frequently contradicted their own and each other's testimony.

When I read Cushing's deposition several weeks after her testimony I noticed she also had committed perjury, but to a lesser extent than Rivera and Sherfinski. She testified she evaluated me before the layoff and gave me a written performance evaluation which showed I "partially met" the expectations of my job. In what simply became two "dog ate my homework" stories by Cushing and Rivera, Cushing stated that immediately prior to leaving the PDU following her layoff, she put my performance evaluation and those of her other staff members into a dumpster and they were shredded. She also testified that she evaluated Glowacki, and her performance evaluation was superior to mine.

Rivera testified that although she couldn't "recall" whether or not she ever saw Glowacki's performance evaluation, but she was "sure" one had been created for her. She also claimed that following her layoff, she left my performance evaluation and those of other PDU employees in a desk drawer in her office, and she did not know what happened to them thereafter.

A reasonable-minded judge or jury was supposed to believe that these two veteran human resources professionals had made "executive decisions" to destroy the performance evaluations of their entire staff. The purported performance evaluations were not destroyed; they did not exist. Cushing and Rivera were lying under oath—through their teeth! At no time during my tenure with the PDU did I receive a written performance evaluation from Cushing or any other manager. In fact, performance evaluations for the period in question were not produced for a single employee in the PDU's department of Training and School Support, which was the unit in which Sherfinski, Glowacki, I, and several others had worked. Rivera and Cushing did not and could not produce performance evaluations for *any* employee because they simply did not exist, and they never had existed.

Later during the lawsuit, the Board's attorney, Sabrina Haake, backed away from Rivera's and Cushing's fairy tales regarding my fantasy performance evaluation, and instead, she began to suggest that I had received a performance evaluation which was "not in writing." Haake also claimed I admitted during my deposition that Cushing had given me a performance evaluation. I made no such admission. I merely stated Cushing claimed she was in the process of creating performance evaluations for her staff; therefore, there might have been a "draft or a page" of the performance evaluation in my emails or hers.

My rationale for stating this during my deposition was, although I did not recall seeing any such document, I did not want to lie under oath. The Board had possession of Cushing's emails and mine because that was our primary method of disseminating information in the PDU. Therefore, had drafts or any other traces of my performance evaluation or those of any other former PDU employee existed, including Glowacki's, the Board would have been able to produce them during the discovery phase of the lawsuit. Moreover, Rivera and the Board learned of my EEOC Charge in July 2009 and responded to it via their Position Statement and Anderson's declaration on August 10, 2009. Rivera testified that she departed the PDU on August 17, 2009. If Rivera intentionally left my performance evaluation in her drawer after learning I had initiated litigation against the Board, she clearly engaged in spoliation or the destroying of evidence, which is illegal.

Continuing with my former managers' fabricated testimony, Rivera testified that "many emails were going back and forth" between her and Cushing concerning my alleged performance deficiencies. However, she failed to produce a single email throughout discovery concerning my so-called poor performance. She also claimed she believed "the Board erases emails after a year." My attorney asked for and received my emails in August 2010, which was fourteen months after my layoff. Thus, Rivera had no emails regarding my alleged poor work performance for the same reason she had no performance evaluation for me. Like the fantasy performance evaluation, emails regarding my so-called deficient work performance did not exist.

Also during her testimony, Rivera claimed I did not volunteer or take the initiative to perform special tasks or work on special projects, and I was not flexible to work after hours. She claimed it was Glowacki who was willing to work after hours. My attorney presented evidence of numerous instances during which I had worked late and on weekends, and Glowacki specifically testified during her own deposition that she did not generally work after her 4:30 p.m. quitting time.

What I found to be the most comical of Rivera's testimony was when she claimed others told her they had witnessed me sleeping once during a training meeting. When asked to identify the so-called witnesses, Rivera could not "remember" a single name, even though the "witnesses" were members of her own staff and had sat with her at her ten-seat table when I allegedly was snoozing during the meeting. Two of my former colleagues who sat with me during the relevant meeting testified that they never had seen me sleeping while at work. Glowacki, who despite serving as a witness for the Board, testified she never had seen me sleeping on the job at *any* time.

Cushing testified extensively that she literally observed me sleeping during the same training meeting, and like Rivera, she claimed colleagues seated at her table saw me sleeping. When my attorney asked her to provide the names of her so-called witnesses so he could depose them, Cushing also could not "remember" who the witnesses were. Cushing then changed her story and testified that she could not tell for sure if I was asleep during the meeting. I never had heard of the sleeping story until I filed my lawsuit against Rivera, McDonagh, and the Board. Moreover, the Board has a very rigid discipline policy in place for those who sleep on the job, and I was never disciplined or received any type of warning because of my so-called sleeping incident.

To make it appear Glowacki supported NBC as frequently as I had, both Rivera and Cushing testified that there was "not much difference" in the amount of time Glowacki and I had served at the National Board Resource Center. However, as I previously stated, Sherfinski and I supported the work of the Golden Teacher and other PDU programs during the morning, and at noon on Mondays through Thursdays and sometimes on Fridays, we supported the work of the NBC program for the remainder of the day. Glowacki corroborated this during her deposition and also testified that she was hired specifically to support the Golden Teacher program and supported NBC only once a week for three hours.

Data I compiled during discovery showed the following until our final day of work before the June 2009 layoffs:

- Sherfinski and I exchanged hundreds of emails regarding NBC, and neither of us copied Glowacki.
- Hundreds of emails were exchanged between Rivera, Cushing, McDonagh, Sherfinski, and me regarding NBC, and Glowacki was not copied on any of them.
- Hundreds of emails were exchanged between internal and external constituents and Sherfinski and me regarding NBC, and Glowacki was not copied on most of them.

Sherfinski, who lied significantly throughout her entire deposition, also claimed I supported the NBC program only once or twice a week at the resource center. That statement was false, and Sherfinski knew it was false. She frequently forgot what she previously had said and then contradicted her own testimony. For instance, when my attorney asked her questions concerning her knowledge of my writing skills, first she testified that I frequently created letters for teachers inviting them to engage in NBC. Then, she stated she did not know what the writing skills were of people who worked with her. Next, she testified she did not believe I ever wrote anything she saw, and she knew nothing about my writing skills. Finally, she testified that "Joyce is a fantastic writer." She stated she would ask me for input regarding writing-related projects because she knew I had strong writing skills, and Glowacki's writing skills were not as strong as mine. I watched her and listened in amazement to her lies as she testified under oath!

As it further related to my writing skills, Rivera testified that because she had to make a change to a press release I wrote on one occasion, my writing skills were deficient. Cushing testified that she had to edit my written work more often than she had to edit the work of other staff members, and I "needed guidance" on how to write for the NBC program. However, in a letter of recommendation she wrote for me, which I discuss in chapter 9, Cushing referenced twice my "writing talents" and also wrote that my "writing skills are an asset." Moreover, again, because of my strong writing skills, Rivera, Cushing, and McDonagh frequently asked me to write many of the articles and marketing material to publicize NBC and talking points for others, including [then] CEO Arne Duncan and other Board officials. This was corroborated by the deposition testimony of two of my former colleagues who worked with me at the National Board Resource Center before we reorganized in November 2008, and Cushing also included this specific fact as follows in the letter of recommendation she wrote for me: "She [Joyce] also wrote many of the articles publicizing the program and events."

Continuing with my three former managers' fantastic stories, Rivera and Cushing also testified that data and a chart created by management showed I was frequently tardy. According to Rivera, the chart contained no employees' names. At no time during the lawsuit did Rivera and Cushing produce either the data or the chart which contained no employees' names.

As it related to my interpersonal skills and collaboration with my coworkers, Rivera alleged that I did not engage much with staff, I isolated myself from my colleagues, I did not know their names, and I did not interact with them. My attorney produced numerous emails which I had exchanged with my former colleagues and internal and external constituents. The emails showed frequent collaboration on work projects, "thank you" and complimentary messages I received for something I had done for colleagues and others, and numerous messages in which both had expressed their appreciation for work I had performed to ensure the successful completion of the projects on which we had worked together. Rivera presented one fantastic excuse after another during her testimony for my obvious collegiality and collaboration with my former co-workers and others.

Cushing claimed I was "pretty withdrawn from working with others," I "stepped back and tried not to get involved," and I had "poor interpersonal skills." She did not produce a shred of evidence to support her self-serving testimony.

McDonagh claimed I constantly bickered with my co-workers, but they strongly refuted her allegation and she later changed her testimony and stated there was no bickering. McDonagh further testified she received numerous complaints about me from each of my former co-workers. However, they emphatically denied ever complaining to McDonagh about me, and during their individual deposition, each strongly discredited Rivera's, Cushing's, and McDonagh's claims regarding my lack of collaboration.

McDonagh also described me as "disengaged," "lethargic," and "angry." I am unable to comprehend how I could have been "lethargic" if I presented myself as "angry." Also, the hundreds of emails and their attached work products which I presented during discovery certainly did not depict a "disengaged," "lethargic," or "angry" employee. McDonagh's testimony obviously was a contrived attempt to portray me as an "Angry Black Woman," a long-perpetuated, pervasive stereotype, which suggests that anger is an inherent, cultural trait of, is most commonly associated with, and is one of the most ubiquitous beliefs other racial groups (and some black people) have about American black women. Other than my race by association, McDonagh presented nothing which supported her rationale for labeling me with these highly offensive and racist stereotypes.

In another of the defendants' fantastic, implausible, and contradictory stories, the Board claimed Rivera had knowledge of my alleged lack of follow-through with work assignments. Yet, Rivera testified it was Cushing, and not she, who had knowledge of my alleged follow-through on work assignments. Cushing did not testify that I had any such lack of follow-up, and she never produced anything in writing regarding this issue. More important, what was missing were contemporaneous personnel records of discipline, lack of follow-through, poor performance, lack of collaboration, and other work-related deficiencies one would reasonably expect if an employee had poor performance.

The bottom line was this: Rivera, Cushing, and McDonagh failed to substantiate even a single claim they made regarding my so-called workplace deficiencies. These entirely uncorroborated attacks on my job performance were nothing but after-the-fact inspirations triggered by their need to fend off the lawsuit I had filed against Rivera, McDonagh, and the Board.

When my attorney briefly stepped out of the room during Rivera's deposition, Sabrina Haake, the Board's counsel, stood, put her hands on her hips, and without looking at me, she said, "I *wish* we could find something on her! I *wish* we could!" "Her" clearly was me, and as she spoke, Rivera also stood up and with wide eyes, she placed her hands on both sides of her face and looked around the room as if she hoped to find *anything* that would help her and the Board prove their sweeping allegations against me. The court reporter and I stared at Rivera, her attorney, and each other in amazement. Haake also implied I had stolen my performance evaluation from my personnel file in the Board's records department even though she knew it did not exist and never had existed.

With the exception of Glowacki's statement that I was not a team player, her testimony was consistent with what actually had occurred during our PDU tenure. Glowacki and I had worked together on at least one project, and because she only worked with Sherfinski and me once a week for three hours, she knew nothing about the work I was doing and my work relationship with others. Her testimony in this regard appeared rehearsed and simply echoed the depositions of my three managers.

Obviously, Rivera and the Board had not expected me to file a lawsuit against them, as they were unprepared to defend themselves. They had good reason not to expect me to initiate litigation against them. I had no job and no money, and these circumstances alone would have stopped most people in their tracks from filing a lawsuit, particularly when the opposing organization is as large as and has as much clout as the Board. I was shocked to see Rivera and the high and mighty Chicago Board of Education's lawyers so woefully unprepared and looking so amateurish as they tried to defend the school district and themselves against a black woman who had no job, no legal training and no money. Had my entire lawsuit proceedings not been so stressful, traumatic and outrageous, their ineptness and the multitude of lies they told to cover up their illegal discrimination of me would have been hilarious.

The Board also had lots of taxpayer money including my limited income with which to fight me. But I did not care about the Board's size, their clout, *or* the taxpayers' money they had at their disposal. The Board had seized my livelihood and had discriminated against me in the process. I cared about justice, I was ready to fight until it was served, and I was not going to let their size, their lies, their clout, or their money stop me.

In what ultimately was a critical issue during the lawsuit, Glowacki testified that when she arrived home on the day of the layoff, she had received an email from Rivera's assistant in which she was asked to meet privately with Rivera the following morning. She further testified that during the meeting, Rivera told her to "take a few days off," and she believed Glowacki would be "coming back," meaning she would be reinstated. Within one week of our layoffs, Glowacki was rehired and began working with Sherfinski in the National Board Resource Center. Shortly thereafter, the only Hispanic who had been laid off also was rehired. Cushing, who is white, landed a new position in another Board headquarters department, and Rivera was hired as assistant principal at a CPS elementary school.

In late September, my good friend and former PDU colleague, Juanita Jones, moved back home to Springfield. It was a sad day for both of us. She told me later she cried the entire time she drove to Springfield, and I cried the entire day on which she left. Although Springfield is just a few hours' drive from Chicago, it felt as if she had moved to the other side of the world. Juanita was able to get a job fairly quickly after returning to her hometown, and we still communicate quite frequently.

In October 2010, I learned of a job opportunity with a Supplemental Educational Services provider for an instructor to provide training to CPS teachers who would be teaching reading and math to small groups of students during after-school hours. The term "Supplemental Educational Services" refers to free extra academic help, such as tutoring or remedial help which usually is provided to students in literacy and math. This extra help can be provided before or after school, on weekends, or during the summer. According to the US Department of Education, Supplemental Educational Services allow low-income families to enroll their child in such a program if the child attends a Title I school which typically has been designated by their state to be in need of improvement for more than one year. (Title 1 schools have high numbers or high percentages of students from low-income families.) I applied for the position and was hired soon thereafter. The pay was decent and it was a great job, but unfortunately, I was scheduled to work only once a week during a four-week period. Therefore, I basically remained unemployed.

I also applied for the position of Senior Educational Consultant with a nationally recognized nonprofit education research and consulting organization. Based in Naperville, Illinois, the organization is a Chicago Board of Education vendor which, at that point, had received millions of dollars in contracts to provide the Board an array of professional services primarily geared to improving teaching and learning. I wanted the position very badly. It was a dream job which required candidates to (a) have extensive teaching experience, (b) hold an advanced degree, (c) be a National Board Certified Teacher, and (d) have other education-related credentials. I met every job requirement.

Shortly after I applied for the position, the organization's human resources assistant called and scheduled me for a phone interview with the human resources chief. It was an excellent interview, and I was scheduled for another phone interview with the director and manager of the department in which I would be working. Following the second phone interview, the human resources assistant asked me to sign a background check form, which I did. I waited nervously for one week and then another to hear from the organization. I had endured this horrible routine numerous times since my layoff, and I had a sick, sinking feeling in my stomach with every passing day I did not hear from the human resources assistant to let me know the status of my job candidacy.

After waiting two weeks, I called the human resources assistant and left a voicemail message asking her to return my call at her convenience and inform me if I was still being considered for the position. She did not immediately return my call, and after I attempted a few more times to reach her, she finally answered her phone. I noticed she was not as enthusiastic as she previously had been, and in a short, curt tone, she told me I should "continue to look for other employment."

As usual, only after conducting a background check of my past employment did the educational institution decide not to hire me. This had happened to me so many times since my layoff I had lost count. Since I had no criminal record, that was not what was keeping employers from hiring me. My friends began telling me what they privately had said to themselves and each other: "The Board is blackballing you." But they were telling me nothing I did not already suspect. By this time, I had been unemployed for most of the sixteen months since my layoff, and with the exception of unemployment benefits, which the government had extended for a maximum of twelve additional months, I had no other income.

During a routine doctor's visit, my physician raised her eyebrows and expressed concern about my very high blood pressure. "What's going on with you?" she asked me. I shared with her the stress I was experiencing due to my continued unemployment and lawsuit. She warned me that my blood pressure was almost at a level that could cause me to have a stroke. In fact, it was at such an elevated level during my visit she refused to allow me to leave the medical center until I no longer was in the danger zone, which was several hours later. I still received COBRA health benefits, so I decided to seek the help of a mental health therapist because I was severely depressed. After receiving a referral from the Board's Employee Benefits Department, I began seeing on a weekly basis a veteran social worker who had her own practice.

NOVEMBER 2010

On November 19, 2010, my attorney sent a letter to the Board's general counsel, Patrick Rocks, and senior assistant general counsel, James Ciesel, whose names had appeared repeatedly in my matters regarding Glass and the CCDOC. In relation to the deplorable manner in which Glass and the Board had treated me while I worked at York Alternative High School, my attorney expressed concern in his letter that (a) eight months after the Settlement Agreement between Chicago Teachers Union and the Board had passed, the "Unsatisfactory" performance evaluation still remained in my personnel file; (b) the Board failed to conduct an investigation into the allegations of Glass and Harrison that I had mistreated and "terrorized" students; (c) Glass had placed documents related to the poor performance of another teacher in my personnel file; and (d) Glass had enlisted teachers and student inmates (in violation of the CCDOC's General Orders), to write letters containing negative information about me, which she ultimately used to discipline me. My attorney demanded the Board do the following:

1) Remove the Warning Resolution which contained my name from its website;
2) Cease and desist from violating its own Grievance Settlement Agreement with the Chicago Teachers Union by failing to remove the "Unsatisfactory" performance evaluation from my personnel file;
3) Purge all information related to the CCDOC matter from my personnel file; and
4) Rescind the discipline imposed upon me regarding Glass' false allegations.

December 2010

In a December 2, 2010 responsive letter, Ciesel "respectfully" rejected the "demands set forth in [my attorney's] correspondence." In other words, according to Ciesel, the Warning Resolution would remain on the Board's website. Ciesel also claimed documents referencing another teacher's performance were not contained in my personnel file. He was right, because I frequently had reviewed the contents of my personnel file and the documents were not in it. The Board had produced the documents to my attorney during the discovery phase of my lawsuit, so obviously, they were contained in a file with my name on it *somewhere*. I later determined the file was retained in the Board's Employee and Labor Relations Department.

The following statements I have underlined, which Ciesel wrote in his letter, disturbed me most: "<u>The Board does not conduct investigations regarding every allegation of misconduct by its employees, for it does not have sufficient resources to do so</u>. Thus, the fact that the Board did not formally investigate this case but instead <u>relied upon eyewitness accounts from Sheriff personnel and York Alternative administrators</u> is more than sufficient to substantiate the claims against Ms. Hutchens."

Harrison had accused me of "terrorizing students on a daily basis," and the Board disciplined me severely because of her allegations. By his response, Ciesel implied that "terrorizing" students, particularly psychologically challenged predominantly minority students, was not serious enough to warrant an investigation, simply because the Board did not have "sufficient resources." Yet, it was serious enough for the Board to give me a Warning Resolution which even today remains on the Internet for the entire world to see, and it was serious enough to besmirch my name and reputation and ultimately destroy my teaching career.

Glass claimed she relied on information from Harrison to substantiate charges against me. She *never* stated in anything she wrote that she had been an "eyewitness" to any allegation Harrison or Student A had brought against me. Ciesel's statement in this regard was patently false. He also wrote that he observed the "Unsatisfactory" evaluation was still in my personnel file, and thanked my attorney for "bringing this oversight to the Board's attention."

Although my attorney had attached to his letter to Ciesel and Rocks the memos Glass had instructed John Bell and Donna Craig to write about me under the guise of using them to mentor her principal mentee, Ciesel did not address that issue in his response. He also did not respond to my attorney's other claim that in violation of the CCDOC's General Orders regarding accessibility and contact with inmates, Glass had instructed students to write negative letters about me which she used to discipline me.

Shortly after my attorney sent his letter to Rocks and Ciesel, the Board finally removed the "Unsatisfactory" performance evaluation from my personnel file, but the damage already had been done. The evaluation had been in my file for seventeen months by that time, and should have been removed eight months earlier when the Board and the Chicago Teachers Union reached the agreement to reverse it. Until it was removed, it was accessible to principals and administrators to whom I had submitted résumés following my layoff. Therefore, it certainly was possible that because the Board had failed to remove the "Unsatisfactory" performance evaluation from my personnel file, I had been denied numerous positions within CPS following my layoff.

Following a disagreement with my attorney in mid-December 2010, he sent me an email on December 20, 2010, informing me he was withdrawing from my case. He also stated he had sent a notice of motion to me with a court date of December 23, 2010, for the withdrawal hearing. A motion is a formal (usually written) request of the court for a ruling. I had not received the notice because my attorney had sent it by US mail. He further stated in his message that because Judge Pallmayer was on vacation, there would be no court hearing on December 23, 2010; therefore, he would let me know the date of the new hearing. The following day, December 21, 2010, my attorney sent another email to me in which he explained he had "assumed there was no court" for Judge Pallmayer that day. He also wrote that earlier that day, he had checked and noticed his motion to withdraw hearing was listed on her calendar as originally scheduled, and it was the only order of business scheduled that day. Therefore, the withdrawal hearing would proceed.

My attorney and Haake, the Board's lawyer, attended the hearing, but I did not. Given the enormously daunting task of finding a lawyer to represent me when I had no job and no money, and summary judgment (which I discuss in the following chapter) was just a couple of months away, I spent most of Christmas Day in bed deeply depressed and curled up in a fetal position.

My attorney had done a good job with the depositions and worked hard on my case. I apologized to him for the dispute which led to his withdrawal and asked him to remain on my case. He did not bother to respond. But later, information I inadvertently discovered regarding a series of questionable occurrences that had transpired before and during his withdrawal hearing, which I discuss in the following chapter, convinced me his departure from my case was not a bad thing for me.

CHAPTER 12

09 C 7931 — Year Two

January 2011

I IMMEDIATELY BEGAN SEARCHING FOR a new attorney to represent me in my lawsuit. I contacted the Chicago Bar Association for a referral, and the organization provided me the name, among others, of one of Chicago's top employment law firms. I knew convincing attorneys at the firm to take my case when I had no money for a retainer's fee would be nearly impossible, but I reached out to them anyway. One of the firm's partners invited me to their law offices for a free consultation. Although he was polite, he made clear his firm neither accepted legal cases on a contingency basis, nor did they have to, for those who retained his firm could afford to pay for their services. He perused my case on the Public Access to Court Electronic Records (PACER) system, which is an electronic public access service that allows users to obtain case and docket information online from federal appellate, district, and bankruptcy courts and the PACER Case Locator. PACER is provided by the federal judiciary and is available to anyone who registers for an account.

After reviewing my case on PACER, the attorney gave me shocking news: Immediately prior to withdrawing, without my knowledge or permission, my former attorney had dismissed from my case defendant Lily McDonagh. The attorney appeared surprised that (1) Judge Pallmayer had allowed him to withdraw from my case without ensuring I had no objections to his withdrawal, and (2) she also had allowed my attorney to dismiss

McDonagh from my case as he withdrew without ensuring I approved of the dismissal.

I knew I had a major problem on my hands and would need the best legal representation I could get. I continued to try to persuade the attorney to take my case on a contingency basis, but I was unsuccessful. As we finished our conversation and I thanked him for his time, I asked him if he thought I should report to the Attorney Registration & Disciplinary Commission (ARDC) my attorney's unauthorized dismissal of McDonagh. "I don't even want to *begin* to go there," he responded. According to its website, as an administrative agency of the Illinois Supreme Court, the ARDC assists the court in regulating the legal profession through attorney registration, education, investigation, prosecution, and remedial action. The agency also investigates and disciplines attorneys for misconduct.

I saw pity in the attorney's eyes and on his face. I had no money, no lawyer, and I was alone in the fight of my life against my former employer, the powerful Chicago Board of Education. But despite my woes, I still had my pride, and I did not want him or anyone else to feel sorry for me. He walked with me and shook my hand as I prepared to leave. As I stepped inside the elevator, he made one final remark: "*I would*," he said, emphatically. I knew what he meant. He was responding to my question and saying to me, "I *would* report to the ARDC what your attorney did if I were you."

I left the attorney's office dismayed and livid! Not only had Fennerty withdrawn from my case, he also had dismissed a defendant from my case during the withdrawal hearing without my permission and without informing me he planned to do so. Nowhere in his motion to withdraw had he even hinted that he intended to dismiss McDonagh from my lawsuit. Although my attorney and I had discussed the likelihood of having to dismiss McDonagh because of information we acquired during several of the depositions, no final decision had been made regarding the dismissal. Moreover, his withdrawal from my case meant any action related to it was no longer his business. I found it suspicious that he would have cared one way or another about what occurred with my case since he was withdrawing.

I immediately purchased the transcript of the December 23, 2010 hearing from Judge Pallmayer's court reporter so I could find out exactly what had been said during the withdrawal hearing. Two specific conversations in the court reporter's transcript immediately caught my attention. One was between the Board's counsel, Sabrina Haake and Judge Pallmayer, and the other was between the judge and my former attorney, Fennerty. The following was taken directly from pages three and four of the court reporter's transcript:

> MS. HAAKE: Before Counsel is dismissed, can I just do one housekeeping issue?
> THE COURT: Sure.
> MS. HAAKE: Counsel and I had agreed after all the depositions were taken, there was no reason to keep individual defendant Lily McDonagh in the case because she wasn't the plaintiff''s supervisor. So, we reached agreement to dismiss her from the case in exchange for the Board's agreement not to proceed against her -- Miss Hutchens, for cost for defense of that suit. And Counsel still agrees to dismiss Lily McDonagh from the case, so I want to make that clear. And the dispositive motions will be only as to the remaining defendants.
> THE COURT: Any problem with that, Mr. Fennerty?
> MR. FENNERTY: No problem.
> THE COURT: Claims against Miss McDonagh are dismissed.
> Mr. Fennerty is granted leave to withdraw. Status is set for January 25th.

Haake had referred to dismissing a defendant from my case as a "housekeeping issue." More important, without asking my attorney if I agreed with McDonagh's dismissal and without directing me to come to court to ensure I approved of the dismissal, Judge Pallmayer simply dismissed McDonagh from my case after asking Fennerty four simple words: "Any problem with that?"

The following was taken directly from pages four and five of the court reporter's transcript:

MR FENNERTY: I'm sorry you had to come here today, Judge.
THE COURT: You know what? I was coming downtown anyway, not quite this early but, hey, it's good to get up and out.
MR. FENNERTY: Thank you. And all three of you have a nice holiday.
THE COURT: You too. All of you.

My attorney apologized to Judge Pallmayer because she *had* to come to court that day.

Although I had worked as a legal secretary for many years before becoming an educator, my work in law firms basically consisted of typing legal documents and performing other clerical duties. However, because I was proceeding *pro se,* (someone who files a civil case and proceeds in the case on his or her own behalf), if I wanted my lawsuit to continue, I would have to represent myself. At that time, I believed serving as my own attorney definitely was out of my league.

On January 10, 2011, my case was reassigned to Judge Edmond E. Chang. President Barack Obama had nominated and the US Senate had confirmed him for a federal judgeship in the US Northern District of Illinois Court one month earlier. I read everything I could find regarding his background and credentials. I noted the 1994 cum laude graduate of Northwestern University Law School and former federal prosecutor had an impressive employment history which included service at the Chicago headquarters office of a global law firm. He was only forty-years-old when President Obama appointed him to the federal court after the US Senate voted unanimously to confirm him for a vacant judicial seat—making him Illinois' first-ever Senate-approved Asian-American federal trial court judge.

I was born and raised in Chicago. I relocated twice and quickly returned to Chicago both times because I love my city; but I am realistic when during my travels people question me about Chicago's reputation for its infamous brand of politics and corruption. That reputation is not baseless. Given Judge Chang's youth, his new appointment to the federal bench, and his federal prosecutorial background, I was excited he was assuming jurisdiction over my lawsuit. I believed he could and would rise above Chicago's politics and be fair and impartial. That precisely was what I needed in my fight against the Board's Law Department which was heavily staffed with attorneys who previously had served in [then] Mayor Richard M. Daley's city hall Law Department, including general counsel, Patrick Rocks. To my knowledge, the Board's two attorneys assigned to my case at that time, Haake and Wu, were not among them.

In relation to Judge Pallmayer's dismissal of McDonagh from my case, I relied on three of my best skills—research, writing, and computer, to move forward. (Remember, Rivera and Cushing claimed during their depositions I had deficient writing and computer skills, even though I had served as a computer teacher at Lincoln Park and York High Schools.) It took less than fifteen minutes of research to determine I needed to have Judge Pallmayer's court order rescinded. To make that happen, I needed to file a motion to vacate dismissal order and reinstate McDonagh as a defendant in my case.

I found examples on the Internet of how to write this type of motion, and I began creating my own. Because of my legal secretarial experience, I knew how many copies I needed and how to file the motion in court. On January 14, 2011, I walked from my downtown residence to the federal court and filed the motion. I also faxed a copy to the Board's counsel, Haake. Less than twenty-four hours later, she called and left a voicemail message asking me not to reinstate McDonagh into my lawsuit. I did not bother to respond.

I continued to work hard to find a new attorney. Fortunately, I accomplished this task very quickly. I had read an article in the local newspaper about another CPS teacher who filed a discrimination lawsuit against the Board shortly after I filed mine, and the article included a quote from her attorney. I briefly researched the attorney, Deidre Baumann, of the Chicago law firm of Baumann & Shuldiner. Afterward, I contacted her via email, told her of my need for new counsel to represent me in my lawsuit, and after a few more email exchanges and an in-person meeting, she agreed to take my case.

She did not request a retainer's fee, and she did not make clear if she would be representing me on a pro bono (free legal services) or contingent fee basis. According to the American Bar Association, with a contingent fee arrangement, the lawyer agrees to accept a fixed percentage (often one third) of the recovery, which is the amount finally paid to the client. If the client wins the case, the lawyer's fee is deducted from the money awarded to the client. I assumed we would clarify those details later, but based on statements she had made, I was certain she wanted to be paid for her work.

Immediately after Baumann became my attorney, I contacted my former counsel's legal assistant and scheduled a date on which I could retrieve the boxes containing my lawsuit documents. I picked them up within a few days and brought most of them to Baumann's office. I also took home two of the boxes which contained information I wanted to review. While going through those boxes, I discovered a five-page Settlement Agreement and Release, which was related to McDonagh's unauthorized dismissal from my lawsuit. I never had seen this document, I did not authorize it, and I did not know it existed. The unsigned agreement had been prepared by the Board's counsel, Haake, apparently in conjunction with my former attorney who had not bothered to tell me about it.

Although I was not a lawyer and had no legal training, I knew a Settlement Agreement and Release should not have been created without my knowledge or permission. I showed it to my new attorney, Baumann, and her law partner, Paul Shuldiner. Both looked at it thoroughly, looked at each other, raised their eyebrows, and handed it back to me.

Because my attorneys had not filed attorney appearances in my case, I was required to continue proceeding *pro se* until they did. During an attorney appearance, an attorney appears in court and informs the judge he or she will be representing the plaintiff or defendant in a case. Once it is established that an attorney represents the person, the attorney may appear in court on behalf of the client on various legal matters without the client being present.

The hearing regarding my motion to vacate and reinstate Lily McDonagh was scheduled for January 25, 2011. Judge Chang was polite and appeared concerned Judge Pallmayer had allowed Fennerty to dismiss McDonagh as a defendant in my case as he withdrew. "So, I am inclined to reinstate the defendant...," Judge Chang stated during the hearing. Haake, the Board's counsel who attended the hearing, responded that there was "no good-faith basis for keeping McDonagh in the claim, which is why Judge Pallmayer dismissed her in the first place," Haake said. She also stated that prior to his withdrawal, she and Fennerty agreed to dismiss McDonagh from the lawsuit. Their agreement was made without my knowledge or input. Judge Chang responded as follows: "I appreciate that. But where a counsel and his client have irreconcilable differences, and then he makes a decision as important as dismissing out a defendant, I pause in enforcing that agreement." However, he warned me I could face court sanctions if I chose to keep McDonagh in my lawsuit without just cause.

Haake asked the judge for permission to speak privately with me, and although I did not want to hear anything she had to say, the judge directed me to speak with her. During our discussion which lasted approximately two minutes, she again asked me not to reinstate McDonagh. I let her know she was wasting my time and hers, so we returned to the courtroom to stand before the judge.

I reported to Judge Chang I had rejected Haake's request, and once again, he said he would reinstate McDonagh if that was my wish. I informed him I had retained a new attorney. He set a date for Baumann to file an appearance in the case, and we agreed McDonagh would not be reinstated until I spoke with Baumann and allowed her to decide if reinstating McDonagh into my lawsuit was necessary or appropriate. (The proper terminology is, he denied my motion without prejudice.) The hearing then concluded.

After we exited the courtroom, Haake approached me in the hallway and again asked me not to reinstate McDonagh into the lawsuit. I ignored her and walked away. I wondered why she was so adamant about dismissing McDonagh and not Rivera from my case. She claimed during our brief discussion it was because Rivera was one of my supervisors and McDonagh was not. (Although McDonagh had been my manager for a brief period while I worked in the PDU, she was not my manager when I was laid off.) But I doubted this was her only reason for wanting to keep McDonagh from being a defendant in the case.

Two days after the motion hearing, I spoke briefly with Baumann and Shuldiner about the reasons my former attorney thought it might be necessary to dismiss McDonagh from my case. The three of us concluded the discussion without reaching an answer as to whether or not McDonagh should be reinstated, and I assumed we would discuss the issue again later.

FEBRUARY—MARCH 2011

On February 8, 2011, Paul Shuldiner, who previously had filed with the court a notice of appearance, attended court on my behalf. I did not attend. He informed Judge Chang Baumann would be filing her formal appearance the following day, and we would not be reinstating McDonagh as a named defendant in my lawsuit. Although it was highly likely I would have agreed with his decision, I was surprised Shuldiner had taken this action without having a final discussion with me. During a conversation we had later, it appeared there simply had been miscommunication between us, and although I decided not to challenge his decision, throughout the remainder of the litigation, it was very unsettling to me McDonagh had been dismissed from my case without my final approval.

The following day, Baumann filed her formal appearance as the lead attorney in my case. Later that week, I provided the ARDC the Settlement Agreement and Release I had discovered and filed complaints related to the agreement and McDonagh's unauthorized dismissal against my initial attorney and the Board's counsel, Haake. In a responsive letter I received from the agency shortly thereafter, I learned the ARDC intended to investigate the matter, and at taxpayers' expense, Haake was being represented by a Chicago law firm which, for several years, had received lucrative contracts from the Board.

On February 15, 2011, the Board filed a motion for summary judgment, a procedural device used during civil litigation to quickly dispose of a case without a trial. By filing such a motion, the movant (the party filing the motion) is claiming all necessary factual issues are resolved or need not be tried because they are so one-sided. The movant also files admissions, exhibits, depositions, and affidavits (statements under oath) to support its motion. The party filing a summary judgment motion must show the absence of a disputed material fact. If this is shown, the burden of proof shifts to the opposing party who must show specific facts which present a genuine issue for trial.

Before issuing a decision on a summary judgment motion, the judge reviews (or is supposed to review) the evidence filed in court and grants summary judgment only when the movant shows there is no genuine dispute as to any material fact, and therefore is entitled to judgment as a matter of law. A genuine dispute as to a material fact exists if "the evidence is such that a reasonable jury could return a verdict for the nonmoving party." Although either party in a lawsuit may file for summary judgment, sometimes both parties do so.

Less than two weeks after I filed a complaint with the ARDC against Haake, Jennifer Wu, the Board's other counsel assigned to my lawsuit, resigned her position with the Board. Since I knew my case far better than my new attorneys, I discussed with them the most critical points and studied relevant documents and case law in order to assist them with preparing my response to the Board's motion for summary judgment which we had thirty days to file.

On Saturday, February 26, 2011, Paul Shuldiner and I worked for several hours on my response. He showed me how to properly respond to the Board's motion for summary judgment. Two days later, Shuldiner died in his sleep. I was shocked and saddened. Baumann, who had served as his law partner for many years, was devastated. Although she was the lead attorney on my case, it was Shuldiner who had worked closely with me, and after his death, I quickly discovered Baumann was not nearly as committed or as interested in my case as he had been. While I had empathy for her because she was grieving her long-time law partner, I also had reached a critical stage in my lawsuit, and there was much work which we still needed to do. But as time passed, I realized I was pretty much on my own, and the very thought of the future of my case terrified me.

Baumann requested and the judge granted her a thirty-day extension in which to file my response to the Board's motion for summary judgment, but she refused to work on my case. I waited patiently day after day and week after week for her to help me with writing the response, but for whatever reason, she would not do it. One day, I asked her if she was interested in my case, and although she claimed she was, the blank look on her face more than told the truth, and I couldn't understand why she had agreed to represent me in the first place.

About one month later, out of sheer frustration and fear I would not be able to file my response to the Board's motion for summary judgment on time—or at all, I sent her an email and told her she needed to communicate with me more often regarding my case. I also stated in the email she should let me know if she was not interested in representing me. "If you do not agree with the way I am handling the case, find another attorney," she responded. That stung. She knew I had no money to pay an attorney, and I had no choice other than to put up with her or proceed in my lawsuit without attorney representation.

I realized then that if I wanted to win my lawsuit, I could not depend on anything but a higher power and anyone but myself. Therefore, I continued to spend countless numbers of hours reading federal district court and appellate court cases and relevant case law. Since I had no job, I read day and night. On the frequent occasions when I would begin my research during evening hours, without intending to do so, I would see the following morning's light of dawn creeping through my blinds when I finally decided to rest for a brief period. I found the laws related to my complaints, particularly Title VII and Section 1983, interesting and fascinating, and I loved reading and learning about both.

My lawsuit consumed me. I worked hard day and night on my responses to the Board's and Rivera's Joint Local Rule 56.1(a)(3) statements and my own Statements of Fact. I became familiar with such phrases as prima facie case; protected class; similarly situated comparator; McDonnell Douglas; cat's paw; scintilla of evidence; pretext; burden of proof; burden of production; direct evidence; indirect evidence; after-the-fact justification; smoking gun; articulated non-discriminatory justification; fact finder; proffered reason; and burden shifting. Over time, I actually began to believe I knew as much about employment and civil rights law as any lawyer who practiced in this field, and I became confident I could win my lawsuit without the help of my attorney.

Although I worked tirelessly on my case, I knew I was disadvantaged. I was the plaintiff in a lawsuit in which the defendants, the Chicago Board of Education, had an entire law department comprised of legal teams who were assigned to specific cases. Most were seasoned attorneys who had nearly unlimited resources with which to fight plaintiffs who were suing the Board. I was forced to handle my case alone while enormously stressed over my continued unemployment; lack of money; inability to pay my bills; overeating; sleeplessness; an increase in illnesses; rapidly mounting debt; no health insurance; increasingly poor credit, and a myriad of other personal problems people experience when unemployed and there is no job on the horizon.

Many nights I worked to the point of exhaustion as I sat at my computer reading case law and applying it to my lawsuit while my attorney and the rest of the world were enjoying a good night's sleep. Despite the numerous résumés I submitted, I remained unemployed but continued to receive unemployment benefits, which thankfully, the federal government had again extended. But those benefits were scheduled to end in June 2011, which at that time was only a few months away.

Because I had attended most of the depositions, I knew the testimonies of my three managers and Sherfinski were largely perjured, and through my research, I learned that false reasons which hide the true intentions or motivations for a legal action in a discrimination lawsuit is considered by the court "pretext for discrimination," or a lie. A finder of fact in the trial of a lawsuit or criminal prosecution is the jury or judge (if there is no jury) who decides if facts have been proven.

The US Court of Appeals for the Seventh Circuit has ruled in numerous cases that when an employer gives one reason at the time of an adverse employment decision, and at trial gives another reason unsupported by documentary evidence, the jury could reasonably conclude the new reason was pretextual, after-the-fact justification. Although I was not on trial, I knew, without a doubt, my managers had provided false reasons for Rivera circumventing my rehiring, and because I was attempting to get to trial, the issue of pretext applied to my lawsuit.

I found the case law applicable to my lawsuit simply by Googling Title VII and Section 1983 cases which had been tried in various federal district and appeals courts. Given the enormous amount of fabricated testimony during the depositions of my three managers and Sherfinski, I knew I could show pretext for discrimination for virtually *every* complaint my three former mangers—Rivera, McDonagh and Cushing— had made about me, and the judge would deny Rivera's and the Board's motion for summary judgment (or so I thought he would). I spent weeks reviewing deposition transcripts to find their lies, and it was an easy task. I found so many lies I stopped trying to count them. Thereafter, I created pages and pages of documents containing those lies which I updated each time I discovered a new lie.

April—June 2011

After completing my responses to Rivera's and the Board's Joint Local Rule 56.1(a)(3) Statements of Fact, I created my own Statements of Additional Facts. A respondent to a summary judgment motion is allowed up to 40 separately-numbered Statements of Additional Facts. All material facts set forth in the statement by the moving party are deemed admitted unless controverted (denied or argued) by the opposing party. When I finished, I asked my attorney to proofread and edit what I had written to ensure I had fulfilled the court's requirement of creating "short, concise statements." I knew many of my statements were neither "short" nor "concise," and I also knew my work needed extensive editing. But my attorney refused to read what I had written.

I also created a memorandum in support of the motion, emailed it to her, and asked her to incorporate the relevant case law. She did not want to do that either, so she told me a memorandum was "not required," and we did not need it. I knew better. It might not have been required, but we needed to put our best foot forward and that meant including a supporting memorandum which explained my responses to Rivera's and the Board's Joint Local Rule 56.1(a)(3) Statements of Fact and my 40 separate Statements of Additional Facts.

I wrote all responses to Rivera's and the Board's summary judgment information, including their supporting memorandum, my 40 additional Statements of Fact and supporting memorandum. I only needed my attorney to incorporate the relevant case law into my memorandum, but she did not want to be bothered. Therefore, she did not incorporate the case law or file my memorandum. She also did not help me as I sifted through the many boxes of evidence my previous attorney and I had acquired during discovery.

As time passed, my attorney and I agreed for various reasons to dismiss Count I and Counts IV through VII of my lawsuit. Although my initial attorney had included those charges so the Board would have to spend time defending them, there was no basis for the age discrimination charge because Glowacki and I were close in age, and I also was an at-will employee who had no contract. Therefore, my attorney was certain, and I agreed, that I would not prevail on Counts I and VII. She also dismissed the retaliation and intentional infliction of emotional distress charges (Counts V and VI). As my lawsuit progressed and I understood my initial attorney's rationale for including those two counts, I became convinced she dismissed them simply because she did not want to spend her time on them, even though I was the one who wrote the brief. She did file my responses and exhibits (supporting evidence) via her court PACER account when I finished and everything was ready for court.

To prove the laundry list of allegations my three former managers had made about me were pretext for discrimination, and also to carry my burden of proof, I filed in court with my responses to the Board's Local Rule 56.1(a)(3) Statements of Fact and my forty additional statements the depositions of four people who had testified during the lawsuit. Their testimony repeatedly corroborated my complaints against the Board and refuted the Board's allegations against me. I also filed twenty-eight exhibits and group exhibits which were comprised of nearly one thousand documents, including, but not limited to the following:

- more than one hundred emails and other documents which showed extensive collaboration between my peers, internal and external constituents, and me;
- more than two hundred emails and other documents which showed I took the initiative on various matters related to the PDU programs I served;
- more than one hundred emails and other documents which showed I followed up on and followed-through with my colleagues and internal and external constituents on matters related to every PDU program I served;
- several emails which showed I frequently worked after-hours and on weekends during the one-year period I served in the PDU;

- at least two dozen emails in which Rivera, Cushing, and McDonagh thanked or complimented me for a job I had done;
- at least twenty emails which showed Cushing, Rivera, and McDonagh had directed me to write an article, speaking points for a school official, or marketing material for the NBC program;
- numerous emails I sent to Cushing informing her of my absences and occasions on which I would be tardy because of work-related matters (in response to the Board's allegations that I was frequently absent without letting my manager know);
- hundreds of emails exchanged between Tabita Sherfinski, my three managers, and me, and others exchanged between Sherfinski and me which showed Glowacki was not copied on even a single email;
- numerous other documents, including the Settlement Agreement and Release related to McDonagh's unauthorized dismissal from my case, Alan Anderson's declaration; the letter of recommendation Karen Cushing wrote and gave to me, an affidavit I created and submitted attesting to the fact that I had not requested a letter of recommendation from Cushing, and various documents comprised of special projects on which I had worked to recruit teachers and market NBC; and
- supportive deposition testimony of two of my former National Board Resource Center colleagues and Glowacki. (Although Glowacki testified for the defendants, her deposition largely was supportive of my allegations.)

Two weeks later, while reviewing the summary judgment responses my attorney had filed in court, I noticed many of the citations were incorrect. I asked her if she had proofread and edited them before she filed my responses. She told me she had not checked my citations, and they must be correct, so I must "focus and fix!" She ended her sentence with a smiley face emoticon. Again, without any help from her, I corrected the citations, and she re-filed my Local Rule 56.1 responses and additional Statements of Fact on June 10, 2011. Then, Judge Chang set a status hearing for July 6, 2011 and took the case under advisement.

July 2011

Judge Chang cancelled the status hearing scheduled for July 6, 2011, and continued my case until August 10, 2011, as the Board's motion for summary judgment remained under advisement. This was the first continuance.

I started a new job as program manager and principal for a five-week summer educational program where I supervised a dozen teachers, teacher's assistants, and support staff. The teachers taught reading and math to low-level students in grades 1-8 who were from disadvantaged homes and communities. Because the position was only temporary, the company which hired me conducted only a criminal and credential background check, so the HR department did not contact the Board for a reference check of my past employment. The pay was not the greatest, but I was glad to have a job of any kind, as my unemployment benefits had recently ended. I absolutely loved the job, and my staff was superb. I called them my "Dream Team." They were committed and hardworking, and the children enrolled in our program were absolutely adorable.

August 2011

Judge Chang cancelled the scheduled August 10, 2011, status hearing and continued my case until September 19, 2011, as the Board's motion for summary judgment remained under advisement. This was the second continuance.

In late August, I acquired a new temporary consulting contract with an organization which focuses on early childhood and family services programs. I was fortunate to get the contract because like most organizations where I had acquired consulting work, this one also did not want the expense of conducting a full-fledged background check. Officials were concerned only with my teaching license and credentials which they could view on ISBE's website and a fingerprint background check to ensure I had no criminal record.

The person who hired me was impressed with my credentials and emphatically stated that although I had very little experience working with Pre-K through second-grade students, which this position required, my

National Board Certification was instrumental in my being hired for the job. The pay was excellent, and I loved what I was doing but I was assigned very few hours to work each week. Therefore, I continued to look for a permanent job. By now, it had been nearly 2½ years since my layoff, and I was hurting financially, emotionally, physically, spiritually and mentally.

SEPTEMBER 2011

Judge Chang cancelled the scheduled September 19, 2011 status hearing and continued my case until October 27, 2011, as the Board's motion for summary judgment remained under advisement. This was the third continuance.

It was not uncommon for me to stop by my attorney's office unannounced to visit her, because I frequently used her office while working on my case. Also, because of my legal secretarial background, sometimes I assisted her with her own matters. One day, despondent because of my unemployment and another of Judge Chang's continuances of my case, I went to see her. Months earlier, my attorney had launched a campaign to become a Cook County Circuit Court judge. After her receptionist announced my visit and she allowed me to enter her office, I told her I was depressed and worried that Judge Chang had continued my case yet again, and I still had no permanent job and very little money. Without showing any concern for me or my emotional state and without looking at me, in a tone that meant "Go away!" she said, "Joyce, you know I'm busy running for judge!" I turned around and walked away.

On September 28, 2011, the Board's general counsel, Patrick Rocks, authorized and the Chicago Board of Education approved the retention of the law office of Sabrina L. Haake to "provide legal advice to the Board relating to legal matters" for a $90,000 contract, which appeared to be no-bid. (Report Number 11-0928-AR3) The contract was for fiscal year 2012. Haake, who remained the Board's counsel on my case, was still being investigated by the ARDC at the time she was awarded the contract in conjunction with my complaint.

Apparently, Haake had either resigned or was terminated while under investigation and immediately was awarded the contract, for she could not or was not supposed to be a Chicago Board of Education employee while receiving a vendor's contract. She had been hired as an employee by the Board effective July 2007 at a taxpayer-funded annual salary of $79,000, and the taxpayer-funded $90,000 contract was equivalent or nearly equivalent to the annual taxpayer-funded salary and benefits she received as an employee.

Court documents Haake filed show she used three different titles on legal documents she prepared and filed on behalf of the Board after becoming a vendor — "counsel for defendant Board of Education," "independent counsel," and the title assigned to her while she served as a Board employee, "assistant general counsel."

Documents she electronically filed in the US Northern District of Illinois Court further show the following: On June 8, 2012, which presumably was at least nine months after her status as a permanent employee ended and she became a vendor, Haake still referred to herself as "assistant general counsel, Board of Education of the City of Chicago, Law Department," the title she was assigned as a permanent employee. However, in a court document she filed three months later, specifically on September 17, 2012, Haake referenced her title as "independent counsel, Board of Education of the City of Chicago." In another court document she filed on November 30, 2012, Haake signed underneath her name on a court document the title of "counsel for defendant Board of Education, c/o Board of Education." Thus, in slightly more than just five months, Haake used at least three different titles in documents she filed in court after she no longer served as an employee for the Chicago Board of Education.

October—November 2011

Judge Chang cancelled the scheduled October 27, 2011, status hearing and continued my case until December 21, 2011, as the Board's motion for summary judgment remained under advisement. This was the fourth continuance.

Because of what had happened with my former attorney, I was determined to remain apprised of all activity related to my case. Therefore, I began visiting the court at least once each week to view my case on the PACER system since at that time I had not opened my own PACER account where I could view cases on my home computer. I also spent hours reviewing discrimination lawsuits filed against the Board by other employees and former employees. I shook my head in amazement at what seemed to be hundreds of race, gender, age, pregnancy, and disability discrimination lawsuits had been filed against the Board during the course of many years. The number was staggering and constantly increased. There appeared to be far more race discrimination lawsuits filed by the school district's employees in federal court than any other form of discrimination, and the suits were filed far more often by black employees and former employees than those filed by any other racial group. Based solely on the cases I reviewed, at that time, it appeared the Board had not lost a single race discrimination case which had been filed against the school district.

December 2011

In mid-December 2011, I was offered a new position as master teacher/instructional coach at a charter school that was included in a network which received funding from the Board to operate its three schools. I was required to provide the educational institution at which I was serving as a consultant one week's notice, which I did. Thereafter, I accepted the position with the charter school. I had applied for the job at least six months earlier after seeing it advertised online. It was a permanent job, but without providing details about the problems I was having with the Board, I convinced the school's CEO to staff me as a vendor rather than a permanent employee. I knew if the school attempted to hire me as a permanent employee, its HR department would contact the Board for a reference, and since I believed the Board was blackballing me, I was convinced I would not get the job.

The pay was 80 percent of what I was earning at the Board when I was laid off, but I was elated when the paperwork was completed and I began working. This was an administrative position in a high school where I mentored and supervised about two dozen teachers. It was interesting and different from any of my previous jobs, and it was the first *real* job I had been able to obtain during the 2½ years since my layoff. I knew I had been hired only because the charter school's HR department did not request a reference regarding my previous employment from the Board.

A few days before Christmas, Judge Chang cancelled the scheduled December 21, 2011 status hearing and continued my case until January 23, 2012, as the Board's motion for summary judgment remained under advisement. This was the fifth continuance. Also, it had been more than one year since I had begun seeing a therapist because of my depression, and I continued my weekly sessions with her even after acquiring my new job.

CHAPTER 13

09 C 7931—Year Three

January 2012
In early January, I received my first paycheck from my new job with the charter school. I sat on the floor of my living room for probably an hour staring at it. It had been so long since I had received a paycheck of this size, I almost did not believe it was real. Meanwhile, Judge Chang cancelled the scheduled January 23, 2012 status hearing and continued my case until February 28, 2012, as the case remained under advisement. This was the sixth continuance.

February 2012
The principal of Truman Middle College contacted me to discuss a permanent job opening at her school. Truman Middle College is a Chicago alternative high school which serves students between the ages of 7-21. It is affiliated with Harry S. Truman College which is one of seven Chicago City Colleges. Like the charter school for which I worked at that time, Truman Middle College receives much of its funding from the Board. I had applied for a position with the school in November 2011. But after my interview, the principal hired another candidate whom she thought would be a better fit for the job. She promised me that if and when she had another opening for which I was qualified she would contact me.

When the principal called me, I was happy with my new job and was not interested in leaving. We agreed to keep in touch, as I remained interested in working for her. I liked the good relationship we had established and did not want to close the door to any future permanent job opportunities at her school because after what I had experienced since my layoff, I was not *about* to take *anything* for granted.

Judge Chang cancelled the scheduled February 28, 2012 status hearing and continued my case until March 28, 2012, as the Board's motion for summary judgment remained under advisement. This was the seventh continuance.

March 2012

I read numerous legal blogs, articles, and court documents which stated that if a judge had not issued a ruling on a motion after six months, it was time to become concerned. By March 2012, it had been more than one year since Rivera and the Board had filed their motion for summary judgment and nine months since my attorney had filed my response to the motion. I was extremely concerned Judge Chang had continued my case for what I perceived was an inordinate number of times, and I began investigating how long it was taking for him to rule on other cases which were under his jurisdiction.

During my investigation, I came across the Civil Justice Reform Act of 1990 (CJRA). According to its website, the CJRA requires the Director of the Administrative Office of the United States Courts, under 28 U.S.C. § 476, to prepare a semiannual report from US district and magistrate judges showing all motions, bankruptcy appeals, social security appeal cases pending more than six months, all bench trials submitted more than six months, and all civil cases pending more than three years. These judicial reporting requirements are designed to help reduce costs and delays in civil litigation in the district courts and the information contained therein also may be used to evaluate demands on the district courts' resources.

Federal judges must provide information detailing cases under their jurisdiction to Washington which becomes publicly available on this report. The report covers data as of March 31 and September 30 of any given year. Although the report contained information regarding many of Judge Chang's other cases, when I viewed them on the federal court's PACER system I noticed there did not appear to be a single case on the report which he had continued as many times as he had mine. The CJRA's website is http://www.uscourts.gov/statistics-reports/analysis-reports/civil-justice-reform-act-report. I strongly encourage litigants who have cases pending in federal courts to peruse this site.

My attorney lost her bid for judge in the Circuit Court of Cook County that month. Judge Chang also cancelled the scheduled March 28, 2012 status hearing and continued my case until April 17, 2012, as the Board's motion for summary judgment remained under advisement. This was the eighth continuance.

April 2012

The CEO of the charter school where I worked was fired in early April 2012. Because he had hired me as an instructional leader, I was concerned the person who replaced him would want to hire his own leadership team and I would be out of a job again, but the charter school did not immediately hire anyone to replace him.

During the latter part of the month, my former York Alternative High School colleague, John Bell, was found dead on the floor of his home. Even before his body was discovered, I suspected he had died. During our last telephone conversation, which had been more than two weeks earlier, he had told me he did not feel well and appeared to be very ill. Bell had been extremely stressed over the loss of his job from York six months earlier for reasons which to this day remain unclear to me. After talking with him for nearly 10 minutes, I asked him to hang up the phone and lie down.

The following morning, I called him but received no answer. Every day afterward, I tried unsuccessfully to reach him by phone. Bell had no family in Chicago, but I was hoping he had gone to visit his out-of-state relatives whom I did not know and for whom I had no contact information. However, I knew it was highly unlikely he was visiting relatives, because he would have mentioned it to me. During the many years we worked together at York, John had adopted me as his "lil sista" and usually kept me informed of his whereabouts. Therefore, I knew something was terribly wrong when time passed and I could not reach him.

I contacted another former York co-worker to try to find out if he knew Bell's address, but he did not. I searched the Internet until I found an address listed with his name, but once I arrived on the block early one Saturday morning, there was no such address. I asked people I saw entering and exiting their homes if they knew him, but no one did. In the spot where I stood at one point, I noticed a beautiful, black, shiny car sitting in a long driveway. As I stared at the car, the strangest feeling came over me, and I felt scared. Again, I contacted my former York colleague. He told me Bell had purchased a new car just before he lost his job, but he could not remember the color of the car.

I returned to my home and tried harder to find Bell's correct address. I spent the remainder of Saturday and most of Sunday trying to find out where he lived. I had not kept in contact with any of my other former York co-workers who might have known Bell's address, and the Internet provided no additional information. Therefore, I decided to wait until Monday and return to the block which I had visited on Saturday. I decided I would ring every doorbell on the block, if necessary, to find out if anyone knew Bell. I was deeply troubled the entire weekend.

On Monday afternoon, as I headed back to the block I had visited on Saturday, my former colleague with whom I had spoken two days earlier called and told me Bell had been discovered dead in his home. He also had begun reaching out to people to try to determine Bell's address, and he contacted a retired York teacher who personally knew one of Bell's neighbors. The retired teacher called Bell's neighbor who had not seen Bell in quite a while and noticed Bell had not moved his car in at least two weeks. It was the same beautiful, black shiny car I had seen in the long driveway where I had stood the previous Saturday. Bell's address which I had found on the Internet was correct. I simply had written it down incorrectly.

After receiving no answer when he rang Bell's doorbell that Monday, the neighbor filed a report with the Chicago Police Department, and an officer contacted the Chicago Fire Department. Firemen forcibly entered Bell's home where they found his body lying on the floor. During the next week, I spoke with Bell's brother who had travelled to Chicago from another city after learning of Bell's death. He told me Bell had died of a heart attack while eating his beloved tangerines. I was enormously sad. Bell's family thanked me later for my efforts to find him, but I always have wished I had done more so he could have been found sooner. He would not have wanted to leave this earth in the manner in which he did.

Bell was a wonderful person. I can say without hesitation that the loss of his job at Consuella B. York Alternative High School absolutely contributed to the stress which caused his death. His legacy is a simple one: He was a loyal friend, and a secret told to him never went any farther. Those who knew him can attest to that. I still miss him terribly.

Judge Chang cancelled the scheduled April 17, 2012 status hearing and continued my case until May 15, 2012, as the Board's motion for summary judgment remained under advisement. This was the ninth continuance.

May 2012

Judge Chang cancelled the scheduled May 15, 2012 status hearing and continued my case until June 19, 2012, as the Board's motion for summary judgment remained under advisement. This was the tenth continuance.

June 2012

Judge Chang cancelled the scheduled June 19, 2012 status hearing and continued my case until July 9, 2012, as the Board's motion for summary judgment remained under advisement. This was the eleventh continuance.

On June 27, 2012, which was only nine months after the Board's general counsel, Patrick Rocks, recommended and the Chicago Board of Education approved a $90,000 contract for Sabrina L. Haake, she was awarded another $90,000 contract. (Report Number 12-0627-AR4) Haake continued to serve as an attorney representing the Board on my case and others, presumably in the capacity of vendor, after either terminating her employment or being terminated by the Board. The contract was for fiscal year 2013, and like the previous contract, it appeared to be no-bid.

Also in late June, I read in one of Chicago's daily newspapers Patrick Rocks was retiring at the end of the month. His name appeared in documents repeatedly during my troubles with Glass. Thus, Rocks ensured Haake received a second $90,000 vendor contract just a few days before his last day of work as the Board's lead attorney. Moreover, as of the date she was awarded this no-bid taxpayer-funded contract with the Board, Haake remained under ARDC investigation which had been ongoing for about fifteen months at that point. Amanda Rivera's former secretary told me later she had learned Rivera also retired the last work day of June 2012.

I am quite familiar with the operations of the ARDC and know that unless the agency deems it highly justifiable to investigate an attorney, a complaint brought against the attorney will be dismissed shortly after it is filed, and the attorney will not be investigated. However, on June 30, 2012, I received two letters from the ARDC dated June 28, 2012, in which the organization informed me it had concluded its investigations into both of my charges and had determined "not to proceed further." Although lack of evidence was the primary reason the ARDC cited in its carefully worded letters, fifteen months after investigating my complaints against my former attorney and Haake, the ARDC claimed it was "proceeding no further" in its investigations of the two. Apparently, it took fifteen months for the agency to determine it had no evidence to proceed.

July 2012

On July 3, 2012, my attorney sent me an email with an attached document she had received from the US Northern District of Illinois Court regarding my case. I knew immediately that after eleven continuances, Judge Chang finally had ruled on my case. For some reason, I knew the news was not good. Because I was still at work, I decided to wait until I arrived home to open my attorney's email.

My work day ended at 4:30 p.m., and I was a nervous wreck during the thirty-minute drive home. I hurried to my computer to read the message as soon as I arrived at my residence, but I could not make myself open it; I just couldn't. I sat at my computer for more than one hour staring at the screen, but no matter how hard I tried, I just could not open the message. I wanted to talk to my attorney and wondered why she had not called me. I believed this also was a sign the message from court was not good and an indication my attorney did not want to discuss what she had forwarded to me.

Two friends and I had planned to go to dinner that evening, and I decided to wait until I returned home before opening the email. When I arrived at the restaurant, I told them I had received what I thought was the court's ruling, and they stared at me as if I had completely lost my mind when I told them I had not opened it. For the next two hours, they repeatedly urged me to open it via my cellphone, but I refused. As we left the restaurant, I promised to call them later that night if I opened the email.

They received no call from me that night because I still did not open the message. However, in the wee hours of the next morning, I opened my attorney's email but not the attached court document. After reading her message, I did not need to open the attachment. The first thing I noticed was the word *"Comments"* in the subject line. I knew this was a huge clue the rest of the message was not good. My attorney stated in the message she was leaving town that day, she would be gone for the remainder of the week, and we had a "short period" in which to file a motion to reconsider. She also asked me to review the judge's ruling and identify any evidence he had ignored. I was deeply hurt she had left town without calling me after I had received such devastating news, so I immediately emailed her and asked her to call me. I knew she would receive my message via her phone, but she ignored it, and I did not hear from her the entire time she was gone.

Recapping everything that occurred between June 27, 2012 and July 3, 2012, which happened to be only five business days: (1) Patrick Rocks recommended and the Board approved Haake's second $90,000 no-bid, taxpayer-funded vendor contract within nine months while she was under investigation by the ARDC. (2) The ARDC sent me two letters informing me there would be no further investigation of my former attorney and Haake. (3) Rocks, the Board's general counsel, retired. (4) Based on information I received from her former secretary, Amanda Rivera, a defendant in my case, also retired. (5) After continuing my case for more than one year, Judge Chang ruled against me and terminated my case two business days after Rocks and Rivera retired.

Despite the glaring and massive number of false statements Cushing, Rivera, McDonagh and Sherfinski had made under oath; despite their repeated inconsistent, implausible, and incoherent testimony; despite presenting not a shred of evidence to corroborate their sweeping allegations against me regarding my so-called poor work performance; and despite the nearly one thousand documents I had filed in court which proved their statements were patently false, Judge Chang granted summary judgment in favor of Rivera and the Board and dismissed my lawsuit.

I called my family and friends and told them the devastating news. Everyone listened in stunned silence and disbelief as I explained that Judge Chang, who wrote in his court order he had "read back and forth" the documents both parties had filed in court, had ruled in favor of the Board and terminated my case. My supporters had followed my lawsuit every step of the way. They knew I had filed a significant amount of evidence to help prove my case and the Board had filed none. They reminded me as they had many times in the past the Board had something I did not have—clout and taxpayers' money with which to fight me.

I walked around in a daze, barely eating and sleeping for nearly one week, and I still had not read Judge Chang's ruling which my attorney had sent via an attached document in her July 3, 2012 email to me. I had read only my attorney's email in which she informed me we had twenty-eight days before filing a motion to reconsider. During that week, my days consisted of going to work, coming home, and heading straight to bed where I stared for hours at the ceiling.

When I finally read Judge Chang's order one week later, I was even more stunned than I was when I opened my attorney's email and learned he had ruled against me. After I had waited for more than one year for him to issue a ruling on the Board's motion for summary judgment, Judge Chang, inexplicably, had excluded from his ruling nearly all of my arguments, the nearly one thousand documents I had filed in my response to the Board's motion for summary judgment, and my forty additional statements. Also, despite the numerous complaints I had brought against Rivera and the Board, and the more than two dozen allegations they and my two other former managers had made against me, Judge Chang granted the Board summary judgment after analyzing only four of those complaints— all of which the Board had presented: my fantasy performance evaluation; the Board's fantasy kronos report containing no employees' names which "showed" I had been chronically tardy; the entirely unsubstantiated sleeping incident; and the "Prison School" issue. Rivera and the Board produced no supporting documentation whatsoever to substantiate even one of those allegations.

As it related to Rivera's and the Board's claims on other issues, such as, I allegedly (a) did not collaborate with my co-workers; (b) did not follow-up on and follow-through with work assignments; (c) had deficient computer and writing skills; (d) did not volunteer with special assignments; (e) did not take the initiative, and (f) lacked even borderline knowledge of NBC, as well as their numerous other complaints about my work performance, Judge Chang did not mention a single one of those claims in his ruling. He also did not mention the significant amount of evidence I had filed in court which proved those claims were false. Also missing from Judge Chang's order were other far more critical claims than the four he analyzed, including, but not limited to Glowacki's superior salary, the letter of recommendation my former manager had written and given to me, and my three former managers' massive number of false statements, all of which were claims I had made and presented evidence which strongly supported them.

What disturbed me significantly was the position Judge Chang took on the "Prison School Issue." Labeling the differences in our teaching history an "important distinction," and entirely ignoring my five year teaching history at Lincoln Park High School, Judge Chang ruled that because my "teaching came from a school populated by students in the criminal justice system" and Glowacki's teaching experience did not, the Board's "non-discriminatory justification" for circumventing my rehiring was valid, and not pretext (a lie) for discrimination.

Like any law-abiding citizen, I appreciated and supported the judge's understandable aversion to criminal activity. However, as an English teacher at York Alternative High School, my exclusive role in the criminal justice system, or the "Prison School" was to teach my students to read, write, and speak properly. Therefore, I was confused as to how this non-issue became an issue on which the judge focused extensively during his ruling, simply because I had taught inmates in a CPS school located within the Cook County Jail for a period during my teaching career.

Although my teaching history at York Alternative High School was one of the issues Judge Chang used to rule in favor of the Board, his judicial colleague had ruled nearly two decades earlier the students at the "Prison School" were entitled to the same educational opportunities as students who were "not in the criminal justice system." To wit, in 1993, when Consuella B. York Alternative High School was named the Cook County Jail School, (but still was one of the Chicago Public Schools), Judge John Albert Nordberg of the Northern District of Illinois Court ruled that all school-aged current and future pretrial detainees confined in Cook County Jail were or would be entitled under state or federal law to the same free regular or special education services as other CPS students, or those who were not "in the criminal justice system."

Judge Nordberg issued the ruling after 23 Cook County Jail inmates who attended the school filed a lawsuit in which they sought the same educational opportunities as those provided to students who were not incarcerated. *Donnell C. v. Illinois State Board of Education, Docket/Court 92 C 8230 (N.D. Ill.)* Interestingly and ironically, the lawyers who filed the lawsuit on behalf of the students worked for Northwestern University's Legal Clinic. Judge Chang attended Northwestern University's Law School at that time, it is the school from which he graduated in 1994, (one year after Judge Nordberg's ruling) and where, as of this writing, he teaches civil rights law.

I strongly believe the aggregate rhetorical effect of Judge Chang's words regarding the "Prison School" issue, was this: Because I had taught incarcerated students during my CPS employment, my teaching record was sullied and my inherent intelligence obviously was inferior to Glowacki's. To be clear, in contrast to Glowacki, who held an Illinois elementary teaching license and a master's degree, and whose prior teaching experience had been in parochial and CPS elementary schools, I held an Illinois multi-subject, multi-grade teaching license, two master's degrees, and 21 additional graduate hours at the time of my layoff. Although I had more college degrees than Glowacki and my credentials were superior to hers, it did not automatically mean I was more intelligent than her. The fact that she is white and I am black also did not automatically mean she was inherently more intelligent than me.

Since Judge Nordberg's ruling, the U.S. Department of Education, the Illinois State Board of Education, the County of Cook and the Chicago Board of Education have recognized that students attending Consuella B. York Alternative High School are entitled to receive the same quality of education as that which other CPS students receive.

An issue far more critical than my teaching experience at the "Prison School" exists here. Job Bulletin Number 111, which was the job posting for Curriculum Facilitator, listed the following requirements for the position: A Bachelor's Degree from an accredited college or university, (a Master's Degree was preferred); a valid Illinois teaching certificate was preferred; a National Board Certification and/or high school teaching experience, and 5-7 years of experience in education, training, or human resources. According to the job bulletin announcement, the position opened and applications were to be accepted beginning October 22, 2008, and the position closed on November 5, 2008.

As of the November 5, 2008 closing date for the curriculum facilitator's position, documents show I achieved NBC on November 9, 2007—one year before the job was even posted, and Glowacki achieved on November 21, 2008—three weeks **after** the position's closing date. As illustrated by the following chart, Glowacki also did not hold a high school teaching certificate which was required in lieu of NBC.

My Credentials as of the November 5, 2008 Closing Date to Apply for the Curriculum Facilitator's Position	Glowacki's Credentials as of the November 5, 2008 Closing Date to Apply for the Curriculum Facilitator's Position
Two Master's Degrees from an accredited university and 21 additional graduate hours.	One Master's Degree from an accredited university
A valid Illinois State teaching certificate in English Language Arts and Journalism, and endorsements in Business Marketing and Management	A valid Illinois State teaching certificate in elementary education
A Master Teaching Certificate (National Board Certification)	Elementary and Middle School Teaching Experience
High School and Middle School Teaching Experience	11 years of experience in education
11 years of experience in education	

Based on the requirements of the position listed in the job bulletin, and as shown in the chart, I met *every* requirement for the job when the position opened in 2008. In fact, I exceeded the requirements. However, Glowacki DID NOT meet either of the two most critical requirements for the position during the period it was posted—a high school teaching certificate and National Board Certification. Moreover, the Board produced not a shred of evidence Glowacki had ever applied for the position in the first place. Despite my attorney's repeated requests to the Board during discovery in 2010 for the résumé Glowacki submitted in response to the job opening, the Board submitted nothing. There also was nothing contained in court records which showed Glowacki produced a résumé or any type of application in response to Job Bulletin Number 111, dated October 22, 2008, for the curriculum facilitator's position.

As it related to the Board's four allegations which Judge Chang used to rule against me, Rivera and the Board produced no evidence which supported a single allegation they had made about me. Because of the nature of those claims, it simply was my word against the Board's, and the burden of proof was on me, the plaintiff, in the lawsuit. When Judge Chang excluded my evidence nearly in its entirety in his court ruling, it was impossible for me to carry my burden of proof and receive a fair trial by a jury of my peers—if I had been able to make it to trial, which I had not. Moreover, in relation to the Board's numerous other claims against me, which by my preponderance of evidence I proved were false, Judge Chang neither addressed in his ruling those claims, nor the evidence I had filed in court to refute them.

Shockingly, every evidentiary ruling and major conclusion Judge Chang reached was contradicted by evidence, or lack thereof, on the court's record, including his determination that there were no factual disputes between the Board and me, which must be the case before a party is granted summary judgment. Yet, the "non-discriminatory" motives the Board articulated and the heavily-contested rebuttal evidence I filed in court created disputes regarding *every* issue on which Judge Chang relied to grant the Board summary judgment, and the numerous other issues he failed to analyze and include in his ruling.

A person reading Judge Chang's order who was unfamiliar with my case, could easily have surmised there existed no genuine factual disputes (also called genuine issues of material fact) between the Board and me. The *only* reason it might have appeared there were no factual disputes was because Judge Chang excluded nearly all of my arguments and evidence in his ruling.

Thereafter, he dismissed my lawsuit for lack of the very evidence he excluded and ultimately claimed I was lacking.

Because of Rivera and the Board's complete lack of evidence for their sweeping allegations against me, and the significant evidence I filed in court to prove they had lied, my attorney and I were certain Judge Chang would deny them summary judgment. Therefore, we were shocked to learn we had to file a motion to reconsider judgment. I assumed my attorney would file an appeal in the US Court of Appeals for the Seventh Circuit because I knew of no other remedy. She informed me we could file a motion to alter, amend, or reconsider judgment, which, under the Federal Rules of Civil Procedure, Rule 59(e), is the accepted vehicle for requesting judges to reconsider their ruling in federal court. This procedure allows judges to correct their own errors and avoid unnecessary appeals by the involved parties.

My attorney had twenty-eight days after Judge Chang ruled on my case (which was July 3, 2012) in which to file my motion to alter, amend, or reconsider judgment. I knew this meant I would have to begin writing all over again. Therefore, citing the judge's exclusion of nearly all of my evidence and his other errors, I began preparing my motion. My attorney did not bother to tell me the motion could not exceed fifteen pages, so I wrote a twenty-nine-page motion which she reviewed only briefly. She did not mention to me after I completed it that in violation of court rules, the motion contained far too many pages. On July 31, 2012, my attorney filed the motion to alter, amend, or reconsider exactly twenty-eight days after Judge Chang issued his ruling on the Board's motion for summary judgment.

August 2012

The Board filed a Bill of Costs in the amount of $4,724.38 on August 1, 2012, seeking payment from me for certain deposition costs and copying fees the school district allegedly incurred during the lawsuit. It is common for the winning party in a civil lawsuit to file such bills, and the losing party typically must pay, at a minimum, a portion of the bill. Although my attorney should have filed a response to it, she filed nothing, and you will see it came back to haunt me two years later.

Judge Chang was displeased, annoyed, or both, for on August 7, 2012, he filed a minute entry in which he appeared to be scolding my attorney for the twenty-nine-page motion because he probably believed she had written it. A minute entry is a legal document which is recorded in the minutes of a court session and frequently is the court's response to a party's request. Judge Chang warned my attorney that the reply motion to the Board's response to my motion to alter, amend or reconsider must not exceed the fifteen-page limit, and it must be filed on time.

In late August, Truman Middle College's principal contacted me again to discuss another job opening with the school. I thanked her but refused the offer to join her staff. Both my principal and assistant principal at the charter school where I was working had resigned over the summer, and I was needed to provide some semblance of stability and leadership to the charter school's young teaching staff.

September 2012

On September 4, 2012, my attorney forwarded me an email she had received from Haake who still served as the Board's lead counsel on my case. She wrote that there was "no good-faith basis" for us to file the motion to alter, amend, or reconsider, and "in interest of economy, defendants offer to withdraw the bill of costs against plaintiff as settlement of this matter, in lieu of briefing the motion and any appeal." She also warned my attorney the $4,724.38 I allegedly owed the Board "will likely result in a financial judgment against your client."

The words "any appeal" in Haake's message immediately caught my attention. I concluded the Board did not want me to file an appeal which Haake realized most likely would happen if the judge did not rule in favor of my motion to alter, amend or reconsider. Using unladylike language which I will not share, I asked my attorney to deliver a special message to Haake. "Thought that is what you might say," she replied. However, she did not send Haake the very special response I had created especially for her. Two weeks later, Haake filed the Board's response to my motion to alter, amend, or reconsider, and on September 25, 2012, my attorney filed my reply. Judge Chang then took my motion under advisement and scheduled a status hearing for October 30, 2012.

October 2012

Shortly after a new CEO was hired, I was laid off from my position as master teacher/instructional coach at the charter school where I had worked since December 2011. The budget for the new school year required one master teacher to be laid off, and although there were three other people who served in the same capacity at the two other schools in the charter school's network, I was the only person who had been staffed as a consultant rather than a permanent employee. Therefore, it made sense to lay me off instead of one of the master teachers who had been staffed as a regular, full-time employee.

You might recall I had asked the previous CEO to hire me as a consultant because I did not want the school's HR department to conduct a reference check of me. I feared the Board would provide a negative reference regarding my employment as retaliation for my legal proceedings against the school district. During the remainder of my employment with the school, I was not re-staffed as a permanent employee because after the CEO was fired, things became crazy until his replacement was hired. The charter school network gave me two months' severance pay which it did not have to do since I was a consultant, and we parted on friendly terms.

I immediately reached out to the principal of Truman Middle College who, by this time, had contacted me three times during the previous two years to discuss job opportunities with her school. I told her of my availability and asked if she had job openings for which I might be qualified. She told me of an opening for the part-time position of instructor/tutor and asked me to submit my résumé for consideration. After I applied for the position, she invited me to the school to formally interview with her and a school district administrator, and she hired me the same day.

I signed the paperwork necessary for Truman Middle College's HR department to conduct a background check and underwent a drug test. I was hired before Truman received the background check results with the understanding that if it revealed negative information, I could be terminated. Although I was concerned that a reference check with the school's HR department would result in a negative reference for me if Truman Middle College contacted the Board, I pushed those concerns aside because I had no choice. Like any other self-supporting person, I needed to work.

By the end of October 2012, I had completed Truman's new employee orientation and had been staffed as a permanent part-time employee in an instructor's position at the school. The principal told me she would hire me into a permanent full-time position when or if funds became available.

Meanwhile, Judge Chang cancelled the scheduled October 30, 2012 status hearing and continued my case until January 16, 2013, as my motion to alter, amend, or reconsider judgment remained under advisement. This was the judge's first continuance after my attorney filed my reply motion on September 2012.

November—December 2012

In early November 2012, after studying Glowacki's Salary Recommendation Form once again, which incorrectly listed her job title as "teacher training specialist," I discussed with my attorney the initials *LM*, which had been written immediately next to Amanda Rivera's signature, authorizing the title and salary. As I noted in chapter 11, although Glowacki and I were hired as curriculum facilitators, the Salary Recommendation Form which reflected Rivera's signature, also contained the initials *LM* next to the signature, and Lily McDonagh, who had been one of the defendants in my lawsuit until my attorney's unauthorized dismissal of her from the lawsuit, was the only

PDU employee with those initials who would have been authorized to sign for Rivera.

My attorney sent an email to Sunil Kumar who also was a Board attorney assigned to my case in a supervisory capacity, but only received court filings related to the lawsuit. He did not respond in writing. My attorney later informed me that during an in-person conversation she had with him shortly thereafter, he asked her to discuss the matter with Haake, the Board's attorney who was representing Rivera in the lawsuit. Haake also represented McDonagh until my former attorney dismissed her from my lawsuit as he withdrew. My attorney sent Haake an email asking if the initials on the form were McDonagh's. She also asked Haake why those initials appeared on the form when McDonagh had testified under oath during her deposition that she knew nothing about Glowacki's salary until she heard details about it during Rivera's testimony. Haake did not respond to my attorney's email, and we did not hear a word from Kumar regarding this issue.

On Sunday, November 4, 2012, Flo, my friend for more than twenty-five years, died. She had not told me before she died that just a few weeks earlier, she had learned she had cancer. She succumbed to it less than one month after being diagnosed. I will forever believe the 2008 loss of her job as an administrative support employee in the Board's HR department was a significant contributing factor to her illness. She never got over losing her job, and she was unable to find another permanent one. She was entirely self-supporting, so this caused her extreme stress. Thus, during a seven-month period, I lost two close friends, John Bell and Flo. Both had lost their jobs with the Board, neither had gotten over the loss of their jobs, both developed critical health issues, both died soon after losing their jobs, and the deaths of both have caused everlasting voids in my life.

The following day, November 5, 2012, was my first day of work at Truman Middle College. The pay was low, the job was only part-time (twenty hours each week), but at least I was working, and I loved the school and students. Because Truman Middle College is an alternative high school, the students had many of the same issues as those of my former York Alternative High School students. The principal and I had discussed the possibility of me serving as director of a writing center she wanted to open in the future. I was elated about the possibility of becoming staffed in a permanent position with the school and doing what I loved most—teaching students to write.

Two days after I began my new job at Truman Middle College, the principal held an after-school meeting which all staff attended. She introduced me as someone she hired, among other reasons, because I had "excellent classroom management skills." I was happy to be part of an academic team once again, and I was excited about my new job.

On Friday, November 9, 2012, my fifth day of work at the school, I asked the principal if she had a specific student with whom she wanted me to tutor or a particular project on which she wanted me to work the following week. She was typing on her computer when I entered her office, and she neither answered my question nor did she look at me. I waited for at least twenty seconds before asking her again, and she still did not respond. "Do you want me to wait until I hear from you about my duties for next week?" I asked her. "Yeah; wait until you hear from me," she said. Her tone and demeanor were unfriendly and very different from what I had become accustomed during the previous year when she had contacted me repeatedly to try to persuade me to work at her school. I walked away from her office with that old familiar sick feeling in the pit of my stomach—the feeling that surfaced each time I suspected the Board had prevented me from getting a job.

By now, I had been laid off from the Board for 3½ years, and because of the difficulty I had had getting jobs since my layoff, I immediately suspected the Board had told her or the person checking my reference something negative about me. Since Truman Middle College received a significant amount of its funding from the Board because of its status as one of the school district's charter schools, I believed, without a doubt, I never would work at Truman Middle College again.

Later that night while perusing job openings online at Chicago City Colleges, I noticed Truman Middle College had posted an advertisement the same day for what appeared to be a new position which had a different job title and a salary that was less than what I had earned as an instructor/tutor. Like the job I had held, this position also was part-time, and the description was almost identical to the job for which I had been hired. I was even more convinced the Board had blackballed me again, and I was absolutely certain I had worked my last day at Truman Middle College.

The following Monday, I waited for the principal to call me to return to work, but she did not. Days passed, and she still did not call me. When I did not hear from her for a full week, on November 16, 2012, I sent her an email asking her if she would please tell me the status of my work schedule, if there was one. She did not respond. Eventually, two weeks and then a full month had passed since my first and only week at work, and I still had heard nothing from her. I wondered why this was happening to me, but I knew it had nothing to do with my job performance. For the mere five days I worked at Truman Middle College, my performance had been excellent, and I had established good relationships with the students and staff.

Despite hiring me as a permanent employee and although she did not tell me I was terminated, with the exception of a December 3, 2012 email in which she stated "There is a possibility I might need you today," the principal did not contact me to return to work at Truman Middle College for the remainder of 2012. I heard nothing more from the principal on December 3, and the email she sent me that day was on a string of messages which included the November 15, 2012 email I had sent, in which I asked her to apprise me of my work schedule, to which she did not respond. This was undisputed evidence she had seen the message. I concluded—and this is only my opinion—that after Truman Middle College received a reference for me from the Board, the principal and HR department decided not to allow me to continue to work for the school.

Neither I nor anyone else I know had ever heard of a person being hired for a job, working a few days, and without being fired, that person was not allowed to return to work. However, after nearly one year of contacting me to work for her, that precisely is what happened to me; the principal of Truman Middle College would not allow me to return to work after I had served as instructor/tutor for only five days, and she did not extend me the professional courtesy of an official termination and/or explanation.

I told my attorney I had lost my job at Truman Middle College and explained what had happened. She looked at me with pity and made a pouty mouth, but she made no effort to contact the principal or to do anything else to find out why I had not been allowed to return to work. I did not want to believe this madness, but I had to face reality. I was unemployed again solely because I had filed a lawsuit against the Chicago Board of Education, and I was sick and tired of it.

CHAPTER 14

09 C 7931—Year Four

January 2013

I BEGAN 2013 THE SAME way I ended 2012—unemployed. I renewed my job search and began submitting résumés in every profession for which I was qualified. I applied online for a part-time position as proctor for test preparation with The Princeton Review Chicago on January 1, 2013. My responsibilities in that capacity would have been to assist CPS students at assigned high schools with preparing for ACT exams in the English Language Arts content area.

The day after I applied for the job, I received an invitation from The Princeton Review to engage in a teaching audition which was to be held on Saturday, January 12, 2013. With two other job candidates, I auditioned at The Princeton Review's Chicago headquarters. Two days later, I received a follow-up letter from Robert Hennen, The Princeton Review's operations manager. He expressed the organization's continued interest in my job candidacy and requested that I complete an online application which would be used to "learn more about your education and employment history." In other words, The Princeton Review would conduct a background check of my previous employment and education to determine if I had a criminal record. I completed and submitted the online application to Hennen on January 15, 2013.

Later that month, I sent to the US Department of Justice, the Illinois State's Attorney, and the Board's inspector general, a letter accompanied by several documents the Board had submitted to my attorney during the discovery phase of my lawsuit. The documents appeared to depict a payroll fraud scheme involving Glowacki's salary. The main document was the Staffing Recommendation Form I previously mentioned which reflected Glowacki's position as a "teacher training specialist" when, in fact, she had been hired as a curriculum facilitator. I ensured that each of the agencies I contacted knew the Board's two attorneys who were assigned to my case, Wu and Haake, had been made aware of this scheme in March 2010 when my attorney requested information regarding Glowacki's questionable salary. I was blowing the whistle on what I believed was malfeasance.

On January 9, 2013, Lisa Dreishmire, the Board's new assistant general counsel, who had filed an attorney appearance in my case on January 4, 2013, filed defendant Amanda Rivera's motion to withdraw appearance for attorney Sabrina Haake and substitute attorney Lisa Dreishmire as lead and trial counsel. In the carefully worded motion, Dreishmire wrote that Haake "is transitioning from her role as counsel for the Chicago Board of Education," whatever that meant. The motion made no reference to what position, if any, or to where Haake was "transitioning." However, a January 24, 2013 email exchange between Haake and another Board attorney shows Haake continued to handle legal matters for the Board, and she used the same taxpayer-funded CPS email address she used as a permanent employee. This was exactly two weeks after she supposedly had "transitioned from her role as counsel for the Chicago Board of Education." Court records also show that on June 28, 2013, which was more than five months after Dreishmire filed the Board's motion regarding Haake's "transition," Haake electronically filed court documents in which she still identified herself as "counsel for defendant Board of Education."

On January 15, 2013, Judge Chang granted Dreishmire's motion, cancelled the scheduled January 16, 2013 status hearing, and continued my case until February 26, 2013, as my motion to alter, amend, or reconsider judgment remained under advisement. This was the second time the case was continued after my attorney filed the reply motion in September 2012.

In mid-January, I was hired as a tutor for another after-school Supplemental Educational Service provider which had a contract with the Board. I was assigned to an elementary school to provide after-school reading and math instruction. Although the pay was decent, like so many other positions I had acquired, I only worked a few days each week for two hours at a time, and the job ended within a few months. I also was hired for a one-month temporary assignment by a charter school where I proctored exams for elementary school English Language Learners. The pay was awful, but the job was fun and I loved the students. Therefore, I had two "job fragments," as I called them, which provided me two paychecks for a brief period. Even combined though, the pay was barely a fraction of what I had earned before I was laid off by the Board. My inability to pay my monthly bills and my stress mounted.

On January 29, 2013, I received an email from The Princeton Review's operations manager, Robert Hennen, in which he wrote, The Princeton Review had "completed the process and decided to move forward with other candidates who better meet our qualifications and needs at this time." I sent the following responsive email:

Thank you, Mr. Hennen, for your response.
Please clarify Princeton Review's specific "qualifications and needs" that I did not meet in this regard.
Sincerely,
Joyce Hutchens

Hennen did not respond. Of the three candidates who had participated in the teaching audition, I was the only one who had actual high school teaching experience, which was a "preferred qualification" for the position. The Princeton Review also had extended job offers to me several years earlier when I taught at York Alternative High School. Despite a very successful teaching audition and overall interview process, and despite being highly qualified for the position, following a background check which most likely included a reference check of my past employment with the Board, Hennen rejected me for the job.

The Princeton Review is a Chicago Board of Education vendor which has for many years received a significant number of contracts and funding from the Board; hence, the reason I would have provided educational services to CPS students had I been hired.

February 2013

In early February 2013, I drafted a letter to Truman Middle College's principal, asking her to explain why she did not allow me to return to work after I had completed only five days in my new position. I wrote the letter because I knew that asking my attorney to write it would have been a waste of time. After I finalized the letter, I asked her to review it to determine if any additional information should be added and to print and sign it on her firm's stationary when she had time. As usual, she refused. I still had no job and no money and Truman Middle College would not allow me to return to work, but my attorney was "too busy" to help me.

In early February 2013, with $275 I borrowed, I paid another attorney to do what my attorney would not. A friend had referred the attorney to me, and within two days after I met with her, she had revised the letter where she believed it was necessary, printed it on her law firm's stationery, signed it, and sent it to the principal of Truman Middle College. I loved her attention to detail and diligence and wished I could afford to hire her as the attorney who handled my lawsuit.

In her two-page letter to Truman Middle College's principal, the attorney wrote of the "inexplicable series of events" which had a "severe adverse impact on Ms. Hutchens' livelihood." She explained that she was reaching out to the principal to "ascertain clarification with respect to Ms. Hutchens' employment status with Truman Middle College, together with an explanation of the complete lack of communication regarding the same." She also wrote that I had a right to be informed if Truman Middle College had terminated my employment.

As of the date she wrote the letter, which at that time had been more than three months since my last day of work at Truman Middle College, I had not heard from the principal or anyone else at the school regarding my employment status. Because I had been hired as a permanent employee, this certainly was inexplicable. The attorney concluded the letter by informing the principal she could either reach out to either of us if she wished to respond. She sent the letter to the principal via email and US mail.

Less than 24 hours later, the principal called and left me a voicemail message claiming she had staffed me in a "temporary substitute position" with the understanding she would call me "as needed." In a follow-up email in which she explained she was writing to "clear up any confusion with this position," the principal reiterated that I had been hired as a substitute teacher for Truman Middle College, and since my last day of work for the school, my services had not been needed. She also wrote that if I did not wish to continue working for the school on an as-needed basis, I was "more than welcome to resign from the position" if it did not meet my needs. In other words, the principal wanted me to resign because she had no reason to fire me, and if I resigned, the school would not have had to concern itself with me filing a lawsuit for wrongful termination. I neither responded to her message nor did I resign. Instead, I continued my status as what I called an "Employee without a Job." It made no sense.

Truman Middle College had paid for me to take an expensive drug test, required me to engage in its new employee orientation, and enrolled me into its pension plan. I cannot begin to imagine why the school would have done any of those things if I had been hired as a temporary employee or on an "as needed" basis. Clearly, I had been hired as a permanent employee, and I believed that because Truman Middle College had been told by the Board not to allow me to work, the principal was attempting to make it appear that I had been hired only on an "as needed" basis. By this time, I had been without permanent employment for nearly four years. The positions I had been able to acquire were only temporary, and I was grossly underpaid and underemployed for each.

Judge Chang cancelled the February 26, 2013 status hearing and continued my case until March 25, 2013, as my motion to alter, amend, or reconsider judgment remained under advisement. This was the third time the case was continued after my attorney filed my reply brief on September 29, 2012.

March 2013

My financial situation had deteriorated so badly by this time, I was seriously in debt. My friends and family constantly encouraged me to file for bankruptcy, but I refused. I discussed this matter with my attorney who asked me why I was so adamant about not dissolving my debts through bankruptcy. "I believe I will be able to pay my creditors at the conclusion of my lawsuit," I told her and everyone else who asked me the same question. I had become almost totally reliant on others for my existence. The health club, which for decades had been a critical part of my life, became a thing of the past. I preferred eating and then lying in bed in a fetal position most of the time. My blood pressure and weight ballooned out of control. My health deteriorated so drastically I had four bouts with bronchial pneumonia during a twelve-month period. Food and sweets became my best friends, and I consumed them constantly in a desperate attempt to find *anything* that would make me feel better, even temporarily. Depression was a frequent visitor in my life, and even when the sun would shine the brightest, my days were filled with darkness. I was a miserable woman.

After struggling mightily each month to pay my bills and never having enough money to buy even life's most basic necessities, I applied for food stamps with the Illinois Department of Human Services in March 2013. The caseworker repeatedly shook his head in disgust as he reviewed my income for the prior one-year period on the computerized system and listened as I told him of the problems I had encountered during my job search. When he finished, the caseworker approved me for two hundred dollars in monthly food stamps. "After what I just saw I only wish I could do more for you than this," he said, obviously referring to my 2012 and 2013 incomes which he had reviewed on the State of Illinois computerized system.

This was the new reality for me. I was a three-time college graduate, but I had to pay for my food with a government-issued "Link Card" in order to eat. A Link Card serves the same purpose as the former food stamps, and according to the Illinois Department of Human Services, the Link Card is part of the Supplemental Nutrition Assistance Program (SNAP). I never had applied for or received welfare in my life, but I was so happy to finally be able to buy food without spending my very limited income, it did not matter to me that the same grocery store cashiers who for years had seen me pay for food with cash, were seeing me purchase it with food stamps. That was my life's new reality.

My belief that the Board was blackballing me continued, particularly after what had happened with Truman Middle College and the Princeton Review. Therefore, in March 2013, I hired Allison & Taylor, Inc. to conduct an employment verification and reference check of my past employment with the Board. Allison & Taylor identifies itself as a nationally recognized job reference and background-checking firm.

According to information contained on the Board's Employment Verification Form, "requests will be processed and mailed within three to five business days" after the Board receives a signed and notarized authorization form from an employee or former employee. Therefore, I sent and Allison & Taylor received my signed and notarized authorization form on March 29, 2013. An employee in the Board's Employee Records Department acknowledged receiving the form from Allison & Taylor the same day.

In a report an Allison & Taylor consultant issued to me after she contacted the Board numerous times to obtain information regarding my past employment, she wrote that on April 10, 2013, the Board's records department employee, "Maria," informed Allison & Taylor that Gina Morrow was handling my verification request, was doing "research" on it, and "it could take ten days" before Morrow concluded the research regarding my past employment with the Board. The Allison & Taylor consultant responded to "Maria" that it already had been more than ten days since the Board had received my employment verification request, but the Board still would not provide the consultant with information regarding my employment history.

I had worked for the Board twelve years when I was laid off. Therefore, there was no reason for anyone at the Board to "do research" regarding my employment. I knew if the Board's employees were responding to calls from my prospective employers in this manner, which included putting the Allison & Taylor consultant on hold for as much as seventeen minutes during one call, this certainly would raise questions and cause concern about my employment with the Board from those who were interested in hiring me.

More than two weeks after the Board's Employee Records Department received my reference checking authorization form, Allison & Taylor issued a written report to me which contained the following message: "We are closing out this case, as it is apparent the reference is not motivated to respond to our messages or provide the information as requested. Further attempts to reach the reference could be perceived by them as either unduly persistent, or suspicious (or both)." The Allison and Taylor consultant recorded on the form step-by-step efforts she had made to acquire information regarding my employment history from the Board, and also wrote the following:

> Please note that we have made every effort to obtain information regarding your previous employment there, have faxed the information as requested by them and have attempted to contact them on the status of the information due to me. Regrettably, they have not seen fit to mail, call, or fax back the information and ongoing efforts on our part may simply antagonize them. The conclusion we must draw is that they have no desire or intention of speaking with us or with any prospective employer who attempts to contact them regarding your references. While we are constrained to close your case, note again that the reference's refusal to speak with us (or by extension, with a prospective employer) is instructive in itself.

Although the Board provided the information Allison & Taylor requested shortly thereafter, I believe the conduct exhibited by employees in the Board's Employee Records Department was indicative of the same behavior the Board repeatedly had shown toward each of my prospective employers since my June 2009 layoff. Therefore, my inability to acquire a single permanent position, my extended periods of unemployment, and my multiple periods of underemployment were a direct result of the manner in which the Board had handled reference calls regarding my employment verification and work history, and I knew it was time for me to do something about it.

Judge Chang cancelled the scheduled March 25, 2013 status hearing and continued my case until April 25, 2013, as my motion to alter, amend, or reconsider judgment remained under advisement. This was the fourth time the case was continued after my attorney filed my reply brief on September 29, 2012.

April 2013

The Allison & Taylor incident was the final straw and enough to convince me that what I had feared all along was true; the Board was blackballing me to prospective employers as retaliation because I had filed a charge of discrimination against Rivera and the school district. I also believed the retaliation was because I had implicated Board employees in a payroll fraud scheme involving Glowacki's salary and because I had filed a complaint with the ARDC against Sabrina Haake, the Board's lawyer. Therefore, on April 17, 2013, I filed with the EEOC a charge of retaliation against the Chicago Board of Education. I knew I ultimately would sue the Board again, so I asked the EEOC not to investigate my charge, and instead, to submit it to the US Department of Justice and request a right-to-sue letter on my behalf, which the agency did.

Initially, I intended only to file a complaint with the EEOC against the Board. However, after stating the reasons I suspected the Board was retaliating against me, including the Truman Middle College issue, the investigator with whom I had filed my complaint said she wanted to know why Truman Middle College had not allowed me to return to work. Therefore, she asked me to also file a charge of retaliation against Truman. I ultimately filed EEOC Charge Number 440-2013-03039 against the Board and 440-2013-03037 against Truman Middle College with the expectation that the EEOC would at least investigate why Truman's principal did not allow me to return to work after I had been hired and worked at the school for only five days.

Less than one week after the Chicago City Colleges' Law Department received my EEOC charge on behalf of Truman Middle College, the principal called me to return to work. I did not respond, but she and her assistant principal continued to contact me by phone several times each week for at least one month and asked me to substitute teach for them. I found out later they maintained a record of each call, and I received those records later during the discovery phase of the second lawsuit I ultimately filed against the Board in September 2013.

I also learned they sent several messages to an email address the school had established for me. Since I had worked for Truman Middle College only a few days, I was entirely unaware I had an email address. Because of the manner in which the principal had behaved toward me after she hired me, I refused to return to work for Truman even though I still had no job and desperately needed one. I wanted nothing else to do with her or Truman, so I did not bother to respond to her calls or those from her assistant principal.

After receiving the Chicago City Colleges' Position Statement, the EEOC decided not to proceed with its investigation against Truman Middle College. My primary concern was to sue the Board again and at that time, I did not believe I had enough evidence to initiate and prevail in a lawsuit against the school. Therefore, I did not proceed with my charge against Truman Middle College after the EEOC chose not to investigate my complaint.

Judge Chang cancelled the April 25, 2013 status hearing and continued my case until May 30, 2013, as my motion to alter, amend, or reconsider judgment remained under advisement. This was the fifth time the case was continued after my attorney filed the motion.

May 2013

Despite the motion Dreishmire filed on January 9, 2013, in which she wrote that Sabrina Haake was "transitioning in her role as counsel for the Chicago Board of Education," on May 22, 2013, the Board's general counsel, James Bebley, (who replaced Patrick Rocks when he suddenly retired in 2012), recommended and the Chicago Board of Education approved a $50,000 contract for Sabrina L. Haake. (Report Number 13-0522-AR5) As of this date, Haake had received two previous contracts totaling $180,000, both of which appeared to be no-bid, while being investigated by the ARDC in conjunction with my 2011 complaint against her and my former counsel.

Like the $90,000 June 2012 contract she was awarded, the $50,000 contract also was for fiscal year 2013. Thus, Haake received during an eleven-month period two taxpayer-funded contracts totaling $140,000 for fiscal year 2013, which included the new $50,000 contract she received after "transitioning in her role as counsel for the Chicago Board of Education." Haake's contracts raised the following questions:

1) If Haake assumed the role of "counsel for the Chicago Board of Education" as of the date Dreishmire filed the motion to substitute attorneys, which was January 9, 2013, why had Haake referred to herself as "independent counsel" in court documents filed on behalf of the Board since 2011? Dreishmire did not indicate in her motion that Haake was transitioning from her role as "independent counsel." She wrote that Haake was transitioning from her role as "counsel for the Chicago Board of Education."

2) If Haake "transitioned from her role as counsel for the Chicago Board of Education," effective January 9, 2013, why did she continue to refer to herself in court documents as "counsel for defendant Board of Education" months after her purported "transition?"

3) If Haake did, in fact, "transition" from her role as "counsel for the Chicago Board of Education" in January 2013, why was the $50,000 apparent no-bid contract she received on May 22, 2013, still charged to the Board's Law Department for professional services under Budget Classification 10455-115-54125-231101-000000, which was the same budget classification number used when she was awarded the September 2011 and June 2012 contracts for the respective fiscal years identified in the Board Report?

4) Following her termination in 2011, why did Haake use four different titles — "independent counsel," "counsel," "counsel to the Board," and "assistant general counsel" on legal documents she created and filed on behalf of the Board? Which title was accurate?

5) Online information published by the Board's procurement office shows Haake received what presumably was another contract for $64,186.00, for the fiscal year ending June 30, 2014, which also would have been after she "transitioned" from her role as the Board's counsel. (http://www.csc.cps.k12.il.us/purchasing/supplier_report_2014.xml), listed as Item No. 2868c is as follows: "All vendors are subject to the procurement spend limits ($10,000 for biddable goods and $25,000 for non-biddable goods or services, but no more than $25,000 in total biddable and non-biddable), unless authorized by a fully executed Board contract." Therefore, why is there no Chicago Board of Education Report like the three others posted online which shows the Board approved a $64,186.00 payout or contract for Haake?

6) Dreishmire filed the Board's motion regarding Haake's "transition" from counsel for the Chicago Board of Education on January 9, 2013. Therefore, where is the Board's motion stating that Haake had "transitioned" back to her role as "counsel for the Chicago Board of Education" or whatever her title was before she received the May 22, 2013 contract or the contract for the fiscal year ending June 30, 2014, during which she ultimately received the $64,186.00 payout?

Chicago taxpayers, including this author, deserve answers to each of these questions.

Also in May 2013, in response to the letter I sent in January 2013 regarding the alleged payroll fraud scheme I discovered regarding Glowacki's salary, I received a letter from the US Attorney of the Northern District of Illinois, informing me his agency would not be conducting an investigation regarding my allegations of a payroll fraud scheme against the Board. The US Attorney also wrote that I should contact the FBI if I suspected federal funds had been used in a payroll fraud scheme. I continued to wait to hear from the Cook County State's Attorney and the Board's inspector general regarding the letters I also had sent to them regarding what I believed was a payroll fraud scheme involving Glowacki's salary.

Judge Chang cancelled the May 30, 2013 status hearing and continued my case until July 18, 2013, as my motion to alter, amend, or reconsider judgment remained under advisement. This was the sixth time the case was continued after my attorney filed my reply motion.

June 2013

In response to the April 17, 2013, EEOC charge I filed against the Board, I received a right-to-sue letter from the US Department of Justice which provided me ninety days in which to file a lawsuit.

July 2013

After applying for a temporary consulting position with Indiana-based Briljent LLC, I was hired to work as an instructional delivery specialist for the company in July 2013. I completed the background check form, but I do not believe Briljent's HR department conducted a background check since this was only a three-month assignment.

Judge Chang cancelled the July 18, 2013 status hearing and continued my case until August 30, 2013, as my motion to alter, amend, or reconsider judgment remained under advisement. This was the seventh time the case was continued after my attorney had filed the motion.

Fed up with Judge Chang's repeated continuances of my case, on July 22, 2013, I wrote a letter to Honorable Reuben Castillo, Chief Judge of the US Northern District of Illinois Court and hand-delivered it to his courtroom deputy. I informed him of Judge Chang's years of repeated continuances, my ongoing unemployment, and my desperate need to have him rule on my case so I could move forward with my life, regardless of the ruling. In a letter dated July 24, 2013, which Judge Castillo sent to my attorney, he responded that he had "no jurisdiction over the cases of any other judge." He sent Judge Chang a copy of his responsive letter. I suspect he also sent Chang a copy of the letter I sent to him.

I wrote the letter to Judge Castillo without my attorney's knowledge, but she did not care, and I knew she would not care. When she received his response, she simply sent me a text message informing me she had received a response to my letter from the chief judge. Most attorneys would have been livid that their client had contacted a judge without their knowledge, but not my attorney. She was entirely unconcerned. When I visited her office to retrieve Judge Castillo's response, she simply handed the letter to me without saying much.

August 2013

Several months after I reported the payroll fraud scheme involving Glowacki's salary, the Board closed the National Board Resource Center which was the subject of my first lawsuit. Glowacki remained employed by the Board in another capacity.

One night in late August, I stood behind a young man in a grocery store who appeared to be in his early thirties. He kept turning around and flirting with me. I was wearing a cap which was pulled down to the point of somewhat covering my face, and either he thought I was younger than I was, or he enjoyed flirting with older women. After a few minutes, I recognized him as one of my former Lincoln Park High School students, but he did not recognize me as one of his former teachers. I asked him, "Young man, what high school did you attend?" "Lincoln Park," he answered, still not recognizing me. "So why are you buying that beer?" I asked him in a stern voice. He turned and looked at me, and after realizing who I was, he moaned, "Ohhhhh Nohhhhh, Ms. Hutchens. I can't believe it's you. Ms. Hutchens, do you know you're the only reason I didn't end up in jail?"

I asked him to explain to me what I had to do with him not ending up in jail, and he said, "Every time I thought about doing something that could make me end up in jail, I remembered how you pointed your finger at us and told us to stay out of trouble, so I stayed out of jail." I asked him if that meant he also had stayed out of trouble since I last saw him. "I didn't say that," he responded. I love seeing my former students, and it is times like these when I am convinced that I had a positive impact on their lives.

Although I had sought help from Judge Castillo, Judge Chang still cancelled the scheduled August 30, 2013 status hearing and continued my case until October 15, 2013, as my motion to alter, amend, or reconsider judgment remained under advisement. This was the eighth time he had continued my case after I filed the motion.

SEPTEMBER 2013

My three-month position with Briljent ended, and once again, I was unemployed. Briljent's HR director told me the company was pleased with my performance, and she assured me Briljent would contact me for more temporary contracts in the future if and when they became available.

Given my ongoing problems with finding permanent employment and my belief the Board was retaliating against me, on September 9, 2013, my attorney and I filed a second lawsuit against the Board in the US Northern District of Illinois Court. Assigned Case Number 13 C 6447, I alleged in the two count lawsuit that based upon my filing and prosecution of *Hutchens v. Board of Education*, Case Number 09 C 7931, as well as my opposition to unlawful discrimination, the Board had continuously retaliated against me in violation of 42 U.S.C. Sec. 2000e-3(a) and the First Amendment to the United States Constitution, by not providing timely, professional references and employment verification information which would allow me to acquire new employment.

Count II of my lawsuit was filed in conjunction with the Illinois Whistleblower's Protection Act 740 ILCS 174/15 (2013) in which I alleged that as a direct result of my reporting what I believed was a payroll fraud scheme to the US Department of Justice, the Illinois State's Attorney and the Board's inspector general, the Board had repeatedly retaliated against me. Because the new lawsuit was related to the first one I had filed which remained "under advisement" due to my filing the motion to alter, amend, or reconsider, the second lawsuit also was assigned to Judge Chang.

OCTOBER 2013

Although my motion to alter, amend, or reconsider had been pending for more than one year, stating, "The Court needs additional time to rule on the motion to alter judgment," Judge Chang cancelled the October 15, 2013 status hearing until November 20, 2013, as my motion remained under advisement. This was the ninth time the case was continued after my attorney filed the motion.

After reviewing numerous court cases, I noted that when litigants file motions to alter, amend, or reconsider, judges generally know soon after the motions are filed how they will rule, because the motions are filed within 28 days after the judge ruled against a litigant. But after getting no help from District Court Chief Judge Rueben Castillo, and with no end in sight to Judge Chang's repeated continuances, on October 23, 2013, I requested assistance from the US Court of Appeals for the Seventh Circuit's Chief Judge, Honorable Diane Wood. In a letter I wrote to her, I explained that my lawsuit was close to the four-year mark, and after initially causing me to wait for seventeen months and through eleven continuances following the Board's filing of its motion for summary judgment, and another fifteen months and nine continuances after I filed my motion to alter, amend, or reconsider, Judge Chang had not ruled on my case and had not held a status hearing on my case since the 2011 appearance hearing of my attorney.

Although I had brought his numerous mistakes and massive omissions of my evidence to Judge Chang's attention when I filed my motion to alter, amend or reconsider, exactly five days after I sought assistance from the US Court of Appeals for the Seventh Circuit, he denied my motion. After I had waited more than one year for him to rule on my motion, the judge explained in a five- page order his reasons for denying some of my complaints against the Board, and in relation to my other complaints, he opined that "None of the other arguments presented by Hutchens merit reconsideration." After reading Judge Chang's court ruling, one of my friends said, "None of the other arguments you presented merit reconsideration? He's telling you to *kiss his ass*!"

I began visiting the Northern District of Illinois Court several times each week to peruse Judge Change's other cases on the Court's PACER system. He was assigned at least 200 cases during that period and I cannot say I reviewed all of them, for he was assigned new cases frequently. However, I did peruse many of the lawsuits assigned to him, and what I learned was Judge Chang already had ruled on cases which either had been filed after or almost the same time I filed my lawsuit.

I reviewed a case in which Judge Chang had ruled in favor of a black plaintiff's religious discrimination lawsuit claim; i.e., *Weathers v. FedEx Corporate Services, Inc.*, a disability lawsuit claim filed by another black plaintiff, *Brenda Myers v. Wickes Furniture Co., Inc.*, and yet another case in which he had ruled in favor of a black plaintiff who alleged her employer had violated the Family and Medical Leave Act (FMLA), *Ballard v. Chicago Park District*. However, was unable to identify even one case in which a black person who filed a lawsuit alleging race discrimination in violation of Title VII had made it past the summary judgment stage and proceeded to trial against their employer when the case was assigned to Judge Chang. It certainly is possible that I overlooked Judge Chang's favorable rulings in this regard.

Weathers v. FedEx Corporate Services, Inc. was filed in September 2009, which was just three months before I filed my lawsuit. However, Judge Chang, who began presiding over Weathers and the aforementioned cases in January 2011, ruled on the Weathers case more than eight months before he ruled on mine. Also, although *Hicks v. Forest Preserve District of Cook County Illinois* concluded while under Judge Chang's jurisdiction, it was Judge David Coar who previously had denied the forest preserve summary judgment and ruled in favor of Hicks, a black plaintiff, in his employment discrimination lawsuit.

As it relates to race discrimination lawsuits Hispanics filed against their employers, in *EEOC v. Lisle Hilton,* Judge Chang issued a consent decree on May 5, 2011, against a suburban Chicago hotel after its executive chef repeatedly harassed and used racial slurs against two Hispanic cooks. In response to the Title VII national origin lawsuit filed by the EEOC on behalf of the Hispanic workers, Judge Chang ordered the hotel to pay

$195,000 to the two Hispanic workers who had filed discrimination charges with the EEOC and also to another employee. The decree also (a) required the hotel to report any further complaints of retaliation or national origin harassment to the EEOC for three years, (b) required remedial training for all employees of the hotel, and (c) mandated that the executive chef receive personal anti-discrimination training. Additionally, the decree included an injunction prohibiting further discrimination on the basis of national origin and barring retaliation for reporting or complaining about discrimination. This lawsuit was filed on September 28, 2009, which was less than ninety days before I filed mine; yet, Judge Chang ruled on the case fourteen months before he ruled on my case in which I alleged the Board and Amanda Rivera, Hispanic, violated my civil rights.

In *Diaz v. Elgin School District U46*, Judge Chang ruled in favor of Hispanic plaintiff Saul Diaz's race discrimination complaint even though on page 2 of his September 22, 2011 court opinion, Judge Chang wrote that "Throughout his employment, Diaz had work performance issues." He also wrote that "a number of managers, administrators, principals and coworkers complained about his work performance," and his former manager "suspended him without pay for five days based on several concerns including '[d]efacing' various documents belonging to the head custodian and poor work performance."

On page 12 of the opinion, Judge Chang wrote "Indeed the record is filled with examples of Diaz's poor work performance." On page 13 of the opinion, Judge Chang wrote. "Diaz's contention that he performed well at his job is refuted by the warning and two suspensions he received that reflected serious work-related deficiencies. Therefore, Diaz has not shown that he was meeting the School District's legitimate expectations."

My former director, Rivera, and former managers, McDonagh and Cushing made allegations regarding my so-called poor performance, but they filed not a shred of evidence to support their allegations. Alternatively, I filed layers of documents in court which refuted each allegation they made against me. Even still, concluding that I could not prevail under the direct *or* indirect methods of proof,

Judge Chang ruled against me twice (on the Board's motion for summary judgement and my motion to alter, amend or reconsider) after repeatedly continuing my litigation before ruling on both motions.

In *Corral v. UNO Charter School*, a case in which a Chicago teacher sued a charter school at which he worked in 2010 allegedly for violating his civil rights, Judge Chang ruled in favor of the Hispanic plaintiff, David Corral, in 2013.

Dora Soto v. City of Aurora was filed in February 2012. Only one year after Soto filed her lawsuit (May 17, 2013) Judge Chang denied the City of Aurora summary judgment on Soto's race discrimination and national origin claims which meant Soto, Hispanic, was able to proceed to trial on those claims.

Although Judge Chang also presided over numerous lawsuits in which black employees complained that their employers discriminated against them and violated their civil rights, I was unable to find a single case in which he ruled in favor of the plaintiff. (See *Deffenbaugh v. BNSF Railway Company; Stanuel L. Thomas v. Norfolk Southern Railway Company; Snorton-Pierce v. State of Illinois; and Sharon Smith v. CNA Financial Corporation and Continental Casualty Company.*)

When Judge Chang dismissed other claims Hispanics in the aforementioned cases had filed in their lawsuits, in *every* instance, he still ruled in favor of them on their race discrimination charges. In every instance Judge Chang ruled against the previously mentioned black litigants' race discrimination claims, with the exception of the claims the litigants voluntarily dismissed, he dismissed every other claim they filed against their employer and terminated their cases, which also is what happened in my case.

Although I found cases in which Judge Chang ruled against at least one Asian and one white plaintiff who filed race discrimination or national origin lawsuits, I was unable to find enough cases under his jurisdiction filed by other plaintiffs of those races to make a comparison of how he ruled in terms of those groups as a whole.

November 2013

The US Court of Appeals for the Seventh Circuit serves the states of Illinois, Indiana, and Wisconsin. It sits in Chicago, Illinois and is located at 219 South Dearborn Street of the United States Courthouse. The Office of the Clerk is in Room 2722. Currently, the Appeals Court has eleven judges, all of whom have chambers in the Chicago courthouse.

My attorney and I agreed to appeal Judge Chang's ruling. The Notice of Appeal for a civil lawsuit must be filed within thirty days after a judge has entered judgment (final ruling) on a case and identifies the aspects of the district court's final judgment the appellant or appellee is appealing. I repeatedly asked my attorney to file the Notice of Appeal, and we still almost missed the filing date. I had miscalculated the last date on which we absolutely had to file the notice, and one afternoon I began counting on my fingers the number of days that had passed since Judge Chang's ruling on my motion to alter, amend or reconsider judgment. I stopped in my tracks when I realized twenty-nine days had passed, and if we did not file the Notice of Appeal that very day, I could kiss justice good-bye.

I called my attorney and told her I would be at her office shortly. We had exactly eight hours (until midnight) to file my Notice of Appeal, and I made clear that if she did not do it, I would. I sat there as she filed it that day. According to federal appellate court rules, the Notice of Appeal must (1) identify the party or parties making the appeal, (2) designate the judgment or order appealed, and (3) name the court to which the appeal is taken.

My attorney wrote in the notice that I (the plaintiff) sought review and was appealing "all aspects of the final judgment entered in this matter on October 28, 2013, including the order of July 3, 2012, granting the defendants summary judgment and all orders and judgment entered in favor of the defendants." She also wrote that the "District Court erred as a matter of law in granting summary judgment where there were significant material facts in dispute between the parties, and erred as a matter of law in making factual determinations." My attorney prepared the Notice of Appeal and the required docketing statement, and I completed an application and supporting affidavit to proceed on appeal *in forma pauperis,* which my attorney filed on November 26, 2013.

Rivera had illegally circumvented me from being rehired to my former position, the Board had prevented me from acquiring new employment, and Judge Chang had continued my litigation for nearly three years. Therefore, by that time, I was entirely out of money. I was rendered indigent, destitute, a poor person.

After earning three college degrees full-time at night while simultaneously working full-time; after having a highly successful career in the corporate arena for nearly two decades; after serving as president of my own company for several years and receiving a Hall of Fame award as a result of the success of my small business; after earning multiple middle and high school teaching certifications which qualified me to teach six subjects; after receiving numerous recognitions and awards for being an accomplished educator; after achieving National Board Certification, the nation's highest teaching credential; and after earning a salary of nearly six-figures for which I had worked hard and deserved every penny, my financial status was so dire I could not afford to pay the required $500 fee to file the Notice of Appeal. (This fee is not required if the appellant or appellee files the appeal *in forma pauperis,* which means the district and appeals courts are authorized by 28 U.S.C. § 1915(a) and Fed. R. App. P. 24 to allow an appeal to be taken without prepayment of fees and costs or security for costs by a party who makes an affidavit that he or she cannot pay those costs.) (See the Federal Rules of Appellate Procedure and Circuit Rules of the United States Court of Appeals for the Seventh Circuit.)

The dictionary defines a pauper as "A person without any means of support, especially a destitute person who depends on aid from public welfare funds or charity." The Latin term *in forma pauperis* or "in the manner of a pauper" is defined by Wikipedia as "someone who is without the funds to pursue the normal costs of a lawsuit or criminal defense." Both of these terms defined my financial status and me in every conceivable way.

December 2013

Judge Chang was responsible for approving my application to allow me to proceed on appeal *in forma pauperis*. Citing my "affidavit, which adequately set out" why I was unable to pay the appellate filing fee, my "intermittent work and inadequate income during the previous years," my "lack of a guarantee of future employment," my "insufficient cash on hand to pay the appellate filing fee," my "monthly and long-term debt," and the fact that my "appeal would not be objectively frivolous given the standard of review and the summary judgment record," Judge Chang granted the motion for me to proceed on appeal *in forma pauperis*. Although I did not mention it in the application I had filed, Judge Chang's repeated continuances in my litigation were absolutely instrumental in my extraordinarily poor financial situation, including my "insufficient cash on hand to pay the appellate filing fee." His inordinate number of delays also contributed to my severe anxiety, depression and serious medical issues.

Sunil Kumar, Susan Margaret O'Keefe, and Brian Flores filed attorney appearances on behalf of the Board in my second lawsuit, 13 C 6447. Flores initially performed the duties related to the case until Dreishmire made an attorney appearance several months later and became lead attorney.

In December 2013, I applied for two positions with the Board: re-engagement teacher, where I would have been working with at-risk students, which, of course, was my passion, and instructional educational specialist, wherein I would have been responsible for designing and implementing teacher and principal evaluation systems. I met every credential requirement listed for both positions.

My opening appellant's brief was due on January 23, 2014. At my attorney's request, the date was rescheduled to February 24, 2014. I knew better than to rely on her to write my brief. Therefore, to learn the appropriate rules and determine how to write appellate briefs, I began reviewing federal civil appeals on the Internet and reading the *Handbook of the US Court of Appeals for the Seventh Circuit*. I spent numerous hours each day studying the Handbook.

Meanwhile, my never-ending unemployment continued. It had become an unwanted and unfortunate way of life for me. With the exception of my three-month assignment with Briljent and the brief temporary consulting jobs I had at the beginning of the year, I did not work at all in 2013. For the fifth year in a row, my Christmas was anything but merry, and 2013 was by far the worst year of my entire life. I was glad when it ended, and I could not imagine that living in hell would have been any worse than the life I was living.

CHAPTER 15

13 C 6447 and 13-3648
Proceeding *pro se* in the District and Appellate Courts

JANUARY 2014

THE SUPPLEMENTAL EDUCATIONAL SERVICE PROVIDER for whom I had worked in 2013, hired me again to tutor CPS students in reading and math during after school hours. I was assigned to work only six hours each week, and the job lasted only three months.

In late January 2014, the charter school which had hired me in January 2013 for a one-month temporary assignment to proctor exams for elementary school English Language Learners hired me again for the same project. During the same week, the Board responded to my second lawsuit, 13 C 6447, denying both of my claims.

In relation to my initial lawsuit, which was on appeal, I began writing a draft of my opening brief. My attorney, who was aware I was writing it, informed me she was preparing for the March trial of a case on which she had been working, and she would not assist me with writing my brief until after it ended. Although I was displeased because my case had been filed long before the case to which she was referring, I kept quiet because I did not want any unnecessary drama which might have resulted in her refusing to write my appellate brief.

In late January, I received an email from a staff member of the Board's Talent Office inviting me to interview for the instructional effectiveness specialist position, one of the jobs for which I had applied in December 2013. I was excited about the interview, and although my excitement was tempered about the thought of returning to CPS after all that had happened, I knew if I was hired I could at least earn a salary which was commensurate with my education and experience. A few of my family members and friends were critical of me because I considered returning to CPS after what I had endured. Most had not offered to pay my bills during my extended layoff, and they still were not offering to pay them if I remained unemployed. Therefore, I told those who had a problem with me possibly returning to work for CPS that they could either pay my bills or mind their own business. They chose the latter.

My interview with several departmental staff members, the executive director, and the manager of the department was held on Friday, February 7, 2014. To my surprise, one of the people interviewing me for the job was someone who had worked with me in the PDU and knew of my first lawsuit against the Board. The Board's attorneys had subpoenaed her for a deposition in my lawsuit, a decision with which I had no input and was not involved. Five years had passed since we had last seen each other, and I did not immediately recognize her. When I realized who she was and acknowledged her, she appeared uncomfortable and avoided looking at me as much as possible.

There were several positions open, and I was happy with how the initial interview had gone. After meeting with the departmental staff members, I engaged in another interview with the executive director and manager of the department. Both seemed impressed with my skills, education, experience, and National Board Certification. At the conclusion of the interview they told me they would make a decision the following week about whom to hire.

Two days later, the HR director informed me via email that the department had "decided to move forward with other candidates." During our communication prior to the interview, she appeared warm, friendly and personable. However, her tone in the email was short, curt and dismissive. "Here we go again," I said to myself. I suspected my former PDU colleague had informed the department's executive director of my lawsuit. I can only surmise the reason I was not hired, but what I do know is by the end of January 2014, I remained unemployed.

February 2014

One day during the beginning of February 2014, I sent my attorney an email requesting information about a court status hearing which she had attended that morning regarding my second lawsuit, but she did not respond. When I received no response after sending her another email in which I wrote, "I can't believe you're ignoring me again," she sent me an email explaining she had entered a scheduling order in the case. She ended the message exactly as follows: "I can't help you if you are going to sweat me over b.s."

On February 24, 2014, my attorney also filed a motion with the US Court of Appeals for the Seventh Circuit to extend time to file my opening appellate brief. The Court granted her motion and extended the due date for the brief until April 10, 2014. I continued to draft the brief, and she continued to prepare for the trial of the other case. She lifted not a finger to help me write the brief, she provided me no directives as to how or what I should write, and when I sent her emails informing her of my progress, she ignored me.

At the end of the month, a staff member of the Board's Department of Strategic School Support Services invited me to interview for a professional development and instructional coaching position, another job for which I had applied in December 2013. I was pleased with the interview. Although there were several openings, immediately afterward, I was notified that I no longer was being considered for the job.

In late February, I interviewed for the position of director of educational services with one of the nation's largest not-for-profit providers of services designed exclusively for people with criminal records. My credentials, employment history, and experience working with inmates at York Alternative High School is what led the organization to contact me after I applied for the job. However, after two interviews and a reference check of my previous employment, I did not get the job.

March 2014

After applying for a part-time English instructor's position with Daley College, another Chicago City College, the departmental director contacted me to interview with her, her boss, and the HR manager. Prior to the interview, the director and I communicated at least three times regarding the hours and days I would be available to work and my preferred work location, as the college had two satellite sites in addition to its main campus. She appeared extremely interested in having me join her staff.

I had an excellent interview with the three of them, and as it concluded, the director asked me to complete a formal job application so I could move to the next step in the process. Two days later, she notified me by email that the selection committee did not choose me "for the current opening." As if she thought I was going to call her after she rejected me, she ended her email as follows: "Please note, due to high volume of applications, recruiters we are unable to accept phone calls." (This is exactly how she wrote it.)

April 2014

Six months had passed since the day my attorney had filed the Notice of Appeal which signaled my intent to appeal Judge Chang's ruling. Other than filing the notice and other required documents, my attorney had made no effort to help me write my opening brief or to find out how much work I had done preparing it. Because of her repeated requests to the Seventh Circuit to allow us more time to file the brief, by this time, it was due on April 8, 2014.

The trial on which my attorney had been working and supposedly had kept her from assisting me with writing my opening brief had ended in early March 2014. More than one month later, she still had neither begun working on my brief nor had she shown any interest in doing so. In fact, just days before my brief was due, she still had not mentioned it to me. During the first week in April I asked her by email if she knew when she would begin working on the brief. She responded that she was not sure because she was "working on three Board projects." Because I had worked closely with her for several years, I knew each of those cases had been filed after mine; therefore, I did not understand why she was putting them in front of mine when the Appeals Court was expecting my appellate brief later that week.

My attorney also had not filed a motion requesting another extension of time in which to file my brief, and the Appeals Court's rule was extension requests must be made at least seven days before the brief was due. In fact, the Court disfavors extension requests, and tardiness can cause the Clerk of the Court to dismiss the appeal. Because I had spent hundreds of hours reading appellate court decisions and the Seventh Circuit's handbook, I knew the rules, so I was aware that most likely, the Court was displeased with my attorney's lack of diligence in filing my brief and my case might have been in danger of dismissal.

I sent my attorney an email reminding her she needed to request another extension of time to file the appellate brief. She responded, "Will do—you are right." But she did not indicate when she would file the request. Clearly ignoring the critical issue we had before us involving my appeal, she asked me to send her information related to my second lawsuit, which I did. Afterward, I again asked her when she intended to help me write my opening appellate brief. I already had spent an enormous amount of time writing the brief as I waited patiently while she worked on other cases and completely ignored mine. She did so knowing I was completely destitute by this time and desperately needed my case resolved. Writing an appellate brief is quite different than writing responses and additional facts for summary judgment, so I was not nearly as confident as I had been during that process. More important, because of my attorney's history of not working on my case, I knew I was in BIG trouble.

After sending her another email and receiving no response, I had had enough of her. I headed to the Appeals Court and asked the *pro se* clerk how I could get the information necessary to properly write the brief myself. The *pro se* clerk was enormously helpful. He patiently walked me through the steps necessary to prepare my brief, but he told me he was not allowed to show me how to write citations. This was a big disappointment, for creating citations was the most important step in the appellate brief writing process to me. I was confident I knew how to write all other parts of the brief. The *pro se* clerk suggested I access PACER and look at other appellate briefs, and I decided I would peruse briefs related to Title VII and Section 1983 race discrimination cases, for those were the two claims my attorney and I had not dismissed. He also told me I could not file a brief unless my attorney withdrew from my case.

When I arrived home, I sent another email to my attorney informing her of my visit to the Appeals Court. I also expressed my lack of confidence in her representing me. I told her I intended to move forward with my appellate brief with or without her help, and I would get whatever help necessary to complete my brief. She sent me a response which I did not immediately read. I learned later that in the message, she asked me if I wanted her to withdraw from my case. I did not read her message because I knew whatever she had written would make me react in a less-than-positive way. I was sick of her, and by that time I was so stressed over the direction in which my appeal and life appeared to be heading, I refused to get into any negative back and forth email messaging with her.

The following morning, I made another trip to the Appeals Court and asked the *pro se* clerk to access PACER so I could find out if anything new had happened regarding my appeal. The Appeals Court is unlike the US Northern District of Illinois Court which is located in the same building. In the District Court, you can go to the twentieth floor where there are several terminals and access PACER yourself. In the US Court of Appeals for the Seventh Circuit there are no specific terminals which the public can access. A clerk must access information on the terminal for you.

I had a gut feeling my attorney had withdrawn from my case, and I was right. Apparently, after she sent me the final email which I had not opened, just two days before my appellate brief was due, she had filed a motion to withdraw from my case. She wrote in her motion that because I had told her I would "acquire the help of civil rights organizations and anyone else if necessary" she "could not ethically" continue to represent me on appeal. According to Lawyers.com, clients have an almost absolute right to hire and fire their attorneys for whatever reason they choose or deem necessary, but attorneys cannot "fire" their clients at whim; they must have a valid reason.

My attorney's alleged issue with me regarding "ethics" was the excuse she used to persuade the Appeals Court to allow her to withdraw from my case because she did not want to be bothered. Although it is true I had told her I would acquire the services of civil rights groups and anyone else to help me if necessary, there absolutely was nothing "unethical" about that. She just did not want to do any work on my case and she never had wanted to do any work on my case. The Clerk of the Appeals Court initially denied her request. That did not surprise me, as courts generally will not allow an attorney to withdraw from a case during important stages of the lawsuit, such as when a critical brief is due.

I returned home and noticed my attorney had sent me another email with an attachment, which I assumed was a motion to also withdraw from my second lawsuit. Again, I assumed correctly, but because I had worked for lawyers and also because of what I had learned during my lawsuits, I knew what I had to do. I began writing my own motion for the Appeals Court in which I stated I did not object to my attorney's withdrawal from my case on appeal. I did not know if it was appropriate to do so, but I explained that my attorney had withdrawn from my appeal simply because, as always, she did not want to do any work on my case. I also requested an extension of time to either find another attorney or to write my own brief, which was about 50 percent completed by that time.

After I filed the motion, the Clerk allowed my attorney to withdraw from representing me on appeal and granted me the five-week extension I had requested. In the meantime, Judge Chang refused to allow her to withdraw from my second lawsuit until I appeared before him on May 1, 2014, which I discuss later in this chapter.

Lisa Dreishmire, the Board's attorney assigned to my case, called me shortly after the Appeals Court granted my extension. In a congenial, concerned tone, she left me a voicemail message stating that she wanted to "assure [me] for [my] peace of mind in case [I] was unaware that the Seventh Circuit had granted [me] the extension I had requested." I thought it was odd she would call me, and I smiled as I said to myself that she probably thought I was a "poor *pro se*," who was about to get my butt kicked by the Board now that I did not have an attorney. But in reality, even when I *had* an attorney, the Board was kicking my butt.

Initially, I was afraid when my attorney abandoned me. Although I knew better than to rely on her when I needed her, I never, ever thought she would walk away from me two days before the due date of a document as crucial to my case as my appellate brief. My family, friends, and other supporters were absolutely livid when she withdrew from representing me on appeal, but as time passed, I was not. I was just happy to have her out of my life and out of my way. I felt relieved and free for the first time in years. There would be no more missed deadlines, no more kissing her butt to get my work done (which still did not happen even when I kissed up), and above all, I could do things MY WAY, and they would be done correctly and on time.

The first few days after she withdrew, I searched for a new attorney, even though I knew my search efforts probably would be fruitless. I contacted a few law school clinics and asked them to help me. I also reached out to several lawyers I personally knew and requested referrals. It was a waste of time; no one wanted to be bothered with writing an opening and reply appellate brief for me when I had no money to pay them. More important, there was very little time for an attorney to become familiar enough with my case to write two appellate briefs in a few short weeks and also engage in an oral argument. As my search continued, I became filled with despair, and combined with my never-ending unemployment and lack of money, it was almost too much for me to handle. I felt as if I were sinking—fast!

After a law school professor first considered my request to take my case on appeal, but changed his mind ten days later, I decided that regardless of the obstacles which stood in my way, I was going to continue my fight for justice. That night I stood in my living room, pointed above and said aloud, "God, it's just you and me."

I relaxed and got a good night's sleep the night before I began researching the proper format for writing my brief and relevant citations. Earlier that evening I had taken a long walk. and as I strolled near my home I found a ten-dollar bill lying on the ground in a nearby parking lot. An interesting thing about me is I have found money in all denominations my entire life. But as I picked up the ten-dollar bill that day, there seemed to be a special reason or purpose for me finding it. I felt as if it had good luck or an omen attached to it. Never before had I had such a feeling about money I found. Although I definitely needed it, I placed the ten-dollar bill in a side compartment of my purse and decided to hold onto it at least until my appeal had ended.

The following day was Friday, the day on which I began transforming the very rough draft I had created of my brief into a final document I could file with the Appeals Court. I cannot explain how happy I was that I had had the foresight to begin writing the brief months earlier, for it made all the difference in the world. Using the Seventh Circuit's Handbook and the checklist the *pro se* clerk had given me during one of my visits to the Appeals Court, I carefully researched other briefs I found on the Internet and the court's PACER system to learn how to write each required section of the brief.

I determined the most critical issues I needed to prove to the three-judge appellate panel who would decide my case was Judge Chang's exclusion of my evidence was prejudicial and legal error, and the "non-discriminatory justifications" articulated by Rivera and the Board's other witnesses were pretext. Therefore, those were the issues on which I spent the most time researching, writing, and finding relevant case law, which I found on the Internet by searching Seventh Circuit and other appellate and district court opinions. I did not use Westlaw, which is considered America's primary online legal research services for lawyers and legal professionals, or any other related service when conducting my research. I viewed numerous Title VII and Section 1983 race discrimination cases which had been decided in the Seventh Circuit and the twelve other appeals courts, and various cases which had been decided in the ninety-four US district courts. I read cases in which the plaintiffs had won so I could determine what they had done and what evidence they presented which caused their successful outcomes. I also read cases in which plaintiffs had lost, in order to determine what they had or had not done which caused their unsuccessful outcomes.

Finding cases in which a person filed their appeal *pro se* and won a race discrimination case in a federal district or appeals court was nearly impossible. Although there might have been numerous cases in which a *pro se* won a race discrimination case on appeal, despite my extensive research, I was able to find only one such case, and it involved a white appellant in another city who filed his appeal in the Second Circuit Appeals Court. (*DiPetto v. U.S. Postal*

Service) I knew I had a major challenge on my hands, but there was no way I even considered giving up my important fight for justice.

May 2014

May was an extremely busy month in relation to my two lawsuits. First, I attended a District Court hearing on my attorney's motion to withdraw from my second case, for as I mentioned, Judge Chang (who remember, also had been assigned to my second case) refused to allow her to withdraw until I appeared before him. My attorney and I and both of the Board's attorneys, Lisa Dreishmire and Brian Flores, attended the hearing. However, because Judge Chang determined the matter regarding my attorney's withdrawal was attorney/client privileged information, he did not allow the Board's attorneys to remain in the courtroom during that part of the hearing.

Before Judge Chang ordered them to wait in the hallway outside of the courtroom, Flores reported to him that my attorney had failed to comply with his repeated requests for information and attempts to schedule me for a deposition in relation to my second case, which I had filed in September 2013. In fact, Flores remarked he had provided my attorney dates on which he wanted to depose me in the case, but she did not respond. This surprised me, as she had not mentioned anything to me about a deposition. In fact, she had told me very little about the second case, the one in which she told me I was "sweating [her] over b.s." when I asked her what had happened during a related court hearing. What I knew is what I learned when I visited the court and accessed my case on the PACER system. Information regarding depositions usually are not contained on the system unless the depositions are mentioned in various documents which have been filed in court.

As I had done with the Clerk of the Appeals Court, I stated emphatically to Judge Chang I did not object to my attorney withdrawing from my second lawsuit. He attempted to quell what he conjectured was a "misunderstanding" between my attorney and me, but I insisted I no longer wanted her as my attorney. As far as I was concerned, there was no way I could perform any worse on my case than she had, but more important, no longer would I have to be bothered with her. After trying unsuccessfully to change my mind, Judge Chang granted her motion to withdraw from my lawsuit in the District Court.

I continued to work hard day and night writing my opening appellate brief. Because I do my best writing during the wee hours of the morning, I usually began writing between 2:00 a.m. and 3:00 a.m. each morning and worked until 6:30 a.m. Then, I would stop writing and get ready for work, as I had secured another temporary consulting assignment with a Washington-based firm. My duties were to conduct literacy testing for CPS students. I enjoyed the assignment. It paid a fairly decent hourly wage and it was very interesting, but when it ended one month later, it was the same old story; once again, I was unemployed.

I read every legal document, every published article, and every Internet blog related to Title VII and Section 1983 anti-discrimination laws I could find. I also read the Seventh Circuit's Handbook repeatedly from cover to cover to familiarize myself with appellate brief preparation and requirements. In keeping with the Seventh Circuit's rule to request an extension of time at least seven days before a brief is due, on May 8, 2014, I filed a request for a final extension of 14 days in which to file my brief. I assured the Clerk of the Court I did not anticipate requesting another extension of time, and he approved my request.

The opening brief of the appellant and appellee must comply with the Fed. R. App. P. 32(a)(7)(B), (C) type volume limits, which permits a maximum of fifty double-spaced pages (excluding footnotes and required court documents) or fourteen thousand words. I had much to say in my brief, and although my journalistic education has trained me to be a very concise writer, I needed more than fifty pages to say it. I wanted to tell *everything* about the hot mess which had been labeled a lawsuit. Therefore, when I filed my request for a fourteen-day extension of time, I also asked the Appeals Court for permission to file an "oversized brief," or a brief containing more than fifty pages.

I wanted to file at least sixty pages, but unless the circumstances are extenuating, usually, neither district or appeals courts grant such permission. Although I was aware of this policy, I asked for permission anyway. As I expected, the Clerk granted me the fourteen-day extension to file my brief but denied me permission to file more than fifty pages.

In relation to the required Standard of Review, I immediately found an Appellate Court Standard of Review which was relevant to the main issue in my case—Judge Chang's exclusion of nearly all of my evidence. Apparently, I made the correct choice; after I filed my brief, the Clerk did not notify me that my Standard of Review was incorrect. But I'm getting ahead of myself, so I'll continue explaining how I prepared my brief.

The Statement of the Case is an integral component of the appellate brief. It is comprised of the appellant's summary, facts and procedural history of the case and the issues being presented for review. I took my time and great care when preparing my Statement of the Case, and when I completed it, I felt strongly about it. Taken directly from my opening appellant's brief, the following is the Statement of the Case I filed in the US Court of Appeals for the Seventh Circuit:

STATEMENT OF THE CASE

Plaintiff-Appellant, Joyce Hutchens, challenges and seeks review of the District Court's ("Court") final judgment, including the Court's July 3, 2012 Order granting Defendants-Appellees summary judgment, and, therefore, dismissing each of Plaintiff-Appellant's complaints, and a post-trial motion timely filed on July 31, 2012, during which the Court denied Plaintiff-Appellant's Motion to Alter, Amend or Reconsider Judgment on October 28, 2013.

The Court grossly abused its discretion in its July 3, 2012 Order by silencing Plaintiff-Appellants' "side of the story," almost in its entirety, and refusing to allow her voice to be heard. That is, while the Court included in its Orders the numerous criticisms the Defendants-Appellants proffered regarding Plaintiff-Appellant's numerous alleged work deficiencies, the Court improperly excluded nearly all record-cited facts and supporting evidence Plaintiff-Appellant offered in opposition of the Defendants-Appellant's summary judgment motion which directly controverted those allegations, as well as the claims she brought against the Defendants-Appellees. The evidence raised numerous triable issues of material fact as to whether the Defendants-Appellees' stated reasons for circumventing Plaintiff-Appellant's rehiring to her former position following her layoff were pretextual. More important, the evidence was relevant and necessary to carry Plaintiff-Appellant's burden of proof and, therefore, survive summary judgment. However, as shown throughout this Brief, with her arguments and factual support excluded in nearly their entirety, it was impossible for Plaintiff-Appellant to satisfy her burden of proof and controvert the Defendants-Appellees' numerous allegations against her. The Court, therefore, prejudiced Plaintiff-Appellant, and this violation alone of Plaintiff-Appellant's constitutional rights warrants a reversal of summary judgment.

Case: 13-3648   Document: 31   Filed: 06/20/2014   Pages: 96

The Court also erred when it improperly and prejudicially used personal views to determine that Plaintiff-Appellant's teaching experience at the "Prison School" caused her to be less-qualified or inadequate to traditional standards of performance, value, or production, than her similarly-situated comparator, for her former position in the PDU in which she had already served for one year. Additionally, the Court erred when it used personal views to rule on issues related to Plaintiff-Appellant's alleged sleeping on the job, performance evaluation and tardiness, when the record-cited, undisputed facts Plaintiff-Appellant presented, demonstrated otherwise. The Court further erred when concluding that Plaintiff-Appellant failed to produce evidence creating genuine issues of material fact on either claim.

The Court's errors were contained in its July 3, 2012 Order granting the Defendants-Appellees summary judgment. When Plaintiff-Appellant brought the massive omissions of her evidence to the Court's attention through the filing of her Motion to Alter, Amend, or Reconsider Judgment, the Court compounded those errors by ruling that her arguments "did not merit reconsideration," even though Plaintiff-Appellant proved that the Court had failed to consider relevant evidence and manifestly erred as a matter of law.

The factual record is lengthy and nearly all statements are disputed. However, the Court excluded nearly every record-cited argument and all supporting evidence Plaintiff-Appellant presented, including documentation which demonstrated the Defendants-Appellees' irrefutable and inexplicable salary disparity between Plaintiff-Appellant and her similarly-situated comparator, and the repeated false testimony of Defendants Amanda Rivera and Lily McDonogh and Plaintiff-Appellant's former manager, Karen Cushing.

But not for the exclusion of Plaintiff-Appellant's evidence, each of the Defendants-Appellees' claims fail, as the Defendants-Appellees produced not a shred of evidence to support

3

their numerous allegations against Plaintiff-Appellant, and although Plaintiff-Appellant controverted each allegation with record-cited evidence and created issues of material fact, the Defendant-Appellees were granted summary judgment, and Plaintiff-Appellant was denied her constitutional rights to due process of a fair trial by a jury.

The Court further erred when granting summary judgment on a retaliation complaint it characterized as based upon a claim of sexual harassment. However, Plaintiff-Appellant filed no such claim and the details outlining the accurate cause for the retaliation claim were contained in her Local Rule 56.1 Statements. Although Plaintiff-Appellant explained the error and directed the Court to the accurate retaliation claim information on her Motion to Alter, the Court refused to alter the inaccuracy. Therefore, Plaintiff-Appellant's name continues to be associated with a sex harassment claim she did not file.

Following two inordinate delays in this litigation, the Court dismissed Plaintiff-Appellant's case as though her claims of discrimination were trivial and unworthy of the Court's fair examination, and inconsequential to our country's important civil rights laws.[1] The successive delays in the Court's rulings, the omission of nearly 100% of Plaintiff-Appellant's admissible evidence, and the Court's repeated ignoring of the Defendants-Appellees' numerous false statements illustrates the Court's unbridled bias of Plaintiff-Appellant, and she believes the Court treated her prejudicially and egregiously. The Court's errors were so prejudicial to Plaintiff-Appellant's constitutional rights, and the judgment was so clearly against logic and

---

[1] The District Court issued its July 3, 2012 Order 17 months and 11 continuances after the Defendant-Appellees filed their Motion for Summary Judgment on February 15, 2011. (Docket No. 75) The Court also issued its October 28, 2013 Order 15 months and 9 continuances following Plaintiff-Appellant's July 31, 2012 filing of her Motion to Alter, Amend or Reconsider Judgment. (Docket. No. 98) Thus, Plaintiff-Appellant experienced a delay of a combined total of 32 consecutive months and 20 continuances before the Court issued the two Orders on her case. There were no extenuating circumstances necessitating this delay, and with the exception of appearance hearings for Plaintiff-Appellant's and the Defendants-Appellees new and substituted counsel, there were no status hearings held during the 32 month period the motions were under advisement.

4

Case: 13-3648　　Document: 31　　Filed: 06/20/2014　　Pages: 96

unjustified by Plaintiff-Appellant's evidence, Plaintiff-Appellant respectfully requests that this Honorable Court reverse the District Court's judgment on Count I, 42 U.S.C § 1981 – Race Discrimination, Count II, Section 1983 – Equal Protection Clause, Race Discrimination; Count III, Race Discrimination –Title VII and Count VI, Intentional Infliction of Emotion Distress charges. Plaintiff-Appellant also requests that this Court modifies Count VII, the Retaliation-Title VII claim, to ensure that the record reflects the true and accurate cause of action as further herein discussed, as Plaintiff-Appellant did not file a retaliation charge based on a claim of sexual harassment.

I filed my opening appellate brief on May 21, 2014, which was nine days earlier than the May 30, 2014 extension date I had requested permission to file it. As I headed home afterward, I felt empowered, happy, and free. I was extremely pleased with the job I had done researching and writing my brief and elated I had completed and filed it so soon after my attorney had withdrawn from my case. Because of the thousands of hours I had spent throughout the many years of my litigation studying Title VII and Section 1983 anti-discrimination laws, I knew, without a doubt, I had addressed the issues necessary to win my appeal.

The following day, I attended a status hearing regarding my second lawsuit. Judge Chang had scheduled the hearing to provide a ruling on my motion for attorney representation, and the Board's counsel, Flores, also attended the hearing. Immediately after my case was called and Flores and I introduced ourselves, Judge Chang informed me he had read my appellate brief which I had filed the previous day. (Apparently, the Appeals Court had transmitted the document to him since he was the District Court's judge on my case.) "I see you filed your brief yesterday; a *fifty-page brief*! I don't agree with everything you said in it, but your brief is impressive," he said. He asked me if an attorney had helped me write the brief, and I assured him I had written it myself.

As if surprised, he then mentioned that I had two master's degrees, and therefore, I was not a "typical" indigent litigant. There was no reason for my education to have been a surprise to Judge Chang. He had served for more than three years as the judge in my first lawsuit, which was now on appeal, and in my summary judgment information which I filed in 2011, I specifically indicated that I had two master's degrees. Judge Chang denied my motion for attorney representation and cited my "advanced education" and "the competency of my *pro se* Seventh Circuit brief" as the reasons for his decision.

There is no constitutional or statutory right for a litigant to have a court-appointed attorney. Most indigent parties in civil litigation must fend for themselves. Judge Chang had volunteered to appoint an attorney for me. I did not request to have an attorney represent me until he asked me to complete the necessary forms so he could appoint an attorney for me after my attorney had withdrawn from my second lawsuit. Ostensibly, however, because he learned I held two master's degrees, he changed his mind. Therefore, if I wanted to continue my lawsuit, I was forced to do it *pro se*, and I was ready to bring it!

Approximately one week later, as I perused my opening brief and a few of my exhibits, something caught my attention in the January 25, 2011 motion to vacate hearing transcripts which Judge Chang's court reporter had prepared. I noticed I had mentioned to Judge Chang during the hearing that I had found what I described as a "Settlement Agreement about which I was entirely unaware, apparently made in secret with my opposing attorneys." This reference was to the five-page Settlement Agreement and Release related to McDonagh's unauthorized dismissal from my lawsuit, which was the basis for my February 2011 ARDC complaint against Haake and my former attorney. I recalled I had brought the Settlement Agreement issue to Judge Chang's attention.

What I had not recalled when I filed my summary judgment information in court was Judge Chang had stated, and the court reporter's transcript showed, he specifically had said to me when I mentioned the settlement agreement and asked if I could show it to him, "I don't need to see that document, because if you are saying it hasn't been entered into—I don't hear the defense relying on any type of Settlement Agreement, and that is not part of this case going forward then, okay?"

Any attorney and litigant who has participated in a court hearing can attest to the fact that it is almost impossible to remember everything said during the hearing. In fact, sometimes it is necessary to retrieve transcripts from the court reporter to clarify what was said. That precisely is what had happened with me. Only after I filed my appellate brief three years after the hearing did I vaguely recall—but only after reading the court reporter's related transcripts—Judge Chang had stated he did not want the Settlement Agreement and Release to be used during the remainder of the lawsuit. Therefore, I gave it to my attorney to file with my summary judgment information as part of my evidence against the Board, which meant it also was being used as evidence in my appeal.

I had not mentioned to my attorney what Judge Chang had said because I did not remember he had told me I was not to use the Settlement Agreement and

Release "going forward." My attorney was unaware of what Judge Chang had said because she was not representing me at the time of the hearing, and I had bought the transcript for myself long after the related motion hearing. The bottom line was this: Judge Chang had made clear he wanted the Settlement Agreement and Release issue to disappear after the motion hearing, but I had given the document to my attorney with the remainder of my summary judgment information, and she had filed it on the court's PACER system.

June 2014

It is likely most *pro se* appellants who represent themselves on appeal and most lawyers who represent appellants wait until the appellee file their responses to the opening brief before they write their reply brief. That is the logical way to proceed because until the appellee replies to the appellant's opening brief, the attorney or *pro se* appellant does not know how to respond to the appellee. In other words, it would have made sense for me to wait for the Board to respond to my opening brief before I wrote my reply brief. However, just one week after I filed my opening brief, I began writing my reply brief.

My rationale for this decision was simple: An appeal is a legal process by which a case is brought before a higher court for review of a lower court's decision, and the parties cannot raise new arguments or present new evidence during the proceedings. Therefore, I knew Rivera and the Board could not—or they were not supposed to—change the stories they presented during summary judgment. They had no choice but to stick to the same fairytales and fantastic stores they had told throughout the lawsuit, so it was easy for me to anticipate what they would say and even easier for me to write my reply brief.

I actually enjoyed writing the reply brief far more than I did the opening brief because this time I knew how to incorporate case law. When I finished, I looked in the mirror and made a bet with myself. I said "Self, I'll bet you there will be nothing in the Board's brief that will stop the three-judge panel from reversing Judge Chang's decision."

July 2014

Rivera and the Board filed a motion requesting an extension of time in which to file their appellees' brief. The Appeals Court granted their request, and I continued writing my reply brief.

August 2014

As I continued to proceed *pro se* in the second lawsuit, I sent a Request to Produce Information to the Board regarding questionable details I found in certain personnel documents I had reviewed after retrieving the boxes containing my lawsuit information from my former attorney in June 2014. In response to my request, Dreishmire sent a letter to me on August 8, 2014, in which she cited my "continuing obligations under the Agreed Protective Order the Court entered in [my] prior lawsuit against the Board." In litigation, a protective order prevents the disclosure of sensitive information except to certain individuals under certain conditions.

Dreishmire claimed I was violating the law by attempting to use in my second lawsuit various documents which had been designated as **"CONFIDENTIAL"** during my first lawsuit. She also appeared concerned I had discovered information contained in those documents which could cause federal and state law enforcement to launch an investigation. Therefore, she "requested" that I do the following by August 15, 2014, or "the Board [would] seek relief from the Court:"

1) Return to the Board all documents the Board produced in Case No. 09-CV-07931 (and any copies you made of such documents, including but not limited to the copies you have attempted to re-use in your current litigation).
2) Confirm in writing that you have not disclosed or provided any documents the Board produced in Case No. 09-CV-07931 (including copies of such documents) to anyone other than the Board.
3) Indicate in writing your understanding of and intent to abide by both the Agreed Protective Order entered in Case No. 09-CG-07931 (Docket #19) and the Parties' Agreed Confidentiality Order in Case

No. 13-CV-06647 (Docket #26, a copy of which is attached for your convenience).

As if she thought threatening to "seek relief from the Court" would scare me to death, Dreishmire ended her letter as follows: "Hopefully, however, we can resolve this issue without the necessity of court intervention."

I reviewed the Protective Order which had been drafted by my initial attorney and Haake when my first lawsuit began in 2009. After reading it, I laughed at Dreishmire *and* her letter. Before my second attorney withdrew from my appeal and second lawsuit in April 2014, she stated in a Rule 26(a)(1) Disclosure she submitted to the Board the following: "Relevant documents are attached to Plaintiff's Complaint, except that the Board has in its possession all documents relevant to the previously filed complaint In *Hutchens v. Board*, Case No. 09 C 7931." Rule 26(a)(1) requires each party in a lawsuit to disclose to the opposing party(ies) the name, and if known, the address and telephone number of each individual likely to have information relevant to disputed facts alleged with particularity in the pleadings (court documents). Dreishmire also stated in her letter, "The [Protective] Order required you to return all confidential documents to the Board within 45 days after the 2009 case closed. However, you did not do so, to my knowledge."

Via my responsive email, I reminded her the Protective Order to which she was referring stated that I had "forty-five days after the conclusion of my lawsuit, whether by jury verdict, court order, settlement or by any other means," to return to the Board's counsel the confidential material produced by the Board. Although Judge Chang had dismissed my lawsuit, it was pending in the US Court of Appeals for the Seventh Circuit, and "conclusion of the lawsuit" would have been when the three-judge panel decided the appeal. Dreishmire knew perfectly well I was entitled to those documents until the Seventh Circuit issued a ruling on my appeal, particularly since the three-judge panel's decision would have decided whether or not my case went to trial and received a jury verdict. In my responsive email, I also stated specifically, "If you wish to get the

Court involved in any matter as it relates to me or to this litigation, that is your prerogative."

After Dreishmire and I exchanged additional emails, she asked me to let her know by 5:00 p.m. on Monday, October 6, 2014, if I would agree that (a) I may not rely on my "later-filed lawsuit or on any documents produced by the Board under a protective order in the 2009 lawsuit," and (b) I would return those documents to the Board within 10 days of the date of her email. I ignored Dreishmire, and she neither contacted me again regarding that issue nor did she and the Board "seek Court intervention" to compel me to return the documents to the Board.

That same month, Rivera and the Board filed a motion in the Appeals Court requesting another extension of time in which to file their appellees' brief. The Court granted their request, and I continued writing my reply brief. Meanwhile, the issue involving the $4,724.38 I supposedly owed the Board was two years old and never had been resolved. My attorney had not bothered to respond to the Board's filing of the bill and Judge Chang had not ruled on it after it was filed in 2012 after he granted the Board summary judgment on all of my claims.

The Board's attorneys were well aware almost every witness who testified on their behalf and Rivera's had fabricated their testimony regarding my so-called poor work performance. Yet, on August 4, 2014, Dreishmire filed another motion in an attempt to force me to pay the bill. Judge Chang ordered me to respond to the motion which I did through my former counsel who had withdrawn during my appeal and second lawsuit. She reentered my case to resolve this issue because although she had withdrawn from my case while it was on appeal, technically she still represented me in the US Northern District of Illinois Court, for she did not withdraw from the case while it was in that court. Therefore, if I won the appeal and it was remanded to the District Court, she was still responsible for representing me unless she withdrew or I fired her. Via a responsive motion, she asked Judge Chang to allow the matter to remain pending until after the Appeals Court issued an opinion on my appeal, and we awaited his ruling on her request.

September 2014

The Board and Rivera again filed a motion requesting an extension of time in which to file their appellees' brief. The Appeals Court granted their request, but made clear no further extensions of time would be allowed "except in extraordinary circumstances." I continued writing my reply brief.

During a court hearing in late September regarding my second lawsuit, when Judge Chang asked how the discovery process was going, Dreishmire responded as follows: (The following is taken directly from the court reporter's actual transcript of the September 24, 2014 hearing.)

```
7   THE COURT: All right. Good morning.
8   How is discovery progressing in this case?
9   MS. DREISHMIRE: I think it is coming along, Your Honor.
10  We have been working with the plaintiff to get complete
11  discovery responses. She just supplemented her production.
12  There are some issues I need to follow up with her on. I am
13  hoping we can avoid a motion to compel all
14  together and schedule her deposition before the end of
15  October.
```

At no time had Dreishmire *ever* told me I was not complying with her requests to produce documents. After the status hearing that day, she also did not contact me regarding this issue. This scene repeated itself several times during the second lawsuit; Dreishmire would allege in court I was withholding documents from her, but she never said a word to me about my supposed non-compliance in this regard prior to or after the court hearings.

During one hearing, we engaged in a heated exchange after she accused me of not providing her certain documents. Dreishmire was wrong. I had mailed her the entire set of documents to which she was referring. She asked Judge Chang if she should file a motion to compel me to produce documents and identify what I supposedly had not submitted to her, and he told her she should. A motion to compel is a request to the court to order an opposing or third party to comply with a discovery request. This type of motion most commonly deals with discovery disputes and typically is filed when a party in a lawsuit believes discovery responses from an opposing party or third party have been ignored or provided insufficient information. However, Dreishmire did not file any such motion, she never again mentioned the so-called documents I purportedly had not provided her, and the judge never asked during future court hearings about documents I allegedly had not produced to her during discovery.

October 2014

There was much activity related to both of my lawsuits during October 2014. First, after the Board and my former attorney filed competing motions regarding the Bill of Costs issue, Judge Chang ruled that the matter would remain pending until after the Appeals Court issued a ruling on my appeal. His rationale was if I won, I would not have to pay the bill anyway. He also remarked that if I lost the appeal, the Board could immediately revisit the issue.

My two lawsuits against the Board, including the second one in which I alleged the Board retaliated against me by preventing me from working, did nothing to stop Dreishmire and the Board's Law Department from continuing to retaliate against me. Briljent LLC, the company which had hired me in a temporary consulting capacity as an instructional delivery specialist in 2013, rehired me in September 2014 as a training facilitator. In this capacity, my duties would have been to train hundreds of CPS teachers in twenty-one schools on a new web-based diagnostic assessment and instructional program which would be used during after-school programs. I signed a contract for the short-term job opportunity with Briljent in September 2014, and it would have ended on December 31, 2014.

The Board had awarded a contract to Curriculum Associates, which according to its website is a research-based, online company that designs educational assessment tools and data management resources. Briljent was the project's subcontractor. Between September 9, 2014, and October 7, 2014, I attended several training sessions and spent an enormous amount of time studying the material provided to me by Curriculum Associates to prepare to train the teachers.

On October 7, 2014, the same day on which I began my new contract job with Briljent, Tammy Brodzeller, Briljent's vice president of Human Resources, contacted me by email and informed me she had received a "bunch of paperwork requests" from the "City of Chicago Schools" and asked me if I could "let [her] know what's going on." The "bunch of paperwork requests" from the "City of Chicago Schools" to which Brodzeller was referring was an Educational and Employment Records Authorization form accompanied by a cover letter from Dreishmire in which she divulged to Briljent I had filed two lawsuits against the Board.

Dreishmire had no reason to request information from Briljent regarding my previous employment because Brian Flores, who initially served as the Board's counsel in my second lawsuit, had issued a subpoena for employee verification information to Briljent in March 2014. In response to Flores' subpoena, Briljent sent a letter dated April 24, 2014, to him stating (1) "With the employee's signature, we will provide income history," and (2) "Briljent does not comment on employees' actions, behaviors, reasons for leaving, or any other information regarding their employment with us." Despite Briljent's unambiguous response, Dreishmire waited six months and then sent the Educational and Employment Records Authorization form to Briljent in which she again requested information regarding my previous employment contract. Remarkably, Dreishmire's request arrived at Briljent's headquarters on October 7, 2014, the same day I began my new contract with the company.

Dreishmire was well aware I had just entered into a new contractual relationship with Briljent and had just begun working for the company when she sent the request for information. In response to the Board's First Set of Interrogatories to Plaintiff, (in relation to my second lawsuit) I wrote that my 2014 employment would again include Briljent from October through December 2014. I submitted my response to Dreishmire on September 15, 2014—just three weeks before my new contract began. I also had previously sent Dreishmire an email on August 28, 2014 regarding another issue and mentioned in that message I had a new consulting contract.

In August 2014, Dreishmire also requested that I meet with her to discuss concerns she had regarding my alleged failure to disclose certain information to her. (Generally, this is referred to as a Rule 37.1 Conference.) During the meeting, I specifically informed her I anticipated receiving additional contracts to work for Briljent and emphatically stated that I did not wish for the Board to contact Briljent again, as Briljent was unaware I had two lawsuits pending against the Board. Dreishmire agreed she would only send Truman Middle College (Chicago City Colleges) a subpoena for information.

On October 2, 2014, Dreishmire informed me by email she had, in fact, contacted Chicago City Colleges to secure information regarding my previous employment. She did not mention she also had contacted Briljent the same day by submitting to Briljent an Educational and Employment Records Authorization form and cover letter informing the company I had filed two lawsuits against the Board. I had signed the form two months earlier, but it was not addressed to any particular company or party. Because the Board already had contacted Briljent and I specifically had asked Dreishmire not to contact the company again, I was not concerned about her communicating with Briljent. Foolish me.

On October 8, 2014, Brodzeller told me during a telephone call that because of my two lawsuits against the Board, Briljent was terminating my contract effective immediately per Curriculum Associates' request. She made clear Briljent's decision to end its relationship with me had absolutely nothing to do with my work performance which obviously had been excellent since the company had re-employed me after my initial contract with them. Brodzeller followed up her phone call later that night with an email which also confirmed the immediate termination of my contract. Thus, after I had worked for only one day, Briljent effectively retaliated against me by terminating my contract solely because Dreishmire also retaliated against me by informing Briljent of my two lawsuits against the Board, which was none of Briljent's business.

I believe Dreishmire intentionally interfered with the performance of my contract and her actions effectively ended my employment opportunities with two companies, as my chances to acquire future temporary or permanent employment with both Briljent and Curriculum Associates ended forever. Because of Dreishmire's illegal retaliation against me, my good professional name was besmirched with Briljent, Curriculum Associates, and my colleagues at both companies.

I immediately revoked the Educational and Employment Records Authorization, which prevented the Board from contacting any other individuals or entities to acquire information about me in the future. After researching my options regarding Dreishmire's retaliation against me, I filed a five-count supplemental complaint to my second lawsuit (13 C 6447), in which I asked Judge Chang to allow me to sue Dreishmire. I did not know if filing the supplemental complaint was appropriate or permissible, but I certainly intended to find out. I also knew the judge would let me know if I could or could not add those claims to my pending second lawsuit. I believed Dreishmire's behavior had gone far beyond egregious, and I indicated in my supplemental claim Judge Chang should hold her and the Board accountable for the loss (again) of my livelihood.

During the court hearing on my supplemental complaint, Dreishmire denied ill-intent as it related to notifying Briljent I had two pending lawsuits against the Board. She claimed she simply was trying to acquire information regarding my employment, and neither she nor the Board "wished to interfere with my income." As I stated in my supplemental complaint against Dreishmire and the Board, had that been true, the Board would not have unlawfully seized my livelihood in the first place, and thereafter, the Board would not have repeatedly prevented me from working. In the Board's Response to Plaintiff's Motion for Leave to Supplement Complaint and Add Lisa Dreishmire As a Defendant, Dreishmire wrote the following:

Plaintiff Likes to Blame Lawyers for her Troubles

Plaintiff has a history of blaming lawyers for her troubles. She filed an Attorney Registration & Disciplinary Commission (ARDC) complaint against Sabrina Haake, one of the Board's counsel in the

2009 Case, complaining of Haake's alleged conduct related to that litigation. The ARDC investigated and dismissed the complaint without further action.

... Plaintiff also implies the Board should have severed its relationship with Counsel Haake (who most recently worked for the Board on a contract basis, not as a full-time employee) due to Plaintiff's ARDC complaint against her. Apparently, this is the result Plaintiff sought, which adds a layer of irony to her proposed claims.

Dreishmire had caused me to lose my job, but she was accusing me of "blaming lawyers for [my] troubles." Moreover, in her own words, she admitted that *"Counsel Haake most recently worked for the Board on a contract basis, not as a full-time employee due to Plaintiff's ARDC complaint against her."* Dreishmire then filed on the US Northern District of Illinois Court's PACER system several documents related to my ARDC complaint against Haake, including a copy of a June 28, 2014 letter Haake's attorney received from the ARDC indicating the agency would not proceed in investigating Haake after I filed a complaint against her regarding the settlement agreement she and my former attorney had created without my knowledge. The ARDC had written in the letter that "Under Illinois Supreme Court Rule 766, this investigation is private and confidential." I was, therefore, shocked that in violation of this rule, Dreishmire had filed the letter on the court's PACER system for the public to see.

As explained in the ARDC's June 28, 2012 letter to me, and according to Dreishmire, after investigating Haake, the ARDC allegedly found no misconduct. But according to Dreishmire, Haake no longer worked for the Board because of my ARDC complaint against her. Either I am delusional or something is wrong with this picture. Dreishmire's statement begs answers to the following questions: (1) If Haake was cleared of misconduct after ARDC investigated, why was she no longer allowed to work for the Board as a permanent employee? and (2) if she no longer was allowed to work for the Board as a permanent employee because of information the ARDC discovered during its investigation, why was she permitted to continue to work for the Board as a vendor and be paid with taxpayer funds—period?

In his December 7, 2014 order denying my motion to supplement my complaint and refusing to sanction Dreishmire for causing me to lose my job, Judge Chang wrote that my supplemental complaint failed to state a claim for relief, which is a defense asserting that even if all factual allegations in a complaint are true, they are insufficient to establish a cause of action, (fact or facts which enable a person to bring an action against another). Judge Chang also made the following points:

1) Post-employment income is relevant to mitigation of damages, and although sometimes it is appropriate to fashion damages-mitigation discovery in a way that does not reveal the lawsuit to a new employer, it is the general practice rather than the exception to allow taking discovery from the new employer (Steffes called it the "direct and natural consequence" of the employee identifying a post-employment position, *144 F.3d at 1076*).

In this regard, Judge Chang was implying that because of the need for me to mitigate my damages, and because of the Board's need to conduct discovery, although it was appropriate for Dreishmire not to reveal my new employer, the fact that Briljent learned of the lawsuits simply was a "direct and natural consequence" of Dreishmire doing her job. Judge Chang also wrote the following in his order:

2) It is also worth noting that retaliatory intent is not plausible in these circumstances, where it is in the Board's interest (and thus Dreishmire's interest) that Hutchens mitigates any damages as much as possible.

In other words, Judge Chang, the same judge who believed it was "implausible" the Board and Rivera had discriminated against me when they had absolutely no evidence to prove their claims against me, and when my evidence clearly proved they were lying, also believed it was "implausible" Dreishmire would retaliate against me. He opined that retaliating against me was not in Dreishmire and the Board's best interest, because it was important to the Board that I mitigate my damages which would minimize the Board's payout to me if I won the lawsuit. In order to mitigate my damages, I had to work. Judge Chang's final point in this regard is as follows:

> 3) Hutchens attempts to increase the plausibility of retaliatory motive by arguing that Dreishmire has engaged in retaliation and discovery harassment of another *pro se* plaintiff against the Board, R. 43 at 1-2, contending that the other plaintiff filed a motion to remove Dreishmire as counsel. Implying that the motion was successful in forcing Dreishmire from the case—and thus implying that the motion had merit— Hutchens states, "Thereafter, Dreishmire withdrew from the case and was replaced by another Board attorney."
>
> The actual facts, revealed by the docket in the other case, show that Hutchens is wrong. In the other case, *Cunliffe v. Chicago Board of Education*, Case No. 12 C 06334, the plaintiff filed the motion to remove Dreishmire in November 2013. Far from being deemed meritorious, the motion was outright denied by the district judge on the recommendation of the magistrate judge. Indeed, the magistrate judge expressed the hope that Cunliffe "will consider carefully any further accusations lacking factual support against the professional reputation and integrity of Board's counsel." This rejection of the challenge to Dreishmire's discovery conduct was in November 2013; it was not until April 2014, around four months later, that Dreishmire voluntarily withdrew because she was reducing her litigation caseload due to her promotion. The Cunliffe case lends no support whatsoever to Hutchens's proposed supplemental complaint.

However, the allegations I wrote in my supplemental complaint as it related to Dreishmire and *Cunliffe v. Chicago Board of Education* were as follows:

During a recent case within the Northern District of Illinois Court, another Former CPS employee filed a complaint against Dreishmire which was remarkably similar to Plaintiff's. Specifically, in *Angela Cunliffe v. Jeffrey Wright, et al., Case No. 12 C 6334,* Plaintiff Cunliffe alleged in a court pleading filed July 31, 2013 that "The Board has already cost me one job, and Dreishmire calls me at work knowing I work with children and cannot answer the phone." Cunliffe asked the judge to sanction the Board for allowing Dreishmire to "harass me in this fashion." She described Dreishmire's behavior as "menacing" and "harassing" and she also had numerous other complaints regarding Dreishmire. Cunliffe ultimately filed a Motion for Disqualification and Removal of Dreishmire and "any Board of Education attorney." Thereafter, Dreishmire withdrew from the case and was replaced by another Board attorney. Like Plaintiff, Cunliffe proceeds *pro se* and filed a Whistleblower lawsuit alleging fraud against Board employees.

Even if Cunliffe's statement and certain information contained in my motion regarding Dreishmire's withdrawal from *Cunliffe v. Chicago Board of Education* were outright false, Judge Chang did not address in his order my claims that Cunliffe made the following three statements in her motion, (1) "The Board has already cost me one job and Dreishmire calls me at work knowing that I work with children and cannot answer the telephone…" (2) "She described Dreishmire's behavior as 'menacing' and 'harassing,'" and (3) "The Board should be sanction [sic] for allowing her to harass me in this fashion."

Cunliffe wrote these statements in court documents after having firsthand experiences with Dreishmire when she proceeded *pro se* in her lawsuit against the Board. Although Cunliffe's complaints in each of these statements were remarkably similar to my own complaints against Dreishmire, Judge Chang did not mention a single word about them in his order, thereby preventing me from using this information to support my claims against Dreishmire.

Judge Chang concluded his written order by remarking that the "tone of the parties' filings was not advancing the litigation and both Dreishmire and Hutchens are professionals who should be able to recognize that no advantage is gained by increasing the animosity in the litigation. And neither the Court nor a jury will find either side more credible based on which side can be more spiteful in the adjectives or adverbs they employ against the other." He did not admonish Dreishmire for causing me to lose my job with Briljent. In fact, he said not a word about it. I could not believe this continuing nightmare.

Following numerous requests for extensions of time, on October 31, 2014, Rivera and the Board filed via the court's PACER system, their appellees' brief. I received their brief and a revised version of it on Saturday, November 1, 2014. I had worked for several months on my response to their reply brief, (even though they had not written and filed it), and by the time I received Rivera and the Board's appellees' brief, I only needed to review it briefly to determine if they had effectively rebutted the arguments I had raised in my opening brief. As expected, based on their responses to my opening brief, I quickly realized I had very little to revise.

As I was required to do with my opening brief, I had to follow certain rules when preparing my reply brief. It could be no longer than fifteen double-spaced pages or comply with the Fed. R. App. P. 32(a)(7)(B) and (C) type volume limits, which allows fifteen pages or seven thousand words, (excluding the required court statements and documents). Although my brief was comprised of twenty-five pages, it contained less than seven thousand words.

Only two business days after I received Rivera and the Board's appellees' brief, I filed my reply brief. When the Appeals Court *pro se* clerk accessed the computer to enter receipt of my brief, he appeared confused that I was filing it so soon after Rivera and the Board had filed their appellees' reply brief. They had not filed the paper copy of their brief by the time I filed my reply brief. They only had filed it electronically.

The US Court of Appeals for the Seventh Circuit's Office of the Clerk reports it currently rejects about 10-15 percent of the briefs tendered for filing because of rule violations. If the brief is deficient, the Clerk issues a notice to counsel or the *pro se* litigant identifying what needs to be corrected, and all corrections must be made within seven days. Consistent and strict compliance with these rules and court orders is required of all attorneys and *pro se* litigants handling appeals in the Appeals Court. Although the Seventh Circuit frequently states in its rulings that it "construes *pro se* briefs liberally and does not hold them to the same standards as those prepared by attorneys," the Court also has made clear it must be able to "discern cogent, legible, and literate arguments in all briefs, including those written by *pro se* litigants." In other words, although the Court provides some measure of special consideration to *pro se* litigants in terms of brief submissions, it cautions them that they should not expect to receive a pass on this compliance simply because they are proceeding *pro se*.

I submitted two briefs on appeal—an opening and a reply brief. I had never written any such legal brief in my entire life. Although I had no legal training, the Clerk's office rejected neither my fifty-page opening brief nor my twenty-five-page reply brief, both of which also contained numerous other pages comprised of documents I had created which were required by the Appeals Court.

In US federal district courts, summary judgment is governed by Federal Rule 56 of the Federal Rules of Civil Procedure, which controls civil procedure (i.e., for civil lawsuits) in United States district (federal) courts. It encompasses rules with which judges are required to comply when analyzing summary judgment information, arguments, and evidence. In my opening and reply briefs, I presented arguments to the Appeals Court that District Court Judge Edmond E. Chang had made significant legal errors in his July 3, 2012 decision granting summary judgment to the Chicago Board of Education, and compounded those errors in his October 28, 2013 order when he denied my motion to alter, amend or reconsider judgment. I also argued that his errors prejudiced, injured, and prevented me from carrying my burden of proof. Therefore, summary judgment for the Board warranted reversal.

Taken directly from my appellate reply brief which also incorporates much of what I wrote in my opening brief are the arguments I presented to prove to the US Court of Appeals for the Seventh Circuit that (1) Judge Chang's July 3, 2012 decision should be reversed because his numerous legal errors prejudiced me and violated my constitutional entitlement to a jury trial, (2) the Board failed to effectively counter even a single argument contained in my opening brief, and (3) the "non-discriminatory" reasons Rivera and the Board presented to the Court in their brief, including paying Glowacki seven thousand dollars more annually than they paid me, were pretext for discrimination:

ARGUMENTS

I. **The procedures the Court employed to grant the Defendants-Appellees summary judgment and deny Plaintiff-Appellant's Motion to Alter, Amend or Reconsider Judgment, were manifestly unjust and extraordinarily prejudicial.**

   A. *Summary judgment for the Defendants-Appellees must be vacated because the Court's exclusion of nearly all of Plaintiff-Appellant's evidence prevented her from presenting her case and carrying her burden of proof.*

Plaintiff-Appellant was unjustly denied her constitutional entitlement to a jury trial after the Court prejudiced her by ignoring nearly all of her evidence, which was relevant and necessary to carry her burden of proof. The Court excluded nearly all of the evidence Plaintiff-Appellant presented to the Court to controvert the Defendants-Appellees claims against her; including arguments, deposition testimony, affidavits; answers to interrogatories, witness statements, hundreds of e-mails and other exhibits. (Opening Brief at 2, 3, 14, 16, 18, 19, 21-23, 27, 30, 33-36; 38-42; 44; 48) To determine whether any genuine issue of fact exists, the Court must pierce the pleadings and assess the proof as presented in depositions, answers to interrogatories, admissions, and affidavits that are part of the record. Fed. R. Civ. P. 56(c) & advisory committee notes (1963 amend). "[w]here an employer acted with discriminatory intent, direct evidence of that intent will only rarely be available, so affidavits and depositions must be carefully scrutinized for circumstantial proof which, if believed, would show discrimination." *Gorzynski v. JetBlue Airways Corp.*, 596 F.3d 93, 101 (2d Cir. 2010)

   B. **Every evidentiary ruling and major conclusion the Court reached, including virtually each issue on which the Court relied to grant the Defendants-Appellees summary judgment, is contradicted by the record.**

Although the Court relied on various issues to grant summary judgment for the Defendants-Appellees, clear contradictions existed between the record and the Court's evidentiary rulings on each of those issues. For instance, when ruling on the Defendants-Appellees' Motion for

Case: 13-3648   Document: 42   Filed: 11/03/2014   Pages: 39

Summary Judgment, in relation to Plaintiff-Appellant's alleged sleeping incident, the Court *insisted* that Plaintiff-Appellant's former manager, Karen Cushing, claimed she "knew for sure" Plaintiff-Appellant was asleep during a meeting. However, Cushing's deposition testimony shows that Cushing made no such statement, and in fact, she changed her statement related to this issue. (Opening Brief at 38)

The Court's conclusion and facts in the record regarding contents of a letter of recommendation Cushing gave to Plaintiff-Appellant following her layoff, also differ. (Opening Brief, 43) Also, in the Court's October 28, 2013 Order on Plaintiff-Appellant's Motion to Alter, the Court opined that the "letter was no different than one Cushing would give to anyone in the Unit who asked for one." However, the record shows that Plaintiff-Appellant stated she never requested a recommendation letter from Cushing, and an affidavit also supports this statement. (Opening Brief at 42)

As it relates to Plaintiff-Appellant's retaliation claim, there is a complete contradiction between the Court's Opinion and the record. (Opening Brief at 49, 50)

As it relates to Plaintiff-Appellant's alleged poor performance evaluation and kronos attendance report which "showed" Plaintiff-Appellant's alleged tardiness, the Court repeatedly insisted that the two documents existed; however, the record shows that the Defendants-Appellees proffered neither a performance evaluation for Plaintiff-Appellant nor a kronos attendance report. (Opening Brief at 18, 29-31, 33) The Court then changed its position after the Defendants-Appellees changed theirs, and concluded that Plaintiff-Appellant received an "informal performance evaluation." (Opening Brief at 31, 32)

As it relates to the Court's contention that Plaintiff-Appellant's teaching experience was at a school "in the criminal justice system," the record shows that Plaintiff-Appellant's teaching

5

experience also included five years as an English and Business teacher at CPS' Lincoln Park High School, where the students are not "in the criminal justice system." (Opening Brief at 6, 27)

As it relates to the salary disparity issue between Plaintiff-Appellant and her similarly-situated comparator, the Court ignored this issue in its July 3, 2012 Order, and in its October 28, 2013 Order on Plaintiff's Motion to Reconsider, the Court stated that the salary information was "new," and could not be considered. (Open Brief at 22, 23) However, the record shows that Plaintiff-Appellant had filed this evidence with her Rule 56.1 materials in April, 2011. (Opening Brief at 23)

Although these and other evidentiary rulings clearly were erroneous, the Court relied on them to grant summary judgment for the Defendants-Appellees, and refused to reconsider them on Plaintiff-Appellant's Motion to reconsider.

C. The Court ruled on only four issues raised solely by the Defendants-Appellees to grant summary judgment, and ignored numerous other issues presented by both parties.

The Court granted the Defendants-Appellees summary judgment after basing its analysis on just four issues, Plaintiff-Appellant's non-existent performance evaluation, a non-existent kronos attendance chart containing no names; Plaintiff-Appellant's alleged one-time sleeping incident, and her teaching experience at the "Prison School." (Opening Brief at 3, 14, 18, 19, 26, 27-33, 36-39, 46) Missing entirely from the Court's analysis was any reference to numerous other critical issues which one could reasonably believe are far more egregious than an unsubstantiated one-time sleeping incident on which the Court focused at length and excluded Plaintiff-Appellant's rebuttal evidence, including the testimony of Plaintiff-Appellant's three witnesses. (Opening Brief at 38)

Case: 13-3648 Document: 42 Filed: 11/03/2014 Pages: 39

Plaintiff-Appellant is not minimizing the seriousness of sleeping on the job, as she views this behavior as so serious, it is incomprehensible that the Defendants-Appellees would have failed to document this misconduct or address the issue with Plaintiff-Appellant. Moreover, although the Defendants-Appellees attempt to justify in their brief (at 45) the "absence of any formal discipline" against Plaintiff-Appellant throughout her PDU tenure despite her alleged continually egregious work performance, as outlined in the Board's Employee Discipline and Due Process Policy, sleeping on the job is viewed as so serious, it warrants either a written reprimand, 1-5 days suspension or a Warning Resolution. (Docket Entry No. 77, pp. 12-13, ¶32)

However, the Court failed to mention in its July 3, 2012 Order other more critical issues the two parties proffered, which, if true, would have been far more serious than an alleged one time, entirely unsubstantiated sleeping incident, and issues for which Plaintiff-Appellant presented significant evidence to controvert the Defendants-Appellees' claims regarding those issues, including Plaintiff-Appellant's (a) alleged failure to follow-through on work assignments; (b) her alleged lack of collaboration with her peers; (c) her alleged poor writing and computer skills; (d) a letter of recommendation Plaintiff-Appellant received immediately prior to her layoff in which her former supervisor lauded her work performance; (e) her alleged lack of interest in and ability to perform her duties; and (f) salary discrimination between Plaintiff-Appellant and her similarly situated comparator. (Opening Brief, 3, 4, 8, 18, 19, 22-25, 29, 40-43, 47) The Court briefly mentioned letters (d) through (f) but only in support of the Defendants-Appellees, to criticize Plaintiff-Appellant, or, in relation to letter (f), merely to justify why it refused to reconsider Plaintiff-Appellant's evidence regarding the salary discrimination issue.

7

D. The Court's substitution of its own views for others as it related to Plaintiff-Appellant's teaching history was prejudicial and improper.

The Defendants-Appellees claimed they were justified in circumventing Plaintiff-Appellant's rehiring to her former position because of her "Prison School" teaching history. (Opening Brief at 26) According to the Defendants-Appellees, Rivera considered Glowacki's teaching experience at a "regular CPS school" more "valuable" than Plaintiff-Appellant's because of her "Prison School" teaching history. (Defendants-Appellees' Brief at 19) Rivera apparently viewed Plaintiff-Appellant's commitment to serving a diverse student population as having less value than other CPS teachers, simply because the students she served for a period during her CPS teaching history, were incarcerated. That, in and of itself, is discriminatory. More important, as a former teacher and administrator in America's third largest public school district, which is charged with providing equal educational opportunities to *all* of its students, Rivera is suggesting that she viewed non-incarcerated CPS students as having greater value than those who were incarcerated. That, too, is discriminatory. It is one thing to believe this in your heart; articulating it to someone else, however, is quite another.

Plaintiff-Appellant's teaching experience at the "Prison School," Consuella B. York Alternative High School, which is located within the Cook County Jail, obviously did not trouble Rivera when she interviewed Plaintiff-Appellant, because Rivera hired her immediately. (Opening Brief at 4, 26) The Defendants-Appellees' "non-discriminatory justification" therefore, backfired, as it unequivocally demonstrates pretext for their discriminatory behavior.

The Court also implied that the Defendants-Appellees were justified in circumventing Plaintiff-Appellant's rehiring to her former position because unlike her similarly-situated comparator, Plaintiff-Appellant had taught students who were "in the criminal justice system," which the Court labeled an "important distinction." (Opening Brief at 27) However, the

Northern District of Illinois Court decided more than two decades ago that Consuella B. York's students were entitled to the same educational opportunities as students who were not "in the criminal justice system.[1]

Additionally, the Court excluded facts in the record which showed that Plaintiff-Appellant's employment history also included five years of teaching CPS students who were not "in the criminal justice system." (Opening Brief, 6-8) ¶ 7)

In contrast to her similarly-situated comparator who held an Illinois elementary teaching license and a master's degree, Plaintiff-Appellant held an Illinois multi-subject, multi-grade teaching license, two master's degrees and additional graduate hours, and she achieved National Board Certification, a prestigious, highly coveted credential, one year before her similarly-situated comparator earned hers. (Opening Brief, 6-8, 11) However, the aggregate rhetorical effect of the Court's words regarding the "Prison School" issue is that the Court injected its personal biases and stereotypical beliefs into its summary judgment analysis and concluded that because Plaintiff-Appellant had taught incarcerated students during her CPS employment, her teaching record was sullied and her inherent intelligence obviously was inferior to her similarly situated comparator. This was improper and beyond the Court's role of employing dutiful impartiality. It is far more difficult and requires far greater teaching skills and abilities to teach highly at-risk teenaged, incarcerated students in the maximum security division of Cook County Jail than it is to teach students at "regular CPS schools" who have the support of family and

---

[1] In 1993, Judge Albert Nordberg of the Northern District of Illinois Court ruled that all school-aged current and future pretrial detainees confined in Cook County Jail were or would be entitled under state or federal law to the same free regular or special education services as those students who were not "in the criminal justice system." (See *Donnell C. v. Illinois State Board of Education*, Docket/Court 92 C 8230 (N. Ill.). Thereafter, the U.S. Department of Education, the Illinois State Board of Education, The County of Cook and the Chicago Board of Education have recognized that students attending Consuella B. York Alternative High School are entitled to receive the same education as other CPS students.

friends at the end of the school day. Therefore, any notion that Plaintiff-Appellant is less qualified than Glowacki because she taught an incarcerated student population during her CPS employment history, is erroneous.

E. The Court's opinion, without explanation, that Plaintiff-Appellant's arguments do not "merit reconsideration," was erroneous and manifestly unjust.

Motions to reconsider "serve the limited function of correcting manifest errors of law or fact or presenting newly discovered evidence." *Cassie Nationalede Credit Agricole v. CBI Indus, Inc.*, 90 F.3d 1254, 1269 *(7th Cir. 1996)* (Opening Brief, 22, 23) Plaintiff-Appellant filed a Motion to Alter, Amend or Reconsider Judgment on July 31, 2012 and informed the Court that it had ignored nearly all of the evidence she had proffered. After characterizing as "new" Plaintiff-Appellant's salary discrimination evidence, without further explanation, without citing authorities, without exhibiting even a modicum of fairness, without attempting to balance the inequities in this case, without showing interest in correcting the manifest errors of law to which Plaintiff-Appellant pointed, and after Plaintiff-Appellant had waited more than one year for the Court to rule on her Motion, as if Plaintiff-Appellant were simply an annoying fly it was swatting away, rather than a human being with a credible cause, the Court opined that Plaintiff-Appellant's arguments "do not merit reconsideration." (Opening Brief at 22, 23)

F. The Court's two inordinate delays in ruling on the Defendants-Appellees' Motion for Summary Judgment, and Plaintiff-Appellant's Motion to Reconsider, were unfair, prejudicial and severely injured and disadvantaged Plaintiff-Appellant.

Filed in 2009, this litigation is five years old. The case was continued nearly one dozen times while under advisement on the Defendants-Appellees' Motion for Summary Judgment and again, immediately thereafter, for more than one year on Plaintiff-Appellant's Motion to Alter, Amend or Reconsider. (Opening Brief, 3, 16, 32, 35, 39) The successive inordinate delays

Case: 13-3648　　Document: 42　　Filed: 11/03/2014　　Pages: 39

adversely affected and disadvantaged Plaintiff-Appellant in the multiple ways it would negatively impact *any* litigant who became and remained unemployed due to unlawful discrimination, filed a lawsuit, waited more than three years for the Court's back-to-back rulings, and remained unemployed, unwillingly, while awaiting the Court's fair resolution. That is, the excessive, consecutive delays severely compounded what already was an extraordinarily difficult time for Plaintiff-Appellant who believes the Court treated her egregiously throughout both processes.

11. **The Defendants-Appellees have failed to counter a single argument Plaintiff-Appellant presented in her opening brief, and their inconsistency continues.**

The principal evidence the Defendants-Appellees proffered regarding Plaintiff-Appellant's alleged poor work performance were the depositions of Plaintiff-Appellant's three former managers whom the Defendants-Appellees claim provided "uncontroverted" and "consistent" testimony that Plaintiff-Appellant's performance was below expectations. (Docket Number 38, p. 5, ¶ 3) (Defendants-Appellees' Brief at 24) However, being consistent becomes problematic when the articulated "non-discriminatory justification" is simply a cover-up for an illegal motivation, for the only consistency Plaintiff-Appellant's three former managers showed throughout this litigation, including their Appellees' brief, is their inconsistency. As illustrated by the following, in every conceivable way, the Defendants-Appellees continue to craft their own doom, as they have, again, recycled the same dishonest methodology and regurgitated the same incoherent and implausible statements and mischaracterization of facts they used when the Court improperly granted them summary judgment.

The Defendants-Appellees falsely contend in their brief (at 6) that the National Board Certification Department ("NBC") was eliminated during the November 2008 reorganization.

However, the NBC Department continued to exist long after both the November 2008 and June 2009 layoffs. (Docket Numbers 47, and 60 (Corrected), p 6, ¶ 23) (Plaintiff-Appellant's Opening Brief at 6, 7) Following the June 2009 layoffs, Rivera simply circumvented Plaintiff-Appellant's rehiring to her former position so that Glowacki could be tapped to fill it.

The Defendants-Appellees also claim (at 9) that Rivera had no input in the 2009 layoffs. However, the Defendants-Appellees then claim (at 11) that Alan Anderson's decision to lay certain individuals off was based on information he received from Rivera.

The Defendants-Appellees site the "common actor:" presumption to suggest that because Rivera hired and fired Plaintiff-Appellant in a short amount of time, "Plaintiff-Appellant cannot overcome this presumption against race discrimination." However, the 7th Circuit has cautioned courts not to place "too strong a reliance" on the inference of nondiscrimination. *Filar, 526 F.3d at 1065 n. 4*. The "common actor" or "same actor" inference is a reasonable inference that may be argued to the jury, but it is not a conclusive presumption that applies as a matter of law. *Blasdel v. Northwestern Univ., 687 F.3d 813, 820 (7th Cir.2012)*. It is misleading to suggest that this skepticism creates a 'presumption' of nondiscrimination, as that would imply that the employee must meet it or lose his case. It is just something for the trier of fact to consider." *Hernreiter v. Chicago Housing Authority, 315 F.3d 742, 747 (7th Cir.2001); see also Waldron v. SL Industries, Inc., 56 F.3d 491, 496 n. 6 (3d Cir.1995)*.

A. The Defendants-Appellees' shifting "non-discriminatory justifications" regarding the salary discrimination between Plaintiff-Appellant and Glowacki is further proof of their inconsistency and pretext.

Under Title VII, an employer may not "discriminate against any individual with respect to compensation…because of such individual's race, color, religion, sex, or national origin." 42 U.S.C. § 2000e-2(a)(1) However, despite Plaintiff-Appellant's superior credentials and equal

Case: 13-3648   Document: 42   Filed: 11/03/2014   Pages: 39

number of years of CPS service as her similarly situated comparator, Deborah Glowacki, the Defendants-Appellees paid Glowacki far more than they paid Plaintiff-Appellant when Glowacki was hired in the PDU six months after Plaintiff-Appellant's hiring. (Opening Brief at 22-25) The Defendants-Appellees proffered four different explanations which shifted over time, for the salary disparity. Two of the explanations were presented during summary judgment and the Defendants-Appellees offered two new reasons in their Response in Opposition of Plaintiff-Appellant's Motion for Summary Judgment. Each reason fails. (Opening Brief at 18, 23-25)

First, according to Rivera, Glowacki's salary when she began working in the PDU in January 2009, was "based on her years of experience and credentials." (Docket Numbers 47, and 60 (Corrected), p 25, ¶ 5, Def. Exh. 4, p. 201 @ 6-12) This argument fails, as Plaintiff-Appellant also was hired into the PDU the same school year, her credentials were superior to Glowacki's, and both had an equal number of years of CPS service. (Opening Brief at 6, 7)

Next, Rivera stated she did not know why Glowacki, who held one master's degree, earned more than Plaintiff-Appellant, and despite interviewing and hiring Plaintiff-Appellant, Rivera claimed she did not know Plaintiff-Appellant held two master's degrees when she hired her. (Docket Numbers 47, and 60 (Corrected), p 25, ¶ 5, Rivera's testimony, Def. Exh. 4 p. 203, @ 8-23). "When a witness repeatedly contradicts himself under oath on material matters, and contradicts as well as documentary evidence likely to be accurate, the witness's credibility becomes an issue for the jury; it cannot be resolved in a summary judgment proceeding. *Perfetti v. First National Bank*, 950 F.2d 449, 456 (7th Cir.1991); *Cameron v. Frances Slocum Bank & Trust Co.*, 824 F.2d 570, 575 (7th Cir.1987)

The Defendants-Appellees claimed in their Reply to Plaintiff's Motion to Alter that Plaintiff-Appellant's three year break in service was responsible for the salary disparity. (Docket

Number 82, pp. 12-13, ¶ 2) However, even when considering Plaintiff-Appellant's three year break in service, both Glowacki and Plaintiff-Appellant had 12 years of service when hired in the PDU. (Opening Brief at 9) Therefore, this argument also fails. This changed story is evidence of pretext and entitles Plaintiff-Appellant to a trial. *Stalter v. Walmart*, 195 F.3d 285 (7th Cir. 1999) (when employer gives one reason at the time of the adverse employment decision, and at trial gives another reason unsupported by the documentary evidence, the jury could reasonably conclude that the new reason was a pretextual after-the-fact justification). See *Perfetti v. First Nat'l Bank of Chicago*, 950 F.2d 449, 456 (7th Cir. 1991), cert. denied, 505 U.S. 1205 (1992)

The Defendants-Appellees' final and new explanation was "Glowacki applied for and was paid according to the Lane III pay band." (Docket Number 82 pp. 12-13, ¶ 2) This was likely the case when Glowacki was a teacher, as lane credits and Collective Bargaining Agreement jargon pertains only to Chicago Teacher's Union ("CTU") members. However, Plaintiff-Appellant and Glowacki were Curriculum Facilitators, or administrators, during the relevant period. (Opening Brief, 24) Moreover, although Plaintiff-Appellant and Glowacki served in the same capacity, Glowacki's Salary Recommendation Form shows she was being paid at an A07 salary band and Plaintiff-Appellant's Salary Assignment Report shows she was being paid at the lower, A06 salary band. (Opening Brief, 24; Docket Number 83, p.13, ¶ 3) The "A" before the numbers denotes an administrative salary. Therefore, this explanation also fails.

In support of this argument, Plaintiff-Appellant proffered a CTU salary schedule for the relevant school year, 2008-2009. (Docket Number 83, p.13, footnote No. 4) The schedule explains salary "lanes" and "steps." "Lane" specifically references a teacher's education, and "Step" refers to the teacher's number of years of teaching experience. Glowacki held one master's degree and had 11 or 12 years of service when hired in the PDU in December 2008. As shown on the CTU salary schedule, a teacher with a Lane III placement (Master's Degree, plus 15 graduate hours) with 11 years of service would have earned $75,911 and a teacher with 12 years would have earned $78,340 during 2008-2009. Glowacki's PDU hiring salary was $97,833, which exceeded by more than $11,000 the highest salary on the CTU salary schedule, which was assigned to teachers who held a PH.D or ED.D, had 14 years of service, and were being paid at Lane VI, Step 14. The Civil Rights Act of 1964 does not require employers to have "just cause" for sacking a worker, see *Pollard v. Rea Magnet Wire Co., 824 F.2d 557 (7th Cir. 1987)*, but an employer who advances a fishy reason takes the risk that disbelief of the reason will support an inference that it is a pretext for discrimination. See *Reeves v. Sanderson Plumbing Products, Inc., 530 U.S. 133, 146-49, 120 S. Ct. 2097, 147 L.Ed.2d 105 (2000)*

Given the above, it is easy to understand why the Defendants-Appellees elected to avoid this issue in its entirety in their brief.

B. The Defendants-Appellees' changed story regarding Plaintiff-Appellant's alleged performance evaluation, also shows inconsistency and pretext.

After insisting for the first two years during the instant litigation that Plaintiff-Appellant was given a written performance evaluation which reflected her alleged poor performance, the Defendants-Appellees changed their story on Defendants' Response In Opposition To Plaintiff's Motion to Alter, Amend or Reconsider Summary Judgment, and insidiously suggested that Plaintiff-Appellant was given an evaluation which was not in writing; the Court accepted the position of both the original version and the Defendants-Appellees' changed story. (Opening Brief at 31)

Several years and two versions later, the Defendants-Appellees have returned to heir original "non-discriminatory" story that Plaintiff-Appellant was given a negative written performance evaluation and Glowacki and Sherfinski were given superior evaluations.

(Defendants-Appellees' Brief at 36) Again, however, the Defendants-Appellees produced said evaluations for neither employee. Despite the Defendants-Appellees' failure to produce an alleged poor performance evaluation for Plaintiff-Appellant, the Court granted the Defendants-Appellees summary judgment. (Opening Brief at 29) From such discrepancies a reasonable juror could infer that the explanations given by [an employer] were pretextual, developed over time to counter the evidence suggesting [discrimination]") See *EFOC v. Ethan Allen, 44 F.3d 116, 120 (2d Cir.1994)*

C. Cushing's changed story regarding Plaintiff-Appellant's alleged sleeping incident, and failure to identify her "witnesses" further proves inconsistency and pretext.

The Defendants-Appellees continue (at 39-41) to insist that Plaintiff-Appellant was sleeping on the job, Cushing testified that she observed Plaintiff-Appellant sleeping and Rivera allegedly learned of the sleeping incident from others. Initially, Plaintiff-Appellant's former manager, Karen Cushing, did, in fact, testify that she witnessed Plaintiff-Appellant sleeping during a training session. (Opening Brief at 37) Cushing then changed her story and testified that she could not tell for sure if Plaintiff was asleep. (Opening Brief at 37) Cushing further claimed that colleagues seated at her table also witnessed Plaintiff-Appellant sleeping; however, she could not "remember" the identity of a single alleged witness. (Opening Brief at 37) Rivera, likewise, could not name one person from the group of people who supposedly told her they saw Plaintiff-Appellant sleeping during the session. (Docket Numbers 47 and 60 (Corrected), pp. 7-8, ¶28)...a finding of pretext is the equivalent of a finding that the employer intentionally discriminated. See *Graefenhain v. Pabst Brewing Co., 827 F.2d 13, 18 & n. 7 (7th Cir.1987)*

D. **The repeated false statements which Plaintiff-Appellant's three managers repeatedly made while under oath, further proves inconsistency and pretext.**

Plaintiff-Appellant's former managers also made numerous false statements under oath and contradicted each other's testimony. (Opening Brief at 21-25, 28-31, 33, 39-41, 45-49) To underscore this point, Plaintiff-Appellant redirects this Court to the incident in which Rivera intentionally circumvented Plaintiff-Appellant's rehiring to her former position. (Opening Brief at 9-12) The Defendants-Appellees falsely claimed that [then] acting Deputy Chief Executive Officer for Human Capital, Alan Anderson, requested that Rivera "recommended" (Defendants-Appellees Brief at 10, 48) who she believed was the superior job performer between Plaintiff-Appellant and Deborah Glowacki so he could rehire that person to Plaintiff-Appellant's former position:

> When asked whose recommended layoff to withdraw, PDU director Amanda Rivera recommended to Anderson that Debbie Glowacki be removed from the layoff list and she did not recommend that plaintiff be removed from the layoff list. Rivera, along with two of plaintiff's previous direct supervisors, observed that Glowacki's skills, attitude and program knowledge exceeded those of plaintiff whom one manager described as "disengaged, lethargic and angry." Thereafter, Anderson made the decision to reverse the layoffs of Deborah Glowacki and Tabita Sherfinski ... (Docket Number 75, p. 4, ¶ 2)

However, when Anderson's testimony is read in context, it is clear he did not ask Rivera who she "recommended." Anderson was unaware Plaintiff-Appellant existed when he restored Glowacki to Plaintiff-Appellant's former position because Rivera intentionally omitted Plaintiff-Appellant's name when Anderson "specifically asked Rivera for the names of those who had served National Board Certification" at the time of the 2009 layoff. (Opening Brief at 11, 12)

In *Malin v. Hospira, Inc., No. 13-2433, 2014, (7th Circuit, August 7, 2014),* this Court criticized Hospira for misrepresenting the record, including repeatedly "cherry-picking isolated phrases from Malin's deposition…" and "presenting evidence which amounted to nothing more than selectively quoting deposition language it likes and ignoring deposition language it does not like." The Court further stated that "Hospira seems to have based its litigation strategy on the hope that neither the district court nor this panel would take the time to check the record," and cautioned litigants who take this approach that they will "often (and we hope almost always) find that they have misjudged the Court." The panel sent notice to defense counsel who employs this type of summary judgment practice that it "quickly destroys their credibility with the court."

Further, the hundreds of e-mails Plaintiff-Appellant proffered during the instant litigation hardly depict a "disengaged," "lethargic" or "angry" employee, and Plaintiff-Appellant is at a loss to explain how she could have been "lethargic" if she presented herself as "angry." The latter label obviously was a contrived attempt by the Defendants-Appellees to portray Plaintiff-Appellant as an "Angry Black Woman," a long perpetuated, pervasive stereotype which suggests that anger is an inherent, cultural trait of, is most commonly associated with and is one of the most ubiquitous beliefs other racial groups (and some African-Americans) have about American Black women. Other than Plaintiff-Appellant's race by association, the Defendants-Appellees presented nothing which supports their rationale for having any such belief about her.

Invoking the "Cat's Paw" theory of liability, Plaintiff-Appellant has a viable Title VII claim for discrimination against the Defendants-Appellees, because although Anderson, as the decision-maker, had no discriminatory intent in laying off Plaintiff-Appellant, he relied on input from Rivera, Plaintiff-Appellant's former manager, to provide him information regarding Plaintiff-Appellant's employment prior to her layoff, which would help him make an informed re-hiring decision. However, Anderson was motivated to unknowingly circumvent Plaintiff-Appellant's rehiring to her former position based solely on the information he received from Rivera. Thus, Anderson, the ultimate decision-maker acted as the conduit of the supervisor's prejudice — his cat's paw. An employer becomes liable under Title VII when the plaintiff "establish[es] that the defendant had a discriminatory intent or motive for taking a job-related action." *Ricci v. DeStefano*, 129 S. Ct. 2658, 2672 (2009) (quoting *Watson v. Fort Worth Bank & Trust*, 487 U.S. 977, 985-86 (1988)) '(internal quotation marks omitted). An employer is liable for an intermediate employee's discrimination when there is proof of a "causal nexus" between the discrimination and the adverse action, *Madden v. Chattanooga City Wide Service Dept, (6th Cir., 2008). Madden,* 549 F.3d at 677, or when the intermediate employee "influences the unbiased decision-maker" to take an adverse action. *Arendale v. City of Memphis,* 519 F.3d 587, 604 n.13 (6th Cir. 2008)

III. Summary Judgment as a matter of law for the Defendants-Appellees, which was unsupported by substantial evidence and reasoned decision-making, constitutes legal error.

Summary judgment for the Defendants-Appellees was unsupported by substantial evidence and "reasoned decision-making," including an examination of the relevant data and a reasoned explanation supported by a stated connection between the facts found and the choice made. *Consumers Res. Council v. Fed. Energy Regulatory Comm'n,* 747 F.2d 1511, 1513 (D.C. Cir. 1984) Other than the "non-discriminatory" justification Plaintiff-Appellant's three former managers articulated for intentionally circumventing Plaintiff-Appellant's rehiring to her former position and instead, rehiring her similarly-situated comparator to Plaintiff-Appellant's position, the Defendants-Appellees proffered nothing. Viewing the record as a whole, no reasonable jury would find that the Defendants-Appellees' mere testimony without supporting documentation was adequate to support the Court's decision. If claims or defenses are factually unsupported, the Court should dispose of them at the summary judgment stage. *Celotex Corp. v Catrett,* 477 U.S. 317, 323-24, 106 S. Ct. 2548, 91 L. Ed. 2d 265 (1986) Summary judgment is appropriate only if "the record taken as a whole could not lead a rational trier of fact to find for the non-moving party . . . ." *Matsushita Elec. Indus. Co. v. Zenith Radio Corp.*, 475 U.S. 574, 587 (1986); *see* Fed. R. Civ. P. 56(c).

There also was no causal connection which justifies the Defendants-Appellees' actions. (Opening Brief at 17-19) Plaintiff-Appellant's departmental employment record contained no evidence of adverse or corrective action her managers had taken against her prior to her layoff, which shows that Plaintiff-Appellant was meeting the Defendants-Appellees' employment expectations. In fact, Rivera stated that Plaintiff-Appellant was performing "the basic job responsibilities that we would expect of any staff member." (Opening Brief at 16) Therefore, no reasonable person could accept what the Defendants-Appellees proffered as adequate to support their articulated "non-discriminatory motives" for discriminating against Plaintiff-Appellant. *Mareno v. Apfel*, 1999 U.S. Dist. LEXIS 8575 (S.D. Ala. Apr. 8, 1999)

Just as the Court examined the Defendants-Appellees' evidence, the Court also had a duty to examine Plaintiff-Appellant's evidence, apply it to the facts contained in the record, and conclude that without substantial evidence, the Defendants-Appellees were not entitled to summary judgment as a matter of law. The Court granted summary judgment to the Defendants-Appellees, whose testimony was largely and glaringly perjured, shifting, self-serving, and unsupported by other evidence. These are distinct legal errors. "Pure legal errors require no deference to agency expertise and are reviewed de novo." *Elec. Consumers Res. Council v. Fed. Energy Regulatory Comm'n*, 747 F.2d 1511, 1513 (D.C. Cir. 1984) (stating that court defers to the agency's expertise, particularly where the statute prescribes few specific standards for the agency to follow, so long as its decision is supported by substantial evidence in the record and reached by "reasoned decision-making," including an examination of the relevant data and a reasoned explanation supported by a stated connection between the facts found and the choice made); *Consumers Union of U.S., Inc. v. Consumer Prod. Safety Comm'n, 491 F.2d 810, 812 (2d Cir. 1974)* Because summary judgment denies the adversary party a trial, [the motion] should be granted with caution. *Colores v. Board of Trustees (2003) 105 Cal.App.4th 1293, 1305*

IV. The Court's conclusion that no genuine issues of material fact existed, is prejudicial error.

The "non-discriminatory" motives proffered by the Defendants-Appellees and the rebuttal evidence Plaintiff-Appellant presented, created disputes regarding every issue on which the Court relied to grant the Defendants-Appellees summary judgment, and on numerous other issues which the Court failed to analyze. The *only* reason it might have appeared there were no genuine issues of material fact was because the Court excluded Plaintiff-Appellant's arguments and evidence, deprived her of the ability to carry her burden of proof, and then dismissed her lawsuit for lack of the very evidence the Court excluded and ultimately claimed Plaintiff-Appellant was lacking. Whether or not a party is entitled to summary judgment ordinarily turns on whether or not there are genuine issues of material fact for trial. *Quick v. Donaldson Co., 90 F.3d 1372, 1376-77 (8th Cir. 1996)* A genuine issue of material fact exists if "the evidence is such that a reasonable jury could return a verdict for the nonmoving party." *Anderson v. Liberty Lobby, Inc., 477 U.S. 242, 248, 106 S. Ct. 2505, 91 L. Ed. 2d 202 (1986)* Summary judgments should seldom be used in cases alleging employment discrimination. *Haglof v. Northwest Rehabilitation, Inc., 910 F.2d 492, 495 (8th Cir. 1990)*

V. The Court erred when it repeatedly failed to view the evidence in favor of Plaintiff-Appellant, the non-movant.

On each issue the Court relied to grant summary judgment to the Defendants-Appellees, and as it related to numerous other issues, including those which the Court ignored in their entirety, the Court failed to view the evidence in the light most favorable to Plaintiff-Appellant, the non-movant, as mandated. This included the alleged sleeping incident during which Cushing's testimony changed and was unsupported by the record (Opening Brief, 36-39) the alleged performance evaluation and alleged kronos attendance chart containing no names which the Defendants-Appellees never produced and which Plaintiff-Appellant successfully rebutted. (Opening Brief, 28-33; 33-36) and the "Prison School" issue on which the Court asserted its personal views and ignored facts in the record. (Opening Brief, 24-28)

For the purpose of summary judgment, the Court views all facts in the light most favorable to the nonmoving party. *Fitzgerald v. Santoro*, 707 F.3d 725, 730 (7th Cir. 2013) Summary judgment is appropriate only if, when viewing the facts in the light most favorable to the plaintiff and giving him the benefit of all reasonable factual inferences, there is no genuine issue of material fact and the moving party is entitled to judgment as a matter of law. See *Leichihman v. Pickwick Int'l*, 814 F.2d 1263, 1268 (8th Cir.), cert. denied, 484 U.S. 855, 108 S. Ct. 161, 98 L.Ed.2d 116 (1987) All the evidence must point one way and be susceptible of no reasonable inferences sustaining the position of the non-moving party. *Holley v. Sanyo Mfg. Inc.*, 771 F.2d 1161, 1164 (8th Cir.1985)

VI. **The record is replete with credibility issues, competing versions of facts and questions which should have been resolved at trial, rather than summary judgment.**

Despite Plaintiff-Appellant's continual insistence that documents related to the Defendants-Appellees' claims never existed, and despite the Defendants-Appellees' failure to proffer any such documents to support their claims, the Court repeatedly made credibility determinations and ruled in favor of the Defendants-Appellees. When considering a motion for summary judgment, the Court must resolve "all permissible inferences and credibility questions in favor of the party against whom judgment is sought." *Kaytor v. Elec. Boat Corp.*, 609 F.3d

537, 546 (2d Cir. 2010). Applying the standards of Rule 56 of the Federal Rules of Civil Procedure, the trial judge's function at summary judgment stage of the proceedings is not to weigh the evidence and determine the truth of the matter, but to determine whether there are genuine issues for trial. *Quick v. Donaldson Co., 90 F.3d 1372, 1376-77 (8th Cir. 1996); Johnson v. Enron Corp., 906 F.2d 1234, 1237 (8th Cir. 1990)*. The Court may not weigh conflicting evidence or make credibility determinations. *Omnicare, Inc. v. UnitedHealth Grp., Inc., 629 F.3d 697, 704 (7th Cir. 2011)*

CONCLUSION

The ultimate question in every employment discrimination case ... is whether the plaintiff was the victim of intentional discrimination." *Reeves, 530 U.S. at 153, 120 S. Ct. 2097*. A court is to examine "the entire record to determine whether the plaintiff could satisfy his 'ultimate burden of persuading the trier of fact that the defendant intentionally discriminated against the plaintiff. '" *Schnabel v. Abramson, 232 F.3d 83 , 90 (2d Cir. 2000) (quoting Reeves, 120 S. Ct. at 2106)*. Because Plaintiff-Appellant produced evidence such that a reasonable factfinder could conclude that the Defendants-Appellees' proffered reasons are false, and raised an inference of racial discrimination, summary judgment for the Defendants-Appellees was more than improper; it was unjust, and severely disadvantaged and injured her.

Plaintiff-Appellant, therefore, respectfully requests that this Honorable Court reverse the District Court's judgment on Count I, 42 U.S.C § 1981 – Race Discrimination, Count II, Section 1983 – Equal Protection Clause, Race Discrimination; Count III, Race Discrimination –Title VII and Count VI, Intentional Infliction of Emotion Distress charges. Plaintiff-Appellant also requests that this Court modify Count VII, the Retaliation-Title VII claim, to ensure that the

23

record reflects the true and accurate cause of action as further herein discussed, as Plaintiff-Appellant did not file a retaliation charge based on a claim of sexual harassment.[2]

The Defendants-Appellees indicated in their Jurisdictional Statement (at 1) that Lily McDonagh is not a "proper party" to this appeal and should not, therefore, be reinstated. Plaintiff-Appellant concurs with this statement, as her only intent was to state the facts in this case and apprise this Court of the method by which McDonagh's dismissal occurred. McDonagh should not have been referenced as "Defendant-Appellee."

---

[2] Plaintiff-Appellant failed to note in her opening brief that although the Court ruled on Plaintiff-Appellant's retaliation claim in its July 3, 2012 Order, and briefly mentioned it again in its October 28, 2013 Order, Plaintiff-Appellant's former counsel had previously waived this claim. (Docket Entry 59, Page 10, ¶ 23) Plaintiff-Appellant is not seeking to have this claim reinstated.

In relation to my three managers' extensive perjured testimony, I cited in my brief the arguments and rebuttal evidence I filed in the US Northern District of Illinois Court during summary judgment, which Judge Chang excluded. Taken directly from my opening appellant's brief, following are the arguments I presented to the US Court of Appeals for the Seventh Circuit in this regard:

X. **The Defendants-Appellees' "non-discriminatory" justifications for circumventing Plaintiff-Appellants' rehiring to her former position were unsubstantiated, shifting, inconsistent, facially implausible, or all of the above. Therefore, a reasonable jury could conclude that their explanations were false, and the true reason they circumvented Plaintiff-Appellant's rehiring was because of her race.**

By establishing a prima facie case, a plaintiff eliminates the most obvious nondiscriminatory explanations for a decision. *(Teamsters v. U.S., 431 U.S. 324, 357-58 (1974).* Accordingly, a factfinder can infer that intentional discrimination motivated the employment decision if it finds that any additional reasons articulated by the defendant are not the true reasons for the decision. See *Reeves, 530 U.S. at 147)* ("a plaintiff's prima facie case, combined with sufficient evidence to find that the employer's asserted justification is false," will ordinarily" permit the trier of fact to conclude that the employer unlawfully discriminated").

Through her Local Rule 56.1 Statements of Fact, Plaintiff-Appellant presented numerous instances wherein the Defendants-Appellees made glaringly false, inconsistent and contradictory statements, including, but not limited to the following: The Defendants-Appellees claimed that all three of Plaintiff-Appellant's managers were disappointed with Plaintiff-Appellant's job performance. (Docket Number 82, pp. 3-5, Sec. III, "All Three Managers were Disappointed in

45

Plaintiff's Performance.") As repeatedly shown, and as herein further discussed, Plaintiff-Appellant's three former managers failed to substantiate a single claim they made regarding Plaintiff-Appellant's alleged poor job performance. (Docket Number 39, ¶¶, pp. 5-8, "Plaintiff's Performance") In fact, their deposition testimony frequently contradicted their own and each other's claims. *(Reeves v Sanderson Plumbing Products, 530 U.S. 133, 143 (2000)*, explaining that the Plaintiff establishes pretext by showing "weaknesses, implausibilities, inconsistencies, incoherencies, or contradictions in the employer's proffered legitimate reasons" such that a factfinder could "infer that the employer did not act for the asserted non-discriminatory reasons."

The Defendants-Appellees alleged that Rivera personally observed Plaintiff-Appellant sleeping on the job. (Docket Number 39, pp. 6-7, ¶ 28) However, Rivera testified she did not observe Plaintiff-Appellant sleeping, but claimed other staff members told her they witnessed the incident. When asked to identify the witnesses, Rivera claimed she could not remember the name of even a single witness, even though the "witnesses" allegedly were members of her own staff and were seated at her table when Plaintiff-Appellant allegedly fell asleep during a training meeting. (Docket Numbers 47 and 60 (Corrected), p. 7 @ 5-6 – p. 8 @ 1-2, ¶ 28)

Rivera also testified that data and a chart created by management which contained no employees' names showed that Plaintiff-Appellant was frequently absent. (Docket Number 39, pp. 6-7, ¶ 28)[9] The Defendants-Appellees produced neither the data, nor the chart, and referenced not a single declaration in Cushing's testimony concerning Plaintiff-Appellant's alleged absenteeism issues during the period Cushing was Plaintiff-Appellant's manager.

---

[9] "I know that in the process of – I don't know if it was prior to or after we did the reorganization, we put together some data on staff absenteeism and tardiness and shared that at the staff meeting. Obviously, I was—we had charts. We didn't have any names on that. And there was a problem with Joyce's attendance."

241

The Defendants-Appellees further claimed Rivera had knowledge of Plaintiff-Appellant's alleged lack of follow-through with work assignments. (Docket Number 39, ¶ 28, pp. 107 @ 20-108 @ 10, Rivera's Testimony) However, Rivera's version of this issue differed. Rivera testified that it was Cushing, not she, who had knowledge of Plaintiff-Appellant's alleged follow through on work assignments.[10] (Docket Number 39, Rivera's testimony, pp.107 @ 20 -108 @ 10, ¶ 28). But, the Defendants-Appellees cited no deposition testimony of Cushing's wherein she claimed that Plaintiff-Appellant failed to follow through on work assignments, and the record is devoid of any such statements, orally or in writing, made by Cushing regarding Plaintiff-Appellant's lack of follow-through.

Rivera alleged that "many e-mails were going back and forth" between her and Cushing concerning Plaintiff-Appellant's alleged work deficiencies. However, Rivera failed to produce even a single e-mail when asked, and at no time throughout discovery did Rivera produce any such e-mails. (Docket Number 47 and 60 (corrected), p. 30, ¶ 21)

Cushing claimed she had to edit Plaintiff-Appellant's written work more than she had to edit the work submitted by other staff. (Docket Number 39, ¶32) However, in her letter of recommendation to Plaintiff-Appellant, Cushing twice referenced Plaintiff-Appellant's "writing talents" and indicated that her "writing skills are an asset." (Docket Number 48, Cushing's Letter, Exhibit 10). There is no evidence contained in the record which supports the Defendants-Appellees' claim that Plaintiff-Appellant's work had to be edited more often than any other staff member.

---

[10] "I mean, the issues that existed were issues that the manager brought to me, and she was able to address them herself. Evidently there were some problems with lack of follow-through on some things with Joyce."

Case: 13-3648   Document: 31   Filed: 06/20/2014   Pages: 96

McDonogh testified extensively that Plaintiff-Appellant continuously bickered with her co-workers; but, Plaintiff-Appellant's co-workers testified that there was no bickering, and McDonogh later changed her testimony and also stated there was no bickering. McDonogh further testified that she received numerous complaints about Plaintiff-Appellant from each of Plaintiff-Appellant's co-workers. However, Plaintiff-Appellant's co-workers emphatically denied ever complaining to McDonogh about Plaintiff-Appellant. (Docket Numbers 47 and 60 (Corrected), p. 10, ¶ 35 @ 1-6). Plaintiff-Appellant was never disciplined for even one of the Rivera's, Cushing's, or McDonogh's allegations. (Id. @ p. 23 @ 8-9, ¶ 68).

Even standing alone, these glaring inconsistencies and outright false statements should have sufficed for Plaintiff-Appellant to have survived summary judgment. Combined, there were, without question, issues of material fact and indisputable evidence clearly demonstrating that Plaintiff-Appellant's three managers were manufacturing false statements solely in response to this litigation. Plaintiff-Appellant controverted each allegation with record-cited arguments and supporting evidence; however, the Court excluded from its July 3, 2012 and October 28, 2013 Orders each of Plaintiff-Appellant's arguments and supporting evidence and each of the Defendants-Appellees' false and inconsistent statements in this regard. In *Atkinson v. Lafayette College, 460 F.3d 447, 454 (3d Cir. 2006)*, the court explained: We have recognized two ways in which a plaintiff can prove pretext. First, the plaintiff can present evidence that "casts sufficient doubt upon each of the legitimate reasons proffered by the defendant so that a factfinder could reasonably conclude that each reason was a fabrication." *Fuentes v. Perskie, 32 F.3d 759, 762 (3d Cir. 1994)*. Second, and alternatively, the plaintiff can provide evidence that "allows the factfinder to infer that discrimination was more likely than not a motivating or determinative cause of the adverse employment action." Id. Just as an employee might be closely questioned as to his or her account of discrimination, so too will an employer's justification for its actions be scrutinized for inconsistencies, including whether that such justification shifts or changes over time. *(EEOC v. Ethan Allen, 44 F.3d 116, 120 (2d Cir.1994)* ("From such discrepancies, a reasonable juror could infer that the explanations given by [an employer] were pretextual, developed over time, to counter the evidence suggesting [discrimination]").

Despite the Defendants-Appellees' glaring and massive number of false, shifting and inconsistent statements, which, as shown, Plaintiff-Appellant brought to the Court's attention through her Local Rule 56.1 Statements, the Court declared that no reasonable jury could infer discrimination, and the Defendants-Appellees' non-discriminatory motives and honesty were unquestionable:

> Whether the evidence is evaluated under an "indirect" method of proof (the "direct" method of proof did not apply), or a more straightforward approach, which simply asks whether a reasonable jury, when viewing the evidence in the employee's favor, could infer discrimination, *Hitchcock v. Angel Corps, Inc., 718 F.3d 733, 737 (7th Cir. 2013)*, the Local Rule 56.1 Statements did not call into question the honesty of the belief that Glowacki should be rehired over Hutchens. To be sure, the honesty of a belief can be called into question if the evidence (viewed in the employee's favor) shows that the explanation is a pretext for discrimination…But the evidence in this case does not cast genuine doubt over the stronger job-performance reviews of Glowacki. (Docket No. 98, pp. 3-4, ¶ 2)

49

Also in late October, I received a telephone call from the Allison & Taylor consultant who had conducted a reference check of my employment with the Board and issued me a follow-up report in March 2013. She informed me Dreishmire had subpoenaed her to speak by phone with her about creating a declaration regarding my employment with the Board. She also said Dreishmire told her it was okay to talk with her because I had "chosen not to obtain an attorney." She sent me an email later that day in which she wrote precisely what she had told me by phone.

Dreishmire had contacted me by letter shortly before calling the consultant and informed me she planned to take the consultant's deposition. She also asked me in her letter to provide her dates on which the consultant and I were available for the deposition, and I had provided her a response. However, without my knowledge, Dreishmire subpoenaed the consultant for the two of them to surreptitiously create a declaration regarding the reference check the consultant had conducted of my past employment with the Board.

After the consultant informed me of the communication between her and Dreishmire, I immediately emailed Dreishmire with the following message: "Please forward me a copy of the subpoena and accompanying correspondence you sent to [the consultant] at Allison and Taylor. In the future, please ensure that I receive copies of everything you send to anyone requesting information regarding me. That includes everything you have sent thus far."

Dreishmire initially did not respond to my email. Several weeks later, she sent me approximately sixty-nine pages of email strings which she and the consultant had exchanged without my knowledge over the course of several weeks. The initial email showed Dreishmire had contacted the consultant immediately after informing me she intended to depose the consultant later that month. The full email string showed Dreishmire and the consultant had communicated repeatedly throughout most of October 2014. I was entirely unaware of the communication between the two of them.

The emails further showed Dreishmire had (a) established a relationship between herself and the consultant, and (b) attempted to overtly and covertly influence the consultant to testify in a manner which would contradict, nullify, or undermine the information contained in the reference report the consultant had created for me in 2013, and which would, therefore, be favorable to the Board.

The consultant clearly appeared uncomfortable with the declaration Dreishmire wanted her to sign. For instance, in one email exchange between the two, the consultant wrote, "Speaking as a person with 11 years of experience" in her industry, what she endured while trying to obtain reference information for me from the Board was "not normal," and had she been a "true potential employer, who contacted the Board to get reference or employee verification information," and had to "go through all the loopholes" that she did, "Ms. Hutchens would not have been considered for the job."

The consultant also wrote, "Something should be said in the declaration about the timeframe of emails and calls" she made while trying to get information regarding me when she contacted the Board. She further wrote in the email the following regarding the declaration she and Dreishmire had created without my knowledge: "I still feel [the declaration] is a negative report and want to reflect so in the information sent to you. Also, where it says Ms. Hutchens did not lose employment over this report, I don't want to agree to that."

Dreishmire and the consultant created three declarations, including two which were drafts of the final version. Afterward, the consultant obviously had second thoughts about communicating with Dreishmire without my knowledge after Dreishmire asked her to sign the final version of the declaration, so she contacted me by phone and email and told me of her communication with Dreishmire.

Because I did not know if Dreishmire had sent me copies of all emails or any other documents she had exchanged with the consultant and each of the declarations the two of them had created, I filed a motion to compel Dreishmire to provide copies of any other correspondence between her and the consultant which she had not provided me. I also asked the judge to prohibit her from using any of the declarations throughout the litigation. During the subsequent court hearing, Judge Chang basically told me the consultant was not my "witness" and had the roles been reversed, I also could have done what Dreishmire did. He also stated that in the future, Dreishmire and I had to provide each other three days' notice before we issued subpoenas to third parties. That was it. He said nothing else.

When I eventually subpoenaed the consultant and requested all correspondence between Dreishmire and her, she sent me a copy of a declaration Dreishmire had not sent to me— even after I filed the motion to compel Dreishmire to provide me all related emails and documents she had in her possession. Obviously referencing the amount of time it took for the Board to respond to her request for information regarding my employment, the consultant had written the following notes on the declaration, describing what had happened when she attempted to acquire information regarding my employment history from the Board's Human Resources Department:

Nobody would have taken that long
Almost 4 weeks
A real potential employer would not have hired

During a December 1, 2014 responsive motion Dreishmire filed in court, she denied that she had told the consultant I had "chosen not to obtain an attorney." In this regard, she specifically wrote the following: "Ms. Dreishmire did not—as Plaintiff claims—tell [the consultant] Plaintiff chose not to obtain an attorney." Rather, when the subject of whether Plaintiff was represented by counsel came up, Ms. Dreishmire said—accurately— that while Plaintiff had originally been represented by counsel, she chose to discontinue that representation and now represented herself."

Dreishmire's statement was not "accurate" even by a stretch. Instead, it was patently false for two reasons: First, as I previously explained, my former counsel chose in April 2014 to "discontinue" representing me and withdrew from my appeal and second lawsuit against the Board. While I did not object when she withdrew, I did not "discontinue the representation." My attorney "discontinued" it herself. Also, when I completed the paperwork necessary for Judge Chang to appoint an attorney to represent me, he denied me attorney representation—AFTER he had volunteered to provide me attorney representation and asked me to complete the paperwork. The consultant and I eventually discussed what had occurred between Dreishmire and her, and our good business relationship remained intact.

November 2014

Judge Chang remarked during a hearing involving my second lawsuit the possibility of my taking depositions of the Board's witnesses or mine. A deposition is sworn out-of-court testimony which is used to gather information as part of the discovery process and may be used at trial. Conducting depositions and buying the court reporter's transcripts is very expensive, and Judge Chang was well aware of my financial situation at that time. I was unable to support myself, so clearly, there was no way I could afford to depose witnesses. Therefore, to obtain the evidence I needed to help prove the Board was retaliating against me, and also to prove my allegation that a payroll fraud scheme had occurred, I relied, instead, on the Subpoena *Duces Tecum*. It is defined by http://www.encyclopedia.com as the "judicial process used to command the production before a court of papers, documents, or other tangible items of evidence litigants generally employ to compel the production of documents which might be admissible before the court."

I knew sending the Subpoena *Duces Tecum* would cost me nothing more than a postage stamp, envelope, and the time it took to travel to the US Northern District of Illinois Court's Office of the Clerk to have it signed and stamped. I also decided that if any individual or entity did not respond to my Subpoena *Duces Tecum*, I would file a motion to compel, take them to court, and force them to explain to Judge Chang why they refused to comply with the requests I had made.

I sent a Subpoena *Duces Tecum* to the schools and other organizations which did not hire me or did not allow me to return to work after they conducted background and reference checks related to my previous employment, including, but not limited to Truman Middle College and the Princeton Review. I requested documents in conjunction with my candidacy for employment with their organizations, such as job applications I had completed and notes they had written while interviewing me, particularly those which explained why they had decided not to hire me. To obtain investigative documents related to the letters I had sent regarding my allegations of a payroll fraud scheme, I also subpoenaed the Cook County State's Attorney and the Board's inspector general. The utter power of the Subpoena *Duces Tecum* surprised me. With very few exceptions, I received what I requested and sometimes more than I anticipated.

A party in a lawsuit must provide an opposing party several days' advanced notice before issuing a Subpoena *Duces Tecum* so the opposing party has an opportunity to object to its issuance. Because I am far more familiar with a classroom than I am a courtroom, I was unaware of this requirement before issuing my first set of subpoenas. Instead of providing Dreishmire advanced notice of my intent to issue them, I hand-delivered copies of the subpoenas to her the same day I issued them to Truman Middle College and the Board's inspector general. Dreishmire immediately contacted me, demanded that I withdraw the subpoenas, and threatened to take court action against me if I did not. I ignored her, and she filed a motion to quash my Subpoena *Duces Tecum*, in which she requested that Judge Chang render them null and invalid.

What I did not learn until later was she also sent letters to Truman Middle College's attorney and the Cook County State's Attorney and asked them to disregard until further notice the subpoenas I had issued to them. In her motion to quash the subpoenas, Dreishmire objected to my hand-delivering the subpoenas and wrote the following: "It appears Plaintiff personally served each of the three subpoenas, which violates Rule 45(b)(1) prohibition on a party serving its own subpoena. The Board tried to verify its understanding that Plaintiff personally served the subpoenas, but she had refused to respond to the inquiry."

Dreishmire could not possibly for one second have believed that I, a person who has spent a good part of my professional career creating lesson plans and teaching students to read, write, and speak properly, rather than a person who practices law, would have known I had violated a law simply by hand-delivering subpoenas instead of issuing them through a "server." I reviewed Rule 45 of the

Federal Rules of Civil Procedure before delivering the subpoenas, and I noted this requirement; but I did not understand I could not be the actual server. The district offices of Truman Middle College (Chicago City Colleges) and the Board's inspector general were located downtown and within walking distance of where I lived, and I truly believed it was perfectly okay to hand-deliver the subpoenas rather than pay to send them by certified mail, which is how I issued it to the Cook County State's Attorney.

As if I wanted to relinquish my wonderful titles of educator and National Board Certified Teacher, Dreishmire also accused me of "falsely personating" an attorney because I inadvertently signed my name in the wrong place on the subpoena. In this regard, she wrote the following in her motion to quash: "Finally, Plaintiff has misled the parties receiving the subpoenas by signing each as if she is an attorney. In doing so, she violated Illinois law: 'False personation; public officials and employees. A person commits a false personation if he or she knowingly and falsely represents himself or herself to be any of the following: an attorney authorized to practice law for purpose of compensation or consideration.'"

Dreishmire did not accuse me of "personating" a movie star, a rock star, or a person I might have considered a hero. She accused me of "personating" an attorney. After observing for nearly a decade the behavior of nearly every "legal professional" who had anything to do with my two lawsuits against the Board and my legal proceedings against Principal Brenetta Glass at York Alternative High School, Dreishmire need not have worried; there absolutely was *no way* I even remotely would have considered "personating" an attorney—*ever*!

In fact, had I been an attorney at any time during my legal proceedings, I would have placed a paper bag over my head and left it there for as long as I had the title of "attorney" attached to my name, for I saw *nothing* that upheld the integrity and reputation of the legal profession as it related to my combined eight years of legal proceedings against the Board. Instead, what I did observe was an extraordinary effort by an inordinate number of "legal professionals" who attempted at every juncture and in every conceivable way to prevent me from getting justice after my character was assassinated and my civil and constitutional rights were violated by those very "legal professionals." Therefore, Dreishmire had no reason to concern herself or bother the court with nonsensical allegations about me "personating an attorney."

December 2014

During the December 8, 2014 court hearing regarding Dreishmire's motion to quash my subpoenas to Truman Middle College and the Board's inspector general, Judge Chang patiently explained to me that the proper line on which I should have signed was below the attorney's signature line. I apologized and responded that I did, in fact, realize this, and my signature on the attorney's line simply was an oversight of which I would be mindful in the future when issuing subpoenas. He appeared satisfied with my explanation and said nothing more regarding this issue.

To his credit, Judge Chang frequently reminded Dreishmire during the hearing I was a *pro se* litigant and not a lawyer who was familiar with the litigation process. When she shook her head in disgust after he refused to sanction me for hand-delivering the subpoenas, he informed her curtly that I had his permission to do so in the future and rose halfway from his seat, reminded her whose courtroom it was, and told her to save her head-shaking "for the office!" With her head hanging almost to her knees, her face the color of a fire engine, and in a small, squeaky voice, she muttered, "I'm sorry, Your Honor." Moments later, Judge Chang denied Dreishmire's motion to quash my subpoenas to Chicago City Colleges (which represented Truman Middle College) and the Board's inspector general. I was so happy I wanted to laugh out loud. It was a marvelous day!

Within fifteen minutes after the judge overruled Dreishmire, I received a telephone call on my cellphone from Assistant Cook County State's Attorney, Jayman Avery. He assured me he would immediately respond to my subpoena and asked me not to file a motion to compel the Cook County State's Attorney to produce the documents I had requested. I had no idea to what he was referring. However, when I hung up, I concluded Dreishmire had contacted the State's Attorney's office after I issued my subpoena and asked the agency not to respond to it. Later, I discovered that this was what had occurred. A few days later I received the documents I had requested via subpoena from Truman Middle College. I realized then Dreishmire also had contacted Truman Middle College's lawyer only minutes after the court hearing ended and informed her Judge Chang had denied her motion to quash. Consequently, Truman Middle College also was responding to my subpoena. I was on a mighty roll!

It might be common practice and perhaps I am not aware of it because I am not a lawyer, but I never have heard of an attorney contacting a party in a lawsuit and asking the party to ignore a subpoena issued to them. I also never have heard of a party disregarding a subpoena simply because an opposing party in a lawsuit asked them to disregard it. I considered Dreishmire's behavior blatantly disrespectful of me as the opposing party in the lawsuit, simply because I was a *pro se* litigant. I cannot begin to imagine she would have done anything even remotely similar to an attorney.

The following day, I issued another Subpoena *Duces Tecum* to Truman Middle College and the Cook County State's Attorney, requesting emails, notes, letters, and anything else the parties had in their possession from Dreishmire in which she asked them not to respond to my subpoenas. Both complied with my requests in a timely fashion.

In response to investigative documents I had requested regarding my allegations of a payroll fraud scheme by Chicago Board of Education employees, (of which at least two of the school district's attorneys had been aware since 2010, and another since 2012), Jayman Avery, the Assistant Cook County State's Attorney who contacted me following the December 8, 2014 court hearing, sent me a letter dated December 2014, which stated, in part: "Please be advised that there is one document responsive to the subpoena, a CL Report consisting of four pages. However, this document contains information protected from disclosure by the attorney work product privilege, the law enforcement investigative privilege, and the deliberative process privilege, among other applicable privileges."

In other words, the Cook County State's Attorney's Office had conducted an investigation regarding my allegations, and what the agency learned was enough to create a four-page investigative report. However, the Cook County State's Attorney was not going to allow me to read it because it was "privileged information protected from disclosure by attorney work product privilege, the law enforcement investigative privilege, and the deliberative process privilege, among other applicable privileges."

Also, over time, I issued the Subpoena *Duces Tecum* several times to the Chicago City College's attorney regarding the Truman Middle College matter. The attorney objected to each one I issued as "overly broad and unduly burdensome," or "not reasonably calculated to lead to discoverable information." I could not have cared less about her objections, as long as she produced to me the documents I requested, which she ultimately did.

The information she sent was extremely helpful. Although it did not prove without a doubt the Board had retaliated against me by having Truman Middle College prevent me from working, it did prove the reason Truman Middle College's principal provided for not allowing me to return to work—I was hired on an "as needed basis as a substitute teacher," was false. The documents I received from Truman's attorney as a result of the subpoena I issued, disclosed the following:

- There were four open positions for instructor/part-time, and I was one of the four people hired for those positions.
- The Position Number was 00002054, and the Job Code was H120.
- I was hired for the grant-funded position of instructor/part-time in Truman Middle College's Department of Dropout Retrieval.
- The work schedule was Monday through Friday from 9:00 a.m. through 4:00 p.m., and I was scheduled to work twenty-nine hours each week.
- There was nothing contained in any of the documents I received regarding the instructor's position which indicated it was created in response to a need for a substitute teacher or a substitute teacher would be hired for the position.
- In relation to the school's need for a person to fill the position, Truman Middle College's principal had submitted and approved the Justification for Position Statement on July 31, 2012. Pages 1 and 2 of the statement listed various reasons for the need to staff the position, including, but not limited to the "mayoral mandate to extend instructional minutes."
- As of September 10, 2012, which was almost two months before I was hired, the position had been approved by Truman's business manager, HR administrator, officer of the District or designee and chancellor

of the City Colleges of Chicago. Moreover, the October 12, 2012, résumé and cover letter I submitted in response to the job posting was for "instructor/part time," and not for a substitute teacher's position.

- A Personnel Action Form showed that on March 25, 2013, which was six weeks after the attorney I hired to write the letter to Truman Middle College's principal, the school's HR manager and the principal "transferred" me to the position of "substitute instructor." This occurred without either of them obtaining my signature on a relevant form, without me working a single day in the new position to which I supposedly was "transferred," and entirely without my knowledge. The new Position Number for the "substitute instructor" was 0009546, and the Job Code was H082. With the exception of an inquiry regarding my paycheck on November 15, 2012, I had heard from neither the principal nor the HR manager since November 9, 2012, and I had received no indication since that day the principal wanted me to work for Truman Middle College again.

I also issued a Subpoena *Duces Tecum* to Briljent, the company which fired me after learning I had sued the Board, and The Princeton Review. I discuss the information I received from both and further efforts to gather information from the Cook County State's Attorney regarding my allegations of a payroll fraud scheme by Board employees in chapter 16.

CHAPTER 16

An Oral Argument, an Appellate Court's Decision, and a Victory!

JANUARY 2015

ACCORDING TO THE *PRACTITIONER'S HANDBOOK for Appeals to the United States Court of Appeals for the Seventh Circuit*, oral arguments are scheduled shortly after the last appellate brief is due. The November 3, 2014 filing of my reply brief signaled the date of the last brief filed on my appeal.

In early January 2015, the Clerk of the Appeals Court sent me a Notice of Oral Argument ordering me to argue my first lawsuit which was on appeal against Dreishmire on March 3, 2015. Each of us was scheduled to argue for ten minutes.

I continued reading the two-page letter, looking for the name of the attorney who would argue the case on my behalf. I had read that if the US Court of Appeals for the Seventh Circuit allows an oral argument to be heard on cases involving a *pro se* litigant, the Court almost always assigns an attorney to argue the case. The Seventh Circuit rarely allows a *pro se* litigant to argue a case against an opposing attorney. But there was nothing in the Notice of Oral Argument regarding an attorney who would argue my case.

I also noticed the letter I received from the Clerk did not contain the names of the judges who would hear my oral argument. Because of information I had read, I understood that each of the 13 appellate courts has its own rules, and to prevent the parties in a lawsuit from tailoring their preparation and presentation for specific judges, the Seventh Circuit does not inform the two parties in a lawsuit of the identities of the appellate panel until the day of their oral argument. I did not let that faze me. I read the biographies, curriculum vitae, and everything else I could find about every judge in the US Court of Appeals for the Seventh Circuit.

Although I knew I had my work cut out for me, I understood I was being afforded the chance of a lifetime to tell my side of the story to three judges this time instead of one, and I intended to take full advantage of it. I was more than a bit nervous at the thought of standing ten minutes before a three-judge panel and convincing them Judge Chang had made errors so critical and so prejudicial to me, his ruling *had* to be reversed by law. I knew that accomplishing this was no small thing, but I was confident I could do it.

After more than five years of litigation in relation to my first lawsuit, I knew all there was to know about my case, and no attorney could argue it as well as I could. Therefore, I began counting the days until March 3, 2015 arrived. I wasted no time preparing for my oral argument. I read numerous online and in print articles and handbooks about how to present my argument, including appropriate attire; what time to arrive; where the appellant sits; what the three lights on the podium means; how to introduce myself; and why those arguing the case should begin their introduction with, "May it please the Court."

Meanwhile, despite having no medical insurance or COBRA, I had continued the weekly sessions with my therapist, a wonderful lady who counseled me during my depression even though I could not afford to pay her one cent. I wrote in documents to the Board that I had continued my therapy sessions throughout my five years of litigation. Consequently, Dreishmire notified me she wanted to subpoena records of the sessions I had had with my therapist.

Because initially, I thought it was a routine litigation process, I did not object. However, my therapist did not believe Dreishmire was entitled to her private records regarding my sessions with her, so she refused to produce them to Dreishmire, who then filed a motion to compel her to do so. The District Court's hearing on the motion to compel was scheduled for January 22, 2015. My therapist, a woman in her late seventies, was extremely nervous about appearing before Judge Chang, so she retained an attorney to assist her in preparing for the hearing and to appear in court with her.

As I did with everything related to my two lawsuits, I began researching what Dreishmire wanted to learn about me from my therapist and her records. I concluded that she appeared to be seeking information associated with claims involving intentional infliction of emotional distress. Although this was one of the claims I had brought against the Board in my discrimination lawsuit, discovery had ended in that case years ago, and it was on appeal. My second lawsuit, which was the one for which Dreishmire was attempting to acquire discoverable information, had only two claims—whistleblower and retaliation. There was no intentional infliction of emotional distress claim, and Dreishmire knew I had no such claim. Yet, citing my "extensive emotional distress claims in the case," Dreishmire attempted to compel my therapist to submit her private records concerning my therapy sessions with her and took her to court so Judge Chang would force her to produce the records.

Immediately after the January 22, 2014 court hearing on Dreishmire's motion to compel began, I informed Judge Chang my second lawsuit had no intentional infliction of emotional distress claim, I was not seeking emotional distress damages in it, and I did not intend to call my therapist as a witness if my lawsuit proceeded to trial. Although he had possession of my filed lawsuit document, he appeared surprised and asked me why I had not informed him earlier. I explained that until I researched the matter, I believed Dreishmire was privy to my private mental health information. Judge Chang immediately denied Dreishmire's motion to compel. However, the legal process caused my therapist who was living on a fixed income unnecessary stress and resulted in her paying an attorney nearly $3,300 to prepare court documents for her and to represent her in court.

Meanwhile, in conjunction with the part-time position for which I had applied in 2013 with The Princeton Review, in mid-January 2015, I received very informative responsive documents to the subpoena I had issued to the organization in late December 2014. The documents disclosed that after I submitted my application, apparently The Princeton Review created a Candidate Tracking Summary which showed that based solely on my credentials and experience, the company assigned me a score of one hundred for the position for which I had applied. Based on their assessment criteria, this exceeded by tenfold the required score of ten to be considered for the job.

The documents also showed that after engaging in a teaching audition on January 14, 2013, I was invited to complete an online application which authorized The Princeton Review to conduct a background and reference check of my past employment. The Candidate Tracking Summary further revealed that on January 29, 2013, Robert Hennen, who at that time was operations manager for The Princeton Review, conducted two telephone interviews apparently in conjunction with my job candidacy. According to the Candidate Tracking Summary, Hennen engaged in one of the phone interviews at 8:00 a.m., and it lasted for one hour. Following the phone interview, apparently Hennen recorded in the "Recommendation" section of the Candidate Tracking Summary, "Do Not Continue." Another box in the "Action" section of the Candidate Tracking Summary showed the words "View Feedback." However, no feedback was provided on the form which I received.

Described on the Candidate Tracking Summary as a "Quick Interview," the other phone interview occurred at 1:10 p.m.; but the duration of the call was not indicated. Apparently, following what also is identified as a "Phone Screen," and again reflecting the name of Robert Hennen, the document contained the words "Hiring Recommendation—Do Not Continue." The Candidate Tracking Summary did not identify to whom Hennen spoke during the phone interviews or show any information contained in the "Feedback" section which caused him not to hire me.

What was clear is that less than one hour after the call ended, Hennen decided that I, a candidate who on paper appeared extremely qualified for the position and whom he obviously considered for the position after I engaged in a teaching audition, was no longer a good fit for the job after he or someone at the Princeton Review conducted a background check of my previous employment. Hennen then sent me an email rejecting my application and thanking me for my interest in the job.

I wasted no time trying to find out to whom Hennen had spoken and what he was told during the two phone interviews after which he provided "Feedback." On January 21, 2015, I filed a motion to compel The Princeton Review to comply with the subpoena I had issued to the organization in late

December 2014. I specifically requested that Judge Chang order The Princeton Review's full compliance with my subpoena by providing me, the Plaintiff,

(a) specific emails which had been exchanged between Hennen and me;
(b) all information related to Hennen's January 29, 2013 phone screens at 8:00 a.m. and 1:10 p.m. concerning my job candidacy. I also stated in the motion to compel that The Princeton Review should include with this information the name of the organization, entity and individual(s) from whom Hennen acquired information and all feedback he received during the two phone screens.
(c) all documents The Princeton Review produced to the Board regarding my lawsuit at any time between January 1, 2013 and January 21, 2015.

The Princeton Review's attorney, Angela Rochester, represented the company in court the day of the motion hearing. Judge Chang denied my motion with the understanding that by February 9, 2015, The Princeton Review would file "an affidavit as detailed in open court by an appropriate Princeton Review representative describing the search for the respective documents."

FEBRUARY 2015

February 2015 was far more difficult and there was far more activity than there had been during any other month in terms of my second lawsuit against the Board. A major snowstorm which began on Saturday, January 31, and ended on Monday, February 2, dumped 19.3 inches of snow on Chicago. I had decided to file charges with the EEOC against Briljent and The Princeton Review because I believed both had retaliated against me after learning I had sued the Board.

Initially, I had not planned to file an EEOC charge against Briljent because I hoped I would get an opportunity to work for the company again. However, after I received documents I had subpoenaed from the company, specifically several emails exchanged among Briljent employees, I realized Tammy Brodzeller, the person who fired me, knew several months before I began my second stint with Briljent that I was suing the Board. She had learned of the lawsuit when Brian Flores, the other attorney who represented the Board in my second lawsuit at that time, subpoenaed Briljent in April 2014 for information regarding my previous employment.

The emails I received from Briljent in response to my subpoena also showed communication about me amongst Briljent employees regarding my lawsuit which offended me. Therefore, I no longer wanted anything else to do with the company. Obviously, the feeling was mutual because after they fired me, I never heard from them again as it related to reemployment. I also believed The Princeton Review had retaliated against me after learning I sued the Board by refusing to hire me following a background check which included engaging in the two phone interviews and receiving feedback.

I had not scheduled a time in advance to meet with the EEOC, but because of the snowstorm, I figured if anyone had made an appointment to file a complaint that day, they would cancel it. Therefore, I headed there to file my two EEOC charges. I was right; there were no complainants at the EEOC's Chicago office, so I was able to meet with an investigator immediately.

I filed EEOC Charge Number 440-2015-02541 against TPR Education LLC D/B/A The Princeton Review, and Charge Number 440-2015-02542 against Briljent. But filing the two EEOC charges was a complete waste of time. Because I had been hired by Briljent as a contractor and not as a permanent employee, I was not protected by Title VII anti-discrimination laws. After receiving Briljent's Position Statement and learning of my contractor's status, the EEOC refused to investigate my complaint and ultimately dismissed it.

The EEOC also refused to investigate and dismissed my complaint against The Princeton Review because the statute of limitations for filing an EEOC complaint had expired. Generally, a charge must be filed with the EEOC within 180 calendar days from the day the discrimination took place. The filing deadline of 180 days is extended to 300 calendar days if a state or local agency enforces a law which prohibits employment discrimination on the same basis. I was aware of the EEOC's time limits, but I had hoped I could file the charge against The Princeton Review under the Continuing Violation Doctrine, which as I understood it, overrides the statute of limitations and is appropriate when an employer engages in recurring acts of discrimination against an employer.

The EEOC either did not want to be bothered with investigating my charge, or I was not entitled to an investigation under the doctrine. Because I was so busy with my two lawsuits against the Board, I did not have time to pursue any action against The Princeton Review. Therefore, I made no further attempt to seek justice against the organization for what I believed and continue to believe was its blatant and unlawful retaliation against me.

In relation to the motion I filed to compel The Princeton Review to produce documents to me, the organization's attorney filed in court on February 9, 2015, two affidavits. The first affiant declared, in part, the following: "Mr. Hennen, the individual who made the decision not to hire Ms. Hutchens, separated from The Princeton Review in or around March 2013, and following a diligent search of The Princeton Review's records, there were no documents or information located reflecting the reason not to hire Ms. Hutchens."

The second affiant stated, in part, the following: "The Princeton Review conducted a search, which included me conferring with our IT department and Human Resources to determine whether responsive documents exist. I understand the only documents located by Human Resources was Ms. Hutchins' [sic] employment application materials and certain related emails, all of which I mailed to Ms. Hutchins by overnight courier on January 13, 2015. I also understand our IT department did not locate any documents which were responsive to Ms. Hutchens' subpoena." I expand more on these two affiants later in this chapter.

In a related matter, Dreishmire sent me an email on February 10, 2015, in which she requested the address and telephone number for Robert Hennen, the former Princeton Review operations manager. I had no information for her because I did not know Hennen's address and telephone number at that time. In fact, I did not know Hennen. Therefore, I ignored Dreishmire's message. Two days later, she sent me another email asking me when I would be providing Hennen's contact information. I continued to ignore her, but her sudden interest in contacting Hennen made me suspicious.

I never even considered discontinuing my fight to obtain the documents on which Hennen had provided his feedback following his two phone calls, so my next step was to retrieve phone records. Through an extensive Google search, I found the name of The Princeton Review's Chicago landline phone carrier and three phone numbers associated with that carrier. Thereafter, I subpoenaed the organization's phone records for the date and a three-hour time period before and after the times the two phone calls had occurred, at 8:00 a.m. and 1:10 p.m. on January 29, 2013.

In mid-February, I informed Dreishmire that unless she objected within three business days, I would issue the subpoena to the phone carrier for The Princeton Review's phone records. She did not object, so I issued the subpoena. I had researched whether it was legal and/or appropriate to obtain phone records without notifying The Princeton Review I intended to subpoena them, and I found nothing in Rule 45 of the Federal Rules of Civil Procedure that made me believe I had to notify the company. Moreover, when I received no objection from Dreishmire, I believed it was legal for me to obtain the phone records without contacting The Princeton Review, because I knew Dreishmire certainly would have objected if I was violating the law.

Approximately one week later, I received responses from the phone carrier for information related to two of The Princeton Review's telephone numbers I had listed in the subpoena. Data for one of the numbers showed that on January 29, 2013, at 11:21 a.m. Chicago time, someone at The Princeton Review spoke with someone at the Chicago Board of Education's central office for ten minutes and fifty seconds. (This was the same date and very close to the time on which Hennen had sent me an email rejecting me for the job.)

The Princeton Review's phone number which appeared in the phone carrier's report was the same phone number that appeared in a January 2, 2013 email I had received from The Princeton Review inviting me to engage in a teacher's audition. I also had listed in my employment application I submitted to The Princeton Review as the number the organization should contact for reference information, the same Chicago Board of Education telephone number which appeared in the report.

The strong suggestion from this circumstantial information is someone from The Princeton Review spoke with someone at the Board's central office shortly before Hennen terminated my job candidacy with the Princeton

Review. Additionally, the time indicated in the phone records circumstantially supported that Hennen's decision not to hire me was based on something he learned after speaking with someone who worked for the Board. This also was supported by the fact that I had provided The Princeton Review the name of only one other reference, which was the charter school at which I had served as a master teacher/instructional coach.

During discovery, I also issued a subpoena to the charter school's HR director and attorney, and the responsive document the attorney provided me (after I was forced to file a motion to compel) showed The Princeton Review had not contacted the school for a reference. The charter school's telephone number also was not shown in The Princeton Review's phone records during the time period in question, and, of course, the Board's telephone number was.

Shortly thereafter, I issued another Subpoena *Duces Tecum* and a Requests for Admission (Request to Admit) which contained thirty-four statements. I sent the requests to Hennen, who by then no longer worked for The Princeton Review. A Request to Admit is a set of statements sent from a litigant to an adversary in order to have the adversary admit or deny the statements or allegations contained therein. Each Request to Admit "question" appears as a declarative statement which the answering party must either admit, deny, or provide details as to why he or she cannot admit or deny the statement's truthfulness.

Requests to Admit are automatically considered admitted in US federal courts if the opponent does not respond or object in a timely manner. I had no idea if sending a Request to Admit to a third party in a lawsuit was permissible, appropriate, or legal, but I intended to let the judge tell me if it was not. (Although much later an attorney who laughed when I told him about the Request to Admit informed me it was, in fact, inappropriate to issue it to a third party, he did not say it was illegal.)

After hand-delivering the Subpoena *Duces Tecum* and a copy of the Request to Admit to Dreishmire and notifying her of my intent to send both to Hennen, Dreishmire immediately objected. She made no other statement in this regard, so I assumed an objection to a subpoena would or should be followed by a formal motion in which I would have to appear before Judge

Chang and explain my reason for issuing the documents to Hennen. After waiting five days for Dreishmire to file a motion objecting to the subpoena and Request to Admit, I sent both to Hennen whose home and work address I had found on the Internet.

Hennen contacted me several days later by phone and left me a voicemail message stating that because he had just received the documents, he could not comply with my request to complete and return them by the due date I had indicated. He also requested a return phone call from me because he had questions regarding the documents. By email the following day, I informed him the documents were related to my January 2013 candidacy for a position with The Princeton Review, when he served as operations manager for the organization. I extended the time by one week for him to respond to my Request to Admit documents and return them to me, but he did not contact me again.

Meanwhile, because Assistant Cook County State's Attorney, Jayman Avery, had denied me the four-page investigative document his agency had created following my 2013 allegations of a payroll fraud scheme involving Glowacki's salary, I filed a motion to compel compliance with my Subpoena *Duces Tecum* and hauled Avery into court in February 2015. He provided Judge Chang the same reasons he provided me—the document supposedly contained privileged information and was protected by various law enforcement and other privileges. Judge Chang ordered Avery to file the document *ex parte* and under seal so he could review the document.

According to Wikipedia, *ex parte* means a legal proceeding brought by one person in the absence of and without representation or notification of other parties. It also is used more loosely to refer to improper unilateral contacts with a court, arbitrator or represented party without notice to the other party or counsel for that party. Also, according to Wikipedia, filing under seal is a procedure allowing sensitive or confidential information to be filed with a court without becoming a matter of public record. The court generally must give permission for the material to remain under seal. During a subsequent court hearing, Judge Change informed me the document did contain privileged information. Therefore, he denied my motion to compel Avery to produce it to me.

Avery's boss at the time was Cook County State's Attorney, Anita Alvarez, who, as I write this, has just lost her bid for a third term in the wake of numerous protests in response to the manner in which she allegedly handled several high-profile matters involving police and the black community, and other issues. Alvarez's office refused to allow me to view its investigative document in response to my letter, and Judge Chang agreed with that decision.

Oddly, after I issued the subpoena and followed up with a motion to compel, the Northern District of Illinois Court included Avery as a recipient of docket entry notifications on my case and did not remove him until after my two lawsuits ended. Therefore, although the Cook County State's Attorney was only a third party in my second lawsuit, for some strange reason, Avery was able to monitor all activity on my case from the time he appeared in court until my two lawsuits ended in October 2015, but neither Judge Chang nor his deputy ever explained why. Because I was so consumed with my lawsuit, it did not occur to me to question them about it at that time.

Interestingly, only a few months before the alleged payroll fraud scheme involving Glowacki's salary had occurred, which was in 2008, the Board's inspector general conducted an investigation of another payroll fraud scheme involving nine black employees who scammed the Board out of $137,000. Alvarez convicted and imprisoned either most or all of them for their crimes. My complaint concerned a scam involving two white Board employees who allegedly bilked the Board out of nearly $100,000 (but apparently only one received the illegal funds).

Because I had no money for depositions, the Subpoena *Duces Tecum* and motion to compel became the primary tools in my fight for justice in my second lawsuit. I called them my "Weapons of Mass Production" and called myself "Queen of The Subpoena *Duces Tecum.*" I ultimately filed more than twenty between November 2014 and the end of discovery in the second lawsuit, which was February 28, 2015. When third parties refused to comply with it by the due date and did not inform me they intended to comply but needed more time, without a second thought I immediately filed a motion to compel. I believe Judge Chang was sick of looking at me as I waltzed into his courtroom almost every week and hauled the Board and/or third parties in the lawsuit into court to stand before him and forced them to explain why they had violated my court order by refusing to provide me the information I requested.

Meanwhile, in a five-hour session which occasionally featured heated exchanges between Dreishmire and me, and during which she frequently raised her voice to the point of screaming at me and shaking her head in disgust as she did in Judge Chang's courtroom as I discussed in chapter 15, on February 19, 2015, Dreishmire deposed me in my second lawsuit. Only minutes after the deposition began, Dreishmire showered me with questions about my former attorney, Deidre Baumann, who had withdrawn from my appeal and second lawsuit in April 2014.

As I previously stated, during the May 1, 2014 court hearing on Baumann's motion to withdraw from my second lawsuit, Judge Chang ordered Dreishmire and her colleague, Brian Flores, to leave the courtroom "because of the need to inquire into the attorney-client relationship" and because the court was holding "an *ex parte* and under seal hearing with plaintiff and plaintiff's counsel regarding the motion." But despite the judge's order that the information was attorney/client privileged and proceedings of the hearing were to remain sealed, in an attempt to find out what had happened during the hearing, Dreishmire repeatedly questioned me during the deposition about Baumann and the hearing. The following was taken directly from the court reporter's transcript of my February 19, 2015 deposition and are some of the questions Dreishmire asked me about Baumann:

- You were once represented by an attorney in this lawsuit, correct?
- That was Deidre Baumann?
- How did you find her?
- And Ms. Baumann actually represented you in your 2009 case against the Board as well?
- Coming on midway in the case?
- Were you satisfied with her representation of you in the 2009 case against the Board?

- And were you satisfied with her representation of you in this case against the Board?
- Did you, in fact, tell the court that you didn't want Ms. Baumann to represent you in this case?
- Did you tell the court you wanted Ms. Baumann to stay on and not withdraw?
- Why does she no longer represent you in this case?
- Did you object to her no longer representing you in this case?
- Do you have a fee agreement with Ms. Baumann related to this case?
- Did you ever have one?
- Have you paid her any money related to this case?
- Does Ms. Baumann represent you in any capacity now?

Initially, I paid little attention to what Dreishmire was asking me about Baumann because I thought she simply was seeking routine discovery-related information. But as she continued to ask questions, there was no doubt she was seeking confidential and attorney/client privileged information from me. At one point, I told her she would have to ask Baumann for the answer. Other notable highlights of the deposition include the following:

- When I made a statement about her repeated failure to produce documents to me in a timely fashion, Dreishmire exclaimed, "Yeah, that's a lie, but that's okay!"
- When I told Dreishmire she needed to stop raising her voice at me, she screamed, "You're not going to lie about me in this deposition, Ms. Hutchens! I'm not going to stand for it!" She also said because the court reporter was tape recording the deposition, there was proof she was not raising her voice. Let me be as clear as I can be: Lisa Dreishmire screamed at me repeatedly during the five-hour deposition. When she learned I had sent the Subpoena *Duces Tecum* and Request to Admit documents to Hennen, former operations manager of The Princeton Review, in what I perceived as a tirade, Dreishmire became *very* upset and screamed at me for several minutes.

- When I attempted to clarify a question Dreishmire asked me, she, in turn, questioned my education and intelligence by asking me if it is true I have two master's degrees; if it is true I have a bachelor's degree; if it is true I graduated from high school; if it is true I have taught the English language to students for many years; and if I feel I'm "able to read and comprehend a sentence like the one that starts with I agree to release and hold harmless…"
- Taken directly from the court reporter's transcript, the following exchange occurred between Dreishmire and me regarding information I allegedly had not produced to her.

  Q. Well, you're obligated to disclose witnesses' contact information –
  A. I gave it to you.
  Q. and I've asked for it multiple times.
  A. I gave it to you in the subpoena.
  Q. You don't get to bury it in a subpoena to someone else that doesn't indicate in any way –
  A. How is it buried? I gave it to you.
  Q. That's ridiculous.
  A. Well, *you're* ridiculous. Buried in a subpoena? In a one-line subpoena?
- In relation to the phone records I obtained from The Princeton Review's phone carrier, I had received them the night before my deposition via a highly secured method that did not allow me to transmit them by email. I had no working printer (which I had discussed several times with Dreishmire); therefore, time did not permit me to have the records for Dreishmire by the following morning's deposition. When I informed Dreishmire I had in my possession phone records showing the Board's phone number close to the time Hennen rejected me for further consideration for the job, in a voice raised to a level of screaming, Dreishmire, who had not objected to me issuing the relevant subpoena, asked me if The Princeton Review knew I had obtained their phone records and if I thought it was "fair or

in compliance with the law" that I would obtain someone's personal phone records without informing the company or giving them an opportunity to object. I responded that I was a *pro se* litigant, (which she knew), and as far as I was concerned, I could use a subpoena to get information from anyone I wished. (My rationale was if the phone carrier believed it was illegal or improper for me to have the records, they would not have released them to me.) Dreishmire was *extremely* upset and continued her tirade for several minutes regarding the phone records which contained the Board's phone number.

- Taken directly from the court reporter's transcript, the following is another exchange between Dreishmire and me regarding the Request to Admit document I had sent to Hennen.
  Q. Okay. How did you send it to Mr. Hennen?
  A. I sent it via subpoena by mail.
  Q. At what address?
  A. At the address on the subpoena.
  Q. Where do you have his telephone number? Have you called him from your cellphone?
  A. I did not call him. He called me and left a message. I did not call him back.
  Q. Did he call you on your cellphone?
  A. Yes, he did.

Dreishmire then asked me if she could "see the history of my personal cellphone," to determine the veracity of my statement that I had not recently spoken with Hennen. Although I knew she absolutely had no business asking to see my cellphone call history and I had every right to refuse to allow her to see it, I actually handed the cellphone to her, because I made up my mind then and there I was reporting her behavior to the ARDC. I knew that everything she was saying was being recorded by the court reporter, and I wanted her to keep running her mouth and behaving as she was because I knew I was going to give a copy of the deposition transcript to the ARDC.

As if I personally knew Hennen, (I did not), Dreishmire asked me how she could reach him, if he still worked for The Princeton Review, when was the last time I had spoken with him, and numerous other questions. She appeared consumed with the fact I had pursued information from Hennen regarding his possible communication with the Board as it related to my job candidacy. Her interest heightened after she learned I had The Princeton Review's phone records which contained the Board's phone number on the same day, at the same number, and near the same time he rejected me for the job.

The deposition transcript shows she referenced Hennen a total of forty-four times and his former company, The Princeton Review, sixty-six times, or a combined total of 110 times she referenced either or both. She referenced Truman Middle College thirty times and another third party in the lawsuit, which I alleged did not hire me after conducting a background check, only thirty-six times.

After learning I had sent the Request to Admit to Hennen, Dreishmire first asked me to "withdraw the deposition on written questions," but I refused. Then, she asked me if I would "rip it up" apparently before she spoke with either Hennen and/or his attorney and learned he had not returned his responses to me. In this regard, taken directly from the court reporter's transcript, the following is the exchange which occurred between Dreishmire while she screamed at me the entire time:

(Exhibit No. 88 was marked for identification.)

BY MS. DREISHMIRE:
Q. You recognize that as a copy of the court order regarding, among other things, the procedure the parties must use in serving subpoenas? And that's at the end of the document, if you want to look at that, the top paragraph on the last page.
A. Yes.
Q. And you received a copy of that order from the court around the time it was issued?

A. I recall receiving it, yes.
Q. You had it before you sent me notice of your intent to issue a deposition on written questions or request of admission to Robert Hennen?
A. Yes, I did.
Q. Okay. If the Board was to propose resolving the issue, which is our concern that you violated a court order in the manner in which you served the subpoena on Mr. Hennen, by ripping up whatever he gives you in response so that you can't use it and then conducting an oral deposition at which both you and the Board could ask him questions, would you object to that?
A. I would object. You can go ahead and file your motion to quash or whatever.
Q. Why would you object to that as a resolution of the issue?
A. Because I'd rather let the judge tell me than you.
Q. You would not -- you don't want -- I'm not telling you. I'm offering you an opportunity to agree to do it.
A. Then I object.
Q. I can't make you do it.
A. I object. You can tell him I object.
Q. You would not agree to do that?
A. No, I would not.
Q. Why not?
A. I don't have to explain to you why. As I just said, I'd rather the judge tell me than you.
Q. You're going to make the Board spend the money to file a motion, even though you clearly violated the order; is that right?
A. Yes. Yes, I am. And I'm going to spend the money to miss whatever day I have with work to come into court, yes, I will.
MS. DREISHMIRE:

Objection; nonresponsive to everything after her actual answer to the question.

Dreishmire repeated "Objection; nonresponsive to everything after her actual answer to the question" so many times during the deposition, I lost count. Although I made clear she could file a motion to quash the subpoena and the accompanying Request to Admit I had issued to Hennen and force me to go to court, for whatever reason, she would not take me to court and did not inform Judge Chang I supposedly had violated a court order.

One final note regarding my deposition: Following a very long break, which Dreishmire stated she needed to take, she returned to the deposition and the first question she asked me was, "Ms. Hutchens, did you provide Mr. Hennen with notice that you were issuing a phone-records subpoena for his personal cellphone?" "I did not," I responded. I suspected she had made a phone call to Hennen's lawyer or possibly to Hennen after I informed her I had found his contact information on the Internet. One week later, despite my unambiguous objection to her taking Hennen's deposition, Dreishmire deposed him at her office. I did not attend; only Hennen, Dreishmire, and Angela Rochester, the attorney who represented Hennen and The Princeton Review, attended the deposition.

Speaking of Rochester, following my deposition she sent me an email informing me she planned to attend the deposition and accusing me of subpoenaing the phone records of Hennen and The Princeton Review without first notifying either. Like Dreishmire, Rochester claimed I had violated the law. By return email I told her what I previously had told Dreishmire: File a motion to quash my subpoena, take me to court, and tell the judge I had violated the law. Also like Dreishmire, Rochester would not do it. In fact, I did not hear another word from her by email.

Hennen did not respond to the Request to Admit document I had sent to him. Either Dreishmire or Hennen informed Rochester of the document after I mailed it to him along with the subpoena. Apparently, Rochester retrieved it from Hennen, responded to it, and returned it to me. She lodged objections to each of my thirty-four statements in the Request to Admit. In the signature block on the final page of the document, she inexplicably represented herself as a Chicago Board of Education attorney, and on the same page, she represented herself as an attorney from the firm at which she actually worked.

Rochester sent a copy of the Request to Admit document to me and presumably to Dreishmire via email and US mail. In a letter attached to the document, she wrote that I was "harassing" Hennen. Rochester's statement was false. While attempting to determine to whom Hennen had spoken on January 29, 2013, during his two telephone "interviews" shortly before he decided I was an unacceptable candidate, I issued two subpoenas to The Princeton Review's phone carrier. In the first subpoena, I requested data from four telephone numbers I identified as assigned to The Princeton Review, and in the other, I requested data related to another telephone number contained in an email I received from Hennen on January 29, 2013, when he rejected me for the position. There was nothing in Hennen's email signature block to suggest the phone number contained in the second subpoena was his personal cellphone number.

In seeking this information, I was not attempting to harass Hennen, I was not interested in harassing him, I did not have time to harass him and I had nothing to gain by harassing him. My sole interest was in learning to whom he had spoken and what they had said which caused him to reject me for the job almost immediately after he completed the phone call and received feedback. Remarkably, despite all of my so-called court violations, neither Rochester nor Dreishmire reported them to Judge Chang—ever. I believe there was a *very* good reason Dreishmire was seriously worried about me communicating with Hennen. I also believe she did not want me to find out what that reason was.

Hennen's quickly-scheduled deposition to which I had objected and did not attend, was held on February 26, 2015, at Dreishmire's office. Unlike my deposition which she had discussed with Judge Chang during numerous court hearings, Dreishmire did not notify Judge Chang she intended to depose Hennen. I was not even aware the deposition had taken place. Although Dreishmire had informed me she intended to depose Hennen, afterward, she did not mention to me she actually had conducted it. To my complete surprise, the EEOC investigator who handled the complaint of retaliation I had filed against The Princeton Review earlier that month, told me of the deposition several weeks later when dismissing my complaint against The Princeton Review because the statute of limitations for filing the complaint had expired.

Apparently, the investigator had learned of the deposition when The Princeton Review's lawyer referenced it in her EEOC Position Statement.

A transcript of the fifty-six-minute deposition, which I acquired months after it had occurred, shows Dreishmire stated the following during the proceeding:

MS. DREISHMIRE:

I'd just like to go on the record to say that Ms. Hutchens, the plaintiff in this case, is not present. She's received notice of this deposition. She's informed me that she would object to it, but not that she would not attend it. And I'd like to give her say, another ten minutes to show up, if that's acceptable?

Two days before Hennen's deposition, I sent an email to Dreishmire in which I informed her I was attempting to work and had several scheduled interviews, so I would not be missing any more days of work to attend depositions.

Taken directly from the court reporter's transcript, Rochester, The Princeton Review's attorney, also stated the following at the beginning of the deposition:

MS. ROCHESTER:

I'm Angela Rochester. "I'm counsel for The Princeton Review, and I'm also counsel for Mr. Hennen for purposes of this deposition. Ms. Hutchens sent me an email this morning in response to objections to purported requests for admission that she sent to Mr. Hennen some time ago. In that email this morning that was addressed just to me, she indicated that she would not -- she may not -- will not be attending a deposition today if it's held at the Chicago Board of education's office. And then the email goes on to address the RFA's that she sent to me."

Rochester was wrong. I did not send the "RFA's" (Requests for Admission) to her. I sent them to Hennen, and to circumvent Hennen's responses to my subpoena and "RFA's" during or immediately after my deposition, either Dreishmire or Hennen alerted Rochester or The Princeton Review I had sent them to Hennen. (Again, I suspect this is what occurred when Dreishmire took the very long break during my deposition,) Hennen no longer worked for

The Princeton Review at that time and had not in quite a while, and although she represented The Princeton Review, Rochester was not an employee of the company.

The court reporter's transcript of Hennen's deposition shows Hennen testified, in part, as follows:

- In response to Dreishmire's question regarding Hennen's employment and educational background, he testified that he worked for The Princeton Review between May 2005 and June 2013 as operations manager, and he resigned in June 2013.
- His duties in the capacity of operations manager were to recruit, hire, train, manage, and in certain cases terminate the pool of part-time instructors employed by the Chicago office.
- With respect to recruiting, his role was to post job ads for instructors and manage and monitor The Princeton Review's applicant tracking system through their website. (This would have been the Candidate Tracking Summary which I previously mentioned had been created in relation to the position for which I had applied with The Princeton Review.)
- Hennen testified he had decided by 8:00 a.m. on January 29, 2013, he would not be moving forward with my candidacy. The Candidate Tracking Summary shows Hennen did not send me an email rejecting me for the position until after he engaged in a 1:10 p.m. "Quick Interview," which was shortly after the Board's central office phone number appeared on the phone carrier's record. Hennen did not address why he engaged in a "Quick Interview" at 1:10 p.m. if he had decided at 8:00 a.m. the same day he allegedly was not going to hire me, and of course, Dreishmire did not ask him that question during the deposition. Also, at 1:12 p.m., which was two minutes after the Candidate Tracking Summary shows what presumably was the end of the "Quick Interview," Hennen sent me an email rejecting me for the position. I was unable to retrieve information from the phone carrier

which showed a phone number in conjunction with the 8:00 a.m. time indicated on the Candidate Tracking Summary.
- Although the deposition transcript shows Dreishmire provided Hennen numerous documents related to my Princeton Review job candidacy during his deposition, he testified that he did not remember why he chose not to proceed with my candidacy for a position with The Princeton Review.
- I just mentioned that Hennen testified he had made the decision by 8:00 a.m. not to hire me and he did not remember why he chose not to proceed with my candidacy. The deposition transcript shows Hennen also testified that he was the one who had decided by 8:00 a.m. on January 29, 2013, he "would not be moving forward with my candidacy." However, the deposition transcript shows he then changed his story and testified that the decision not to hire me was The Princeton Review's. Moreover, as I mentioned earlier in this chapter, on January 21, 2015, I filed a motion to compel The Princeton Review to comply with the subpoena I issued in late December 2014. In response to that motion, The Princeton Review's attorney filed affidavits from two Princeton Review employees. In the first affidavit, the affiant, Kate Eilers, Executive Director of TPR Education, LLC, d/b/a The Princeton Review (The Princeton Review) Chicago Location," stated, in part, "Mr. Hennen, the individual who made the decision not to hire Ms. Hutchens... In the second affidavit, affiant Stephanie Zawalich, who identified herself as "Legal Assistant of TPR Education, LLC, d/b/a The Princeton Review (The Princeton Review)," did not refute Eilers' claim it was Hennen who made the decision not to hire me.
- Hennen made other statements which also show he was the person who had made the decision to "end Ms. Hutchens' candidacy" and "not move someone forward in the process," including the following:
  - Hennen claimed he did not know when he decided I would not advance in The Princeton Review's candidate process.

- According to Hennen, "Feedback Provided" was his own feedback to the system.
- Hennen further claimed "Feedback Provided" and "Do Not Continue" which are words contained in the Candidate Tracking Summary he completed regarding my job candidacy, did not mean he talked with anyone, and the third party who conducted the background check for The Princeton Review could not have input anything into the "Feedback" system; only he could do that.
- Dreishmire did not ask Hennen to identify the information he had input into the "Feedback" system as it related to my Candidate Tracking Summary, and he did not volunteer any information in that regard.

Late in February 2015, I observed oral arguments at the Court of Appeals one week before arguing my own case. Judges Easterbrook, Rovner, and Sykes served on the three-judge panel. Several lawyers argued cases, and I watched intently.

MARCH 2015

March 2, 2015, the day before my oral argument, I compiled the notes I had written and placed them neatly into a white binder notebook. Actually, I did not need the notes because I had read them so many times, I had committed them to my memory. I placed them into the notebook in the order I intended to make my presentation before the three-judge panel. During the many hours I had spent preparing for my oral argument, I learned I probably would not use the notes much because most likely, the three judges would ask me questions I probably would have had to answer without referring to the notes. I was mindful I had only eight minutes for my opening argument and two minutes for my rebuttal (which I had scheduled with the Clerk of the Court ahead of time).

With my white binder in hand, I visited the Appeals Court and because court was not in session, an employee kindly allowed me to enter Room

2712 where my argument against Dreishmire was scheduled to be held the following morning. He was shocked when he learned I was arguing my own case and told me a *pro se* arguing his or her own case is so extraordinarily rare, sometimes years pass without even one *pro se* arguing a case in the US Court of Appeals for the Seventh Circuit. "Your two appellate briefs *really* must have been impressive if the judges are allowing you to argue your own case," he said as he walked out of the room, closed the door, and allowed me to practice my argument. I walked up to the lectern where I would present my argument the following day and stood there quietly for a few minutes. Then, I pretended I was speaking before the panel who would be hearing my case. I practiced my argument for nearly thirty minutes. When I finished, I was ready to stand before the three judges whose identities I still did not know.

I awoke at 4:00 a.m. the next morning and was surprised I had gotten any sleep at all. I reached for my binder which contained my oral argument notes. I had fallen asleep reading them and the binder had fallen on the floor sometime overnight. I was reviewing the notes when I received the first text message: "Good luck today, girl. God's got your back!" The next message came nearly one hour later, "I'll be thinking of you all morning girl; love you!" Both messages were from friends who had supported me throughout my entire litigious nightmare. I received no phone calls, and friends, family and other supporters told me later they did not want to disturb me that morning because they wanted me to focus solely on my oral argument.

I was mindful that the appropriate attire for attorneys is conservative business dress in traditional dark colors (e.g., navy blue or charcoal gray), and I dressed accordingly. The oral argument was scheduled for 9:30 a.m. I left my home at 8:15 a.m. to ensure I had more than enough time for the twenty-five-minute walk and the search by security when I arrived at the federal building which housed the US Court of Appeals for the Seventh Circuit. There had been a light snowfall the previous night, and because it was cold, the snow had turned into a thin sheet of ice, so I took extra care as I headed downtown.

Because of the snow and ice, it took me longer to arrive than it normally would have, and after a five-minute wait in line and the eventual search by US marshals, I stepped onto the elevator and headed for the twenty-seventh floor. I knew every court procedure by that time, so when I arrived, I headed straight for the wall on which a card on the rostrum listed the names of the three-judge panel and the attorneys who were scheduled to present oral arguments that morning. It also listed my name as the plaintiff-appellant who would be proceeding *pro se* in my argument against the Board. I was the only *pro se* presenting an oral argument that day.

When I saw I was scheduled to go first, I almost panicked. I wanted to go last so the attorneys and others in the packed courtroom who had come to hear arguments that morning would be gone by the time my turn came. But there it was posted on the wall—my oral argument would be first. Immediately underneath my name was the title which symbolized my new reality—*in forma pauperis*. I was destitute, indigent, a pauper, a person too poor to pay for my appeal, and it appeared in black print on the wall and the US Court of Appeals for the Seventh Circuit's website for the entire world to see. The pain in my heart was nothing compared to the pain in my soul. But although my pride was shattered, it was not destroyed. My new title and new reality made me all the more determined to prevail against the Board.

There were eight other cases being heard that day. The panel was comprised of esteemed Judge Richard Posner, about whom I had read extensively in *Wikipedia*, on the Internet, and in many legal journals and other publications, and Judges John Tinder and Michael Kanne. I also had read about them, but to a far lesser extent than I had Judge Posner. He is known throughout America as a brilliant judge and a leading figure in the judicial system. I knew all there was to know about my case, and I was ready for this rare *pro se* opportunity and monumental challenge.

I was aware that an attorney or *pro se* arguing a case must sign in with the Clerk's office at least five minutes before presenting their oral argument. When I arrived, for some reason, the person behind the counter knew who I was and why I was there. I had visited the Clerk's office several times when writing my appellate brief and preparing for my oral argument, and although I had seen the gentleman behind the counter a few times, I did not realize he had paid much attention to me. "Sign in right here, Ms. Hutchens," he said as he pointed to the line on which he wanted me to sign my name since I was representing myself that day.

Room 2712 is immediately across the hall from the Clerk's office. I took a deep breath, opened the door, walked in, and sat in the first empty seat I saw. Two friends, John and Jackie, and my therapist, Janese, had insisted on attending my oral argument to support me. I looked around the courtroom, but I did not see them. The time was 9:23 a.m.; I had seven minutes remaining until my oral argument began.

At 9:25 a.m., another worker in the Clerk's office entered Room 2712, carrying the briefs of those who were arguing cases that day. Because of the way mine was bound, I noticed it was on top of his pile. I was five minutes away from arguing my case in front of three judges in the second-highest court in the United States. I couldn't believe what was about to happen; it did not seem real. The door to the courtroom opened, and my therapist walked in and sat in a seat near the door. She did not see me since her seat was several feet away from where I sat.

Attorneys presenting oral arguments must sit at a designated table in the courtroom. The appellant and appellee sit directly across the room from each other. Because of my extensive preparation for the argument, I knew I should sit in my seat at the table before the judges entered the courtroom. Dreishmire and the Board's lawyer who usually handle appeals sat at the table opposite mine. Although the Board has a lawyer specifically to handle its appeals, for whatever reason, only Dreishmire's name appeared on the Board's brief in my case, and she was the person who presented the oral argument against me that morning.

Judges Posner, Tinder, and Kanne entered the courtroom at 9:30 a.m. sharp. After saying good morning, Judge Posner, who was the lead judge that day, called the first case, *Hutchens v. Chicago Board of Education*. "Ms. Hutchens," he added as he looked over at me. I took a deep breath, picked up my white binder, rose from my seat, headed for the lectern, and looked straight into the faces of the three judges.

"May it Please the Court," I said. I had no idea what that meant, but I did know it was an obligatory phrase at the outset of an oral argument, and any other opener suggested the oral advocate was unknowledgeable or inexperienced. Because of the amount of time I had spent preparing for my oral argument, I felt anything *but* unknowledgeable or inexperienced. After saying good morning and introducing myself to the judges, for the next few minutes I explained the basis for my appeal. "Your Honors, I am here this morning because the district court prejudiced me," I began. Within what I believe was no more than two minutes, Judge Tinder asked me, "Ms. Hutchens, what do you want us to reverse?" I told him the claims I wanted reversed in my lawsuit.

Shortly thereafter, Judge Posner asked me a question related to the nearly six years it took to resolve my lawsuit and the judge who had presided over my case during most of my litigation. Although he knew the answer, Judge Posner asked me, "Was it Judge Chang?" "Yes, Your Honor," I responded and continued my argument. Judge Posner asked me several other questions to which I responded before he quietly cautioned me after eight minutes to save the final two of my ten minutes for my rebuttal. Words cannot sufficiently describe how good it felt and how refreshing it was for me to stand before neutral, fair, impartial judges. Each was polite and respectful and they listened attentively as I spoke.

I returned to my seat and looked around the courtroom. I made eye contact with my friend, Jackie, who had entered the courtroom just as I was walking to the podium. She stared at me as if she could not believe what I had just done, and she cried and wiped her eyes as she slowly shook her head from side to side. Next, my eyes met those of my friend, John, who had walked into the courtroom during my argument. He smiled at me, and my therapist also smiled. I felt relieved. I knew I had done a good job, and the looks on the faces of others in the courtroom gallery confirmed it. I had the feeling everyone in the courtroom was on my side after hearing my oral argument.

Dreishmire was next. She recycled the same implausible arguments and fantastic stories Rivera and the Board used since the lawsuit had begun several years earlier. But trying to prove the Board's allegations against me without any supporting evidence was a pretty hard sell which the judges weren't buying, and they wasted no time letting her know it. The following link allows you to listen to the entire oral argument and hear the three-judge panel's scathing responses ("bench slapped" is what they call it in the legal arena), as Dreishmire advanced disingenuous arguments and tried to defend the indefensible. She "put lipstick on a pig," but when she finished her oral argument, it was still a pig. (See https://www.courtlistener.com/audio/11417/joyce-hutchens-v-chicago-board-of-education/).

After Dreishmire completed her ten-minute oral argument, I returned to the lectern for my two-minute rebuttal. Far too soon, it was over. I wasn't ready to stop. I had much more to say, but my time was up. I saw nothing but smiles and thumbs-up signs from those sitting in the gallery as I left the courtroom. "Wow!" Jackie said after my three friends and I exited the courtroom. "Powerful!" my therapist said. Jackie offered to treat everyone to breakfast, and I suggested we go to another floor in the building where we could sit and decide where we wanted to eat.

As soon as we reached the floor, I noticed I had left a bag containing my white binder and other items on one of the chairs outside of the courtroom, so my friends waited while I returned to the twenty-seventh floor to retrieve it. As I walked up to the chair where my bag sat, two gentlemen, presumably attorneys who had heard my oral argument and were standing outside of the courtroom, approached me and shook my hand. "You did a fine job," one of them told me. "You sounded just like a lawyer," the other one said. I thanked them, returned downstairs to my friends, and we headed to a popular restaurant on State Street, where I had the best pancakes I had eaten in a long time. It was a great day!

When I returned home, I headed straight to my computer and accessed the Seventh Circuit's website so I could get an idea of how long it generally took Judge Posner to issue opinions after his panel heard oral arguments. I knew as the lead judge on the panel, most likely, he would write the panel's decision. I reviewed his opinions as far back as 2013 and concluded he usually wrote them within 30 days after hearing oral arguments. Via Internet searches, I also found a couple of articles in which people spoke of Judge Posner's promptness when issuing opinions. This was what I wanted to hear, for it was approaching six years since my 2009 layoff and more than five years since I had filed my first lawsuit. It definitely was past time for this contentious matter to be resolved.

Later that week, as I reviewed documents Dreishmire had provided me during the February 19, 2015 lawsuit of my second deposition, I noticed she had affixed to the following documents the designation of "**CONFIDENTIAL— SUBJECT TO PROTECTIVE ORDER:**"

- Deposition testimony taken in 2010 during my first lawsuit. Designating this information as **"CONFIDENTIAL—SUBJECT TO PROTECTIVE ORDER"** violated the provisions of paragraph 4 of the Protective Order established between the Board and my initial attorney, which stated: "Deposition testimony is protected by this Order only if designated as "**CONFIDENTIAL—**
- **SUBJECT TO PROTECTIVE ORDER**" on the record at the time the testimony is taken." The relevant deposition was not designated as **"CONFIDENTIAL"** when it occurred; therefore, affixing this label five years later, clearly violated the Protective Order.
- The Board's employee rosters and salary information which appeared on the Board's website.
- The five-year-old publicly advertised CPS Job Bulletin No. 111, announcing the position for which I and purportedly Glowacki had applied.

Dreishmire also had placed the **"CONFIDENTIAL— SUBJECT TO PROTECTIVE ORDER"** designation on the following documents my attorney or I had provided her or other Board attorneys during my two lawsuits:

- A facsimile cover sheet my former attorney created and submitted to the Board in 2010 accompanied by his Fourth Request to Produce Documents.

- The Board's response to my attorney's Fourth Request to Produce Documents in which he attempted to retrieve information regarding what I alleged was a payroll fraud scheme.
- The letter I personally created and submitted to the US Attorney and Cook County State's Attorney in January 2013 regarding the alleged payroll fraud scheme I discovered in 2010 and related evidence I had gathered.

On March 20, 2015, I sent a letter to Dreishmire in which I challenged the **"CONFIDENTIAL—**

SUBJECT TO PROTECTIVE ORDER" designation she had affixed to each of these documents. In a March 27, 2015 responsive letter from her, she stated, in part, "The Board agrees to withdraw its 'Confidential' designation for certain documents." She continued, "...otherwise, the Board declines to withdraw its designation." Her reasons included, but were not limited to, my challenge came "too late" because "discovery had closed on February 28, 2015." Therefore, according to Dreishmire, I had waived any objections to the Board's confidentiality designations.

Parties in litigation may agree on their own to limit disclosure of unfiled discovery information to certain individuals during litigation and not to disseminate such information to others; hence the **"CONFIDENTIAL—SUBJECT TO PROTECTIVE ORDER"** designation. At no time had Dreishmire and I made any such agreement about the aforementioned documents. In fact, at no time did we even discuss this issue. Astoundingly, Dreishmire had taken documents the public had every right to see and others I produced to her during discovery, including at least one I created myself, placed **"CONFIDENTIAL—SUBJECT TO PROTECTIVE ORDER"** on them, and thought I would not figure out what she had done. Apparently, she forgot what Judge Chang had said to me during one of our court hearings—I was "not a typical *pro se.* "

During the next few weeks, without fail, I checked the opinions on the Seventh Circuit's website each day following my oral argument. On March 24, 2015, for the first day in quite some time, I had a job assignment and did not have access to a computer. During a morning break, I called my friend John who was checking the Seventh Circuit's website for my ruling just as frequently as I was. He told me he had checked earlier and saw nothing regarding my case. "I'll call you back this afternoon and if there is a ruling on my case, don't tell me; just tell me to go home, and I'll know what it means," I said.

During my afternoon break, I called John again. When I asked him if there had been a ruling on my case, he simply said, "Go home." John did exactly what I had asked him to do, but I did not want him to follow my instructions. I screamed at him, "What do you mean?" I needed more information, but he would not budge. "Go home," he said repeatedly. Finally, I gave up and returned to work. I was substitute teaching at a charter school, and there was only one hour left before school ended for the day.

As soon as I ensured the last kindergartner was safely in the hands of his parents, I dashed to my car and began driving home. The forty-five-minute drive became a twenty-five-minute drive. Within seconds after I arrived home, I accessed the Seventh Circuit's website. The Appeals Court had issued only one opinion that day. The judge who wrote it was Posner and the opinion was for my case. I quickly clicked on the link which led to the opinion, but just as I did when I received my scores following the teacher's exam, I could not read it. I made numerous phone calls and told my friends and family I had received a ruling from the Seventh Circuit, but for two hours I had no idea what the ruling was.

Finally, I called John again and he told me the news: Exactly twenty-one days after my oral argument, and by a unanimous decision with Judge Posner writing, the three-judge panel had reversed Judge Chang's July 3, 2012 ruling on my Title VII and Section 1983 race discrimination claims, which also automatically overruled his October 28, 2013 final judgment on my motion to alter, amend or reconsider judgment. It was a remarkable difference from Judge Chang's inordinate delays and the excruciating wait I had endured for nearly three years, and I was most appreciative of the panel's expeditiousness. Joy finally had come into my life!

Following is the opinion of Judges Richard Allen Posner, John Daniel Tinder, and Michael Stephen Kanne of the US Court of Appeals for the Seventh Circuit, Appeal Number 13-3648, as they reversed the July 3, 2012 opinion of Judge Edmond E. Chang in the Northern District of Illinois Court, Case Number 09 C 7931, *Hutchens v. Chicago Board of Education*:

In the
United States Court of Appeals
For the Seventh Circuit

No. 13-3648

JOYCE HUTCHENS,

Plaintiff-Appellant,

v.

CHICAGO BOARD OF EDUCATION and AMANDA RIVERA,

Defendants-Appellees.

Appeal from the United States District Court for the
Northern District of Illinois, Eastern Division.
No. 09 C 7931 — **Edmond E. Chang**, *Judge.*

ARGUED MARCH 3, 2015 — DECIDED MARCH 24, 2015

Before POSNER, KANNE, and TINDER, *Circuit Judges.*

POSNER, *Circuit Judge.* Joyce Hutchens, the plaintiff in this suit charging racial discrimination in employment in violation of federal law, is a black woman. A large-scale layoff in the Chicago public schools system's Professional Development Unit, where she worked, required the unit to decide whether to retain her or a white woman, Deborah Glowacki, who Hutchens argues was less qualified than she and was retained in place of her only because the unit's director at the time, defendant Amanda Rivera, preferred whites to blacks. The district judge granted summary judgment in favor of both defendants (the other defendant being the Chicago Board of Education) on the ground that they'd presented a justification for the replacement that was not merely a "pretext" — "deceit used to cover one's tracks." *Grube v. Lau Industries, Inc.*, 257 F.3d 723, 730 (7th Cir. 2001).

Hutchens had been a "team leader" in the National Board Certification subunit of the Professional Development Unit. The subunit's job was to help teachers obtain National Board Certification, which "will distinguish you as an accomplished, effective teacher who has met the highest standards in the profession." National Board for Professional Teaching Standards, "Why Certify?" www.boardcertifiedteachers.org/about-certification/why-certify (visited March 17, 2015, as were the other websites cited in this opinion). After a reorganization of the Professional Development Unit, Hutchens was designated a "curriculum facilitator." She continued to assist candidates for National Board Certification (even though the National Board Certification subunit had been abolished in the reorganization), but now she also assisted inexperienced teachers. Her supervisor after the reorganization was Karen Cushing.

Glowacki was hired to be another curriculum facilitator in the Professional Development Unit; her duties were similar to Hutchens'. The two women have basically similar educational backgrounds, but somewhat different vocational backgrounds. Hutchens had taught in public high schools in Chicago for eleven years, the first five of them at Lincoln Park High School (an elite Chicago public school, see "Lincoln Park High School (Chicago)," *Wikipedia*, http://en.wikipedia.org/wiki/Lincoln_Park_High_School_(Chicago)), from 1994 to 1999, and the last six of them at Consuella B. York Alternative High School from 2002 to 2008. York is a public high school administered by the

Chicago Board of Education but located on the grounds of the Cook County Jail; the students are detainees of the jail aged 17 and 21. Cook County Sheriff's Office, *Programs and Services—Education*, www.cookcountysheriff.com/doc/doc_ProgramsAndServices.html.

Between 1999 and 2002 (the interval between her two teaching stints), Hutchens owned and operated her own firm, JDH Training & Communications Group, offering training in "life skills" to professionals and corporations. In that capacity, she was one of three women to receive a Hall of Fame Award from the Women's Business Development Center. See Chinta Strausberg, "Entrepreneurial Summit for Women Slated," *Chicago Defender*, Sept. 7, 2000. She testified that she returned to teaching because she missed the students. The record does not make clear why upon her return to teaching she was assigned to York, though we offer a conjecture later.

As for Glowacki's teaching career, she testified that she had taught second through seventh grades at St. Gabriel's Elementary School (a Catholic parochial school) for four years and then fifth through eighth grades at St. Simons Catholic School for three years. She did not indicate the dates of these teaching stints but testified that her "next job" was teaching at McClellan Elementary School, a Chicago public school, beginning in 1997 or 1998. She further testified that upon going to work for the public school system she had been given two years of credit for her time teaching in parochial schools. For unexplained reasons, her annual salary in the Professional Development Unit exceeded Hutchens' by almost $7,000 even though both had the same jobs in the unit and had been employed by the Chicago public school system for roughly the same length of time. There is no evidence that the "credit" that Glowacki received when she began working for the public school system accounted either for her higher salary or for her rather than Hutchens being retained by the Professional Development Unit rather than laid off.

Glowacki was hired by the Professional Development Unit in January 2009, eight months after Hutchens. In April of that year Alan Anderson, of the Board of Education's Department of Human Resources, was instructed to reorganize the unit. As part of the reorganization both Hutchens' and Glowacki's jobs were abolished and in June the two of them were placed on the layoff list. But later that month, before the layoffs were implemented, Anderson removed Glowacki but not Hutchens from the list and so Hutchens was laid off and Glowacki retained. After receiving a right to sue letter from the EEOC, Hutchens brought this suit.

Other employees in the Professional Development Unit were laid off besides her, but it appears that either Glowacki or Hutchens was going to be retained and the suit charges that Glowacki was retained instead of Hutchens because of her race. The credentials and experience of the two women were similar, but since Hutchens had been employed in the Professional Development Unit longer than Glowacki one might have expected Glowacki to be laid off rather than Hutchens unless Glowacki was the better worker. A reasonable jury could also have found that Hutchens had a stronger resumé than Glowacki, given the standing of the Lincoln Park school and the challenge of teaching jail detainees. And there was more: Hutchens had two master's degrees (journalism in 1987 and education in 1997), while Glowacki had only one (in a combined teaching and leadership program; she didn't indicate the year). Hutchens had 12 additional graduate-level hours in education, and Glowacki did not testify that she had any continuing-education credits. Both were National Board Certified but Hutchens was certified to teach high school English and journalism and middle school language arts, business education, marketing, and management, while Glowacki testified to no certification other than the National Board. An article in the May 15, 2007 edition of the *Chicago Sun-Times* entitled "These Educators Have Something to Teach Us All" discusses the five Chicago public school teachers who had just won the "Unilever Performance Plus Award" by going to extraordinary lengths to make a difference in their students' lives." Hutchens, but not Glowacki, is named as one the recipients of the award. The article states that while at York she had "developed an entrepreneurial training program that teaches students skills needed to start a business."

It's true that Rivera had hired Hutchens, and true too that while Glowacki is Polish-American (Glowacki is a Polish name—if you doubt this, Google the name) and therefore white, Rivera is Puerto Rican. But according to the 2000 Census more than 80 percent of Puerto Ricans consider themselves white and only 8 percent black. See "Racism in Puerto Rico," *Wikipedia*, http://en.wikipedia.org/wiki/Racism in_Puerto_Rico#Contemporary_ Demographics. Rivera in any event is white. See LSNA (Logan Square Neighborhood Association), Issues and Programs, "Rivera, Amanda" (photograph), www.lsna.net/Issues-and-programs/Events/50th-Anniversary/Issues-and-programs/Events/Rivera-Amanda.html.

Having hired Glowacki, Rivera had to choose between the black woman she had hired and the white woman she had hired and she may have picked the white woman on racial grounds in the face of that woman's seemingly inferior credentials. The question is whether a reasonable jury could so find on the basis of the evidence submitted in pretrial discovery. If so, summary judgment should not have been granted in favor of the defendants. Anderson submitted a Declaration to the EEOC in which he said that he'd decided to retain Glowacki because she had "previously supported" and was "knowledgeable in the National Board Certification program," whereas Hutchens, he said, "was not supporting" and "was not as knowledgeable in the National Board Certification program." That was a strange thing to say, given that Hutchens had been hired by the unit that was responsible for that program before Glowacki. In fact, Anderson was misled. He had discussed layoffs with Rivera (who remember was the director of the Professional Development Unit), and she had recommended that Glowacki not be laid off (yet without saying anything about Glowacki's background or qualifications) and had failed even to mention Hutchens, let alone say anything about her background and qualifications.

Thus, in picking Glowacki to survive the cut, Anderson was acting on incomplete information furnished by Rivera. In his deposition Anderson acknowledged that he hadn't known that Hutchens had a National Board Certification—let alone that she'd received it a year before Glowacki had—and further acknowledged that it "would have been useful" to him to have known that. He testified without contradiction that he had never met or even heard of Hutchens even though the Professional Development Unit, where she worked, was part of the Department of Human Resources, where he worked. The district judge acknowledged that this "one particular fact

[Hutchens' earlier receipt of the National Board Certification] would have been helpful [to Anderson] in deciding which employee to retain," but decided that its "significance... paled in comparison to Hutchens's performance problems." We'll see that the evidence that she had such problems was weak, heavily contested, and possibly fabricated—as the judge failed to note.

Anderson further testified that he "absolutely" would have considered, had he known about, e-mails to and from coworkers of Hutchens indicating that right up until she was laid off she was working cooperatively with her coworkers.

Not only was Anderson's decision in favor of Glowacki based on misinformation given him by Rivera, but he admitted that his Declaration to the EEOC that we mentioned had been prepared by the Board of Education's counsel and had been based not on Anderson's personal knowledge but instead on information supplied by Rivera. She was therefore the key witness for the Board, as well as for herself as the Board's codefendant.

She testified in her deposition that she had preferred Glowacki to Hutchens because she thought the former better able to "sell the program and recruit, build relationships, establish rapport, [and] work in collaboration." She testified that Hutchens "isolated herself" during meetings and didn't volunteer to do "anything extra." Cushing, who remember was Hutchens' and Glowacki's supervisor, was also deposed and she testified that Hutchens exhibited poor "interpersonal skills," was "pretty withdrawn from working" (whatever that means), wasn't interested in working "with other people," and "should have known" more than she did but "appeared to not be interested in learning how to do more things," that she had "poor tech skills" and her work "needed more editing" than Glowacki's did and that in evaluating the performance of the two in 2009 Cushing had rated Hutchens as having "partially met expectations" but Glowacki as having "met and exceeded" expectations. Presumably the performance evaluations were written, yet no written evaluations were submitted in discovery (despite which the district judge referred to Glowacki's "comparatively superior performance evaluations"). Cushing thought the evaluations had been destroyed. Hutchens in her deposition denied having seen an evaluation of herself in 2009 and stated that she was not aware of having been formally evaluated.

Another employee, Lily McDonagh, who was Hutchens' supervisor between July and November 2008 (before Glowacki was hired), testified that Timothy Jackson, another employee whom she supervised, complained to her once about "constant bickering" among four other employees, including Hutchens. McDonagh first testified that Hutchens, Carla Vides, and Tabita Sherfinski, as well as Jackson, had all complained about the bickering but later said that Vides and Sherfinski, although they had made some other complaints about Hutchens, had not accused her of bickering. Nor had Yvonne Williams, another member of the unit.

Rivera, Vides, Hutchens, Sherfinski, Jackson, and Williams are all listed as "organizers" on a document Hutchens submitted in discovery called "Unity 2008: Increasing NBCTs [National Board Certified Teachers] of Color for a Diverse Student Population: Proposal to Recruit and Increase the Number of Minority National Board Certified Teachers in the Chicago Public Schools." So the unit was able to collaborate successfully on a project that Hutchens had spearheaded. That project tended also to refute testimony by Rivera and Cushing that Hutchens failed to take initiative on projects, since Unity 2008 was her project. Cushing also acknowledged that Hutchens was very interested in developing strategies to recruit more minority teachers for National Board Certification; the Unity 2008 document emphasizes (at page 4) the racially uneven distribution of National Board Certifications among teachers in Chicago public schools.

Asked at her deposition whether there was any "documentation" of the alleged bickering, McDonagh said no and explained that "documentation wouldn't have been required because it wasn't—there was nothing egregious. It wasn't at the point of discipline. So it was more about an advisory role and working to get them to be more collaborative with one another." Neither McDonagh nor any other witness explained what the bickering was about. McDonagh did testify that when she asked Hutchens about it Hutchens had told her "that she was not going to get involved," "that she was embarrassed that [McDonagh had] been apprised of what was occurring because it was not her style," "that she was not going to be a party to this. That this was between the other people on the team and she was going to rise above it." The team worked in one room, so doubtless there was a lot of chatter some of which could be characterized as bickering.

An odd feature of the bickering issue is that McDonagh did not herself observe bickering; she just listened to complaints about it, apparently making no effort to evaluate the accuracy of the complaints. Hers was thus not the best evidence—in fact was mainly hearsay. Vides, Sherfinski, and Williams also testified. Vides tried to place the bickering issue in perspective by pointing out that "we had a room filled with chiefs, and we didn't have any Indians. ... [B]eing that we were all team leads and then me having to tell team leads what to do and I was equal to them, that was the point of contention within the office. So, it wasn't so much that we didn't get along because we were all so difficult. We were all leaders and we all, literally, had leadership skills and personalities; and so there was, you know, there was bumping of heads, you know, especially like I said if I had to tell people what to do and I had the same title."

Vides further testified that Hutchens had a "strong understanding" of the National Board Certification program, was an "effective collaborator with work colleagues," and had "strong writing skills. ... [S]he had said that she was a journalist; and then she was always asked to write the talking points for Arne Duncan [former CEO of the Chicago public school system, now U.S. Secretary of Education]. And then I [Vides] would always have [Hutchens] edit my work."

Sherfinski didn't testify about bickering, but said that both Vides and Hutchens were "difficult to work with," Hutchens because "she was focused on certain tasks that she wanted to accomplish, but at least I found her willing to help with the work that needed to be done." Sherfinski later worked with both Hutchens and Glowacki. She testified that Hutchens and Glowacki knew "just as much about National Board, which was far less than what I knew." Sherfinski also said that Glowacki was "willing to work" but that Hutchens was "checked out," based on her "body language"—she "leans back; she's closed off; she's [sic] gets a fierce look in her face." Sherfinski added that

Hutchens had "a scowl that means stay away" and was "very, very irritable," though she acknowledged that it was a "good thing" that Hutchens wanted to get more minority teachers National Board Certified.

Williams, on the other hand, testified that Hutchens "got along with people" but would ask Sherfinski to turn her music down, since they were all in one big room; obviously there was no love lost between Hutchens and Sherfinski. Williams also said that Hutchens "communicated with everyone" and "worked well" with her, Vides, and Jackson. She testified that Hutchens "would initiate" birthday celebrations for the members of the team—"something she enjoyed doing was celebrating people's birthdays. ... She communicated with everyone. She helped people when they came into the facility. She worked well with me. ... I've never seen her, you know, kind of be mean to people or standoffish." There was much else in this vein.

Rivera testified that she had known about "issues with tardiness [of Hutchens]." But she did not say how or from whom she had acquired this knowledge. She did not name a single person who had informed her about Hutchens' alleged tardiness, though they would have been Rivera's own subordinates. She referred to a chart that she said showed absences and tardiness by Hutchens, but the chart was not placed in the record. There were references to lost documents that if they had still existed would, the defense witnesses testified, corroborate Rivera's and Cushing's testimony. A reasonable jury might well be skeptical of such a claim.

Cushing testified that on one occasion she had to speak to Hutchens about several late arrivals (by Hutchens) at work. But she conceded that she had been "satisfied" that most of the suspected "tardies" were false alarms because they referred to times at which Hutchens had been working on public school business that required her to be out of her office. Cushing further testified that she thought she recalled seeing Hutchens sleeping during a training session but "couldn't tell you for sure," while Rivera testified that members of her staff had told her that Hutchens was sleeping at work (more hearsay). Yet neither Rivera nor Cushing ever disciplined Hutchens for sleeping during work or even mentioned the subject to her. The judge said that Cushing "knew for sure" that Hutchens' "eyes were closed and that Hutchens was not engaged in the training." But the judge added that Cushing had "conceded that she could not *definitely* say that Hutchens was in fact in a state of sleep" and indeed he scoffed at the idea that she could have known that.

The defense claimed that Rivera knew that Hutchens sometimes failed to follow through on work assignments that she was given. But Rivera testified that it was not she who knew this, but Cushing—but Cushing did not testify to it.

The record contains a rave letter of recommendation that Cushing had written for Hutchens, who having just been laid off was looking for another job. Of course letters of recommendation for laid-off employees tend to exaggerate, yet Cushing testified that the letter was "mostly" true, except when it said that Hutchens "willingly accept[s] new challenges" was a "stretch." The judge said that the "letter was no different than one Cushing would give to anyone in the [Professional Development] Unit who asked for one." We can't find the basis for this statement, and it's almost certainly false, given certain details in the letter, attested as true by Cushing, that (except for the last one) would not have applied to everyone in the unit: that Hutchens "wrote many of the articles publicizing the program and events" (the "program" is presumably the program of the unit); "in addition to her writing talents, she has also supported recruitment of NBC [National Board Certification] candidates by presenting information sessions around the city," "presented trainings for lead mentors and mentors in the GOLDEN Teachers program as well as those for the CPS Excellence in Teaching pilot program," "is well regarded as a facilitator of professional development by her audiences," and "is conscientious and dependable." Cushing did say that she "made the offer [to write a letter of reference] to all the people who worked for me that if they needed a letter of reference that I would provide one," but she didn't say that she wrote the identical letter for everyone.

And remember Cushing's testimony about Hutchens' need for editing? That testimony was in tension not only with Vides' testimony but also with Cushing's having referred twice, in parts of the letter of recommendation that she did not call a "stretch," to Hutchens' "writing talents," adding that Hutchens' "writing talents are an asset." Hutchens appeared pro se in this appeal. Whether because of, or in spite of, not being a lawyer, her two briefs—opening and reply—are indeed well written.

Besides the letter of recommendation and her denial that she had received a formal evaluation, Hutchens presented e-mails by her coworkers to her which indicated that she was cooperative and her work for the Professional Development Unit good.

Remarkably in light of our summary of the record, the district judge, in granting summary judgment said that the honesty of the defendants' beliefs about the relative qualities of Hutchens and Glowacki could not reasonably be questioned. In fact, as our summary of the evidence reveals, there is considerable doubt about the honesty of Rivera and Cushing, the main witnesses for the defense, and Sherfinski, who seems to have had a private quarrel with Hutchens over the loudness of the music in the room in which they both worked. Anderson was just a cat's paw of Rivera, Vides' testimony was on the whole favorable to Hutchens—Williams's even more so—and McDonagh's testimony was hearsay.

The district judge remarked that Anderson is black, as if to imply that Anderson's decision to lay off Hutchens rather than Glowacki could not have been discriminatory. In fact Anderson had never met Hutchens, and there is nothing to suggest that he knew her race. Moreover, he was as we said a cat's paw, which is to say an unknowing tool of Rivera. See, e.g., *Smith v. Bray*, 681 F.3d 888, 897 (7th Cir. 2012). He based his decision to retain Glowacki rather than Hutchens (despite the latter's greater seniority and apparently superior credentials) on what Rivera told him—and as she did not mention Hutchens he had no alternative to retaining Glowacki, which automatically terminated Hutchens.

The judge said that Hutchens' having taught at a "prison school" made her less qualified for a professional development position than Glowacki. There is no reason, let alone evidence, for such a conclusion. The "prison school" in Cook County Jail is a public high school administered by the Board of Education. It differs from other public high schools mainly in the average age and composition of its student body. It must be tough to teach, year after year, inmates many of whom are older than most high school seniors (for remember that the students at York range in age from 17 to 21). The district judge thought it a significant point in favor of the defendants that only 1 percent of Chicago's public schools are "prison schools," and that therefore Hutchens couldn't have been familiar with the Professional Development Unit. But she had been hired into that unit with knowledge of her background, which included not only her time at the "prison school" but also five years of teaching at one of Chicago's very best public high schools. The nature, and significance for the professional-development job, of Glowacki's parochial school and public elementary school careers, were not explored at all. (Of course, zero percent of public schools in Chicago are parochial schools.)

The judge did not remark the surprising fact that the defendants failed to submit a single document that might have corroborated any of the testimony of Rivera or Cushing—testimony, riddled with unreliable hearsay (not all hearsay is unreliable, but this hearsay is), that needed documentary backup. Instead the judge summed up his take on the case by stating that "What is clear is that Defendants honestly believed that Glowacki was the better employee." What is clear is that this was the decision-maker's belief— Anderson's since Glowacki was the only candidate offered to him (as in a Soviet election). What is unclear is whether he based the decision on the honest beliefs of Rivera or on dishonest beliefs, and whether the testimony given by Rivera and Cushing in their depositions had any significant truth value at all.

A reasonable jury could credit Hutchens' evidence while rejecting Rivera's and Cushing's, and impressed by Hutchens' credentials, her seniority over Glowacki, her earlier receipt of National Board Certification, her other credentials superior to Glowacki's, her writing skills, and her toughness in teaching inmates of Cook County Jail year after year, could conclude that she was better qualified for the job than Glowacki. It's true that having found all these facts in favor of Hutchens, that reasonable jury might nevertheless deem Hutchens a victim not of racism but of error, ineptitude, carelessness, or personal like or dislike, unrelated to race. Certainly the Professional Development Unit seems to have been poorly managed, with little effort at recordkeeping despite the befuddled recollections of key members of the unit; Hutchens may have been a victim of incompetence rather than of racism. But equally (so far as one can judge from a record limited to evidence obtained in pretrial discovery) a reasonable jury might deem Rivera's and Cushing's testimony a tissue of lies (the polite term is "pretext"), Hutchens distinctly better qualified for retention than Glowacki (about whom the record contains little information), and the latter's being retained instead of Hutchens a consequence (for why else all the lies?) of a preference for a person of the same race, by the persons who testified against Hutchens. See *Hitchcock v. Angel Corps, Inc.*, 718 F.3d 733, 738 (7th Cir. 2013) ("shifting explanations" for an adverse employment action may give rise to an inference of pretext); *Ondricko v. MGM Grand Detroit, LLC*, 689 F.3d 642, 651 (6th Cir. 2012) (jury could reasonably disbelieve an employer's explanation for a decision inconsistent with the employer's prior conduct); *Vaughn v. Woodforest Bank*, 665 F.3d 632, 638–40 (5th Cir. 2011) (an employee can create a litigable issue by submitting evidence that disputes the employer's charge of "unsatisfactory conduct"); *Holcomb v. Iona College*, 521 F.3d 130, 141–44 (2d Cir. 2008) (a reasonable jury could choose among several possible motives when weighing evidence for and against alleged discrimination). The district judge himself, by emphasizing his belief that the defendants' witnesses had been "honest," implied correctly that if they were liars a reasonable jury could conclude that Hutchens' race had been a decisive factor in the decision to prefer Glowacki over her. But these are factual issues for a jury to resolve.

The district court's judgment as to Count II, alleging racial discrimination in violation of 42 U.S.C. § 1983, and Count III, alleging racial discrimination in violation of Title VII, is reversed and the case remanded for trial on those counts. The district court's dismissal of the other counts is uncontested, and is affirmed.

AFFIRMED IN PART, REVERSED IN PART,
AND REMANDED

CHAPTER 17

The Aftermath

WITHIN TWENTY-FOUR HOURS AFTER JUDGE Posner had issued the appellate panel's ruling, I read the first Internet blog which was written by a Chicago lawyer. (If you use search engines for *Hutchens v. Chicago Board of Education*, 7th *Circuit* results, you can view what initially were at least three dozen blogs regarding the Seventh Circuit's ruling.)

Immediately following my victory, several lawyers contacted me and asked if they could represent me if my case went to trial. I had done the work to get to trial after two lawyers abandoned me, and afterward, no other lawyer wanted to take my case. However, lawyers throughout Illinois offered to represent me on contingency after I won my appeal.

APRIL 2015

On April 7, 2015, Rivera and the Board filed a petition for rehearing with "suggestion for rehearing *en banc*," of the panel's March 24, 2015 decision. According to the Seventh Circuit's Handbook, "A party may file a petition for rehearing within 14 days after entry of the court's judgment. In all civil cases in which the United States or an officer or agency of the United States is a party, the time within which any party may seek rehearing is forty-five days after entry of judgment unless the time is shortened or enlarged by order. Fed. R. App. P. 40(a).

According to Rule 40, petitions for rehearing should alert the panel to specific factual or legal matters the party raised but which the panel may have failed to address or may have misunderstood. It goes without saying the panel cannot have overlooked or misapprehended an issue that was not presented to it. Panel rehearing is not a vehicle for presenting new arguments."

Panel rehearing means only the panel of three judges who issued the original decision rehears the case. Rehearing *en banc* means all appellate judges in an appeals court (or an *en banc* panel) rehears the case. Neither is favored by the courts and few are granted. Rivera and the Board cited several errors the three judges made as reasons for their petition. The following are excerpts taken from the Board's petition for rehearing:

> This is a race discrimination case, but no evidence of racial bias was presented. The record is uncontested that Rivera, who recommended the retention of Hutchens' co-worker over Hutchens, genuinely believed the reasons for that decision. "Snotbot," "LilHelpa," "GoingBatty," and "Woohookitty" were not identified as witnesses and provided no evidence or sworn testimony before the District Court. The appellate panel nevertheless allowed them and/or other nameless, faceless, and/or unsworn *Wikipedia* and Internet contributors to supplement (and even contradict) the record in this case.

> While the panel apparently scoured the Internet for Hutchens' accomplishments, it does not appear to have acted so diligently on behalf of her comparator, Glowacki. Nor does the record show Rivera, who made the retention recommendation about which Hutchens complains, knew about any of these extra record truffles the panel dug up.

Under Federal Rules of Appellate Procedure FRAP 40(a)(3), no party may respond to a petition for rehearing unless an appeals court requests it. This means the party who won the panel's decision does not have an automatic opportunity to respond, but the court will "ordinarily" not grant the petition for rehearing without asking for a response. The three judges who decided my case did not ask me to respond to the Board's petition for rehearing, and on April 30, 2015, the US Court of Appeals for the Seventh Circuit issued the following order:

> On April 7, 2015, the Defendants-Appellees filed a petition for rehearing and rehearing *en banc*. All the judges on the original panel have voted to deny rehearing, and none of the court's active judges has requested a vote on whether to rehear the case *en banc*. The petition is therefore **DENIED**.

To be honest, I was somewhat disappointed to learn I would not have an opportunity to argue my case again before the three-judge panel or before the entire Appeals Court. The first time had been so much fun, I wanted to do it again! The judicial panel remanded the case to Judge Chang who assigned an attorney to represent me pro bono to prepare for trial.

August 2015

Both lawsuits, 09 C 7931 and 13 C 6447, were settled in the Northern District of Illinois Court on August 20, 2015. Even after the cases had settled, according to my newly assigned attorney, Dreishmire contacted him and said the Board wanted to know if I would "agree not to be re-employed by the Board as part of the settlement." Supposedly, this was in conjunction with my "underlying behavior" regarding the matter involving my former principal, Brenetta Glass, at York Alternative High School. Also according to my attorney, Dreishmire told him if I signed such an agreement, my two cases could settle then and there. However, if I did not, she would have to re-appear before the Chicago Board of Education and CEO at another Board meeting the following month to discuss my settlement again.

This was not an issue on which the Board and I had agreed during settlement negotiations. In fact, it was not discussed during the negotiations. Therefore, I refused to sign *anything,* and the CEO and Board approved the settlement anyway. Dreishmire and likely other attorneys in the Board's Law

Department were attempting to ensure I remained unemployed, and they definitely did not want me to work for the Chicago Board of Education again. They were attempting these tactics only after the settlement negotiations had ended.

I appreciate that Dreishmire, who questioned my education and ability to comprehend English during my deposition because I attempted to clarify a question she had asked me, was unable to add my case to her court victories she proudly displays on her Avvo webpage. (Avvo describes itself as an online legal service marketplace.)

April 2016

In mid-April, I filed with the ARDC thirty pages which encompassed eight complaints I made against Dreishmire. The complaints were based on her actions and behavior precisely as I have described them. To support my allegations, I provided the ARDC sixty-five sets of multi-page exhibits which corroborated each of the eight complaints I lodged against her. Many of those exhibits contained layers of evidence for the allegations I had made against Dreishmire.

I also filed a complaint with the ARDC information I acquired during my lawsuit concerning Haake's no-bid contracts. This included the one for $64,186.00 she received but for which there was no published Chicago Board of Education Report as required by the Board's Spend Authorization Policy which required the Board to make public vendors who received more than $25,000 from the Board. The Board did not, of course, do that in relation to this specific contract for Haake, their former attorney employee.

I was unaware when I filed the complaints against Dreishmire that she had applied—and had been accepted to become—a part-time ARDC hearing board lawyer member while maintaining her employment as a Board attorney. According to its website, the ARDC hearing board panels "preside over the hearing of disciplinary, disability, and reinstatement cases." Thus, Dreishmire, whose inappropriate behavior and misconduct I highlighted throughout this case study, was assigned to the ARDC hearing board to preside over disciplinary hearings for lawyers who engaged in inappropriate behavior and misconduct.

When a person files an ARDC complaint against an attorney, the agency submits the complaint to the attorney and allows a response. Once the ARDC receives the attorney's response, the agency almost always sends it to complainants and provide them an opportunity to refute information contained therein. However, on April 15, 2016, I received a response to my complaints from an attorney who described himself as the "ARDC Special Counsel." He wrote that he, rather than another ARDC staff person, was responding to my complaint letter because Dreishmire was an ARDC board member.

Despite my 30-page well documented complaint and the sixty-five sets of multi-page supporting evidence I provided the ARDC, the "ARDC Special Counsel" also wrote in his letter "There is insufficient basis to charge Dreishmire with professional misconduct under the Rules." He further wrote that I should submit additional evidence within 14 days, otherwise the ARDC did not intend to discipline Dreishmire for the allegations I had brought against her regarding the behavior she exhibited during my lawsuit."

The ARDC "Special Counsel" did not forward with his letter the response to my complaint of Dreishmire's taxpayer-funded attorney. (It is my understanding the Board's Law Department usually either hires an attorney or designates an attorney or law firm with which it already does business to represent their attorneys when serious ARDC charges have been filed against them.) Moreover, the "ARDC Special Counsel" did not mention a single word about my complaint that Haake received numerous no-bid contracts after she was no longer allowed to work for the Board as an employee (as written by Dreishmire in the 2014 motion she filed in court alleging "Plaintiff Likes to Blame Lawyers for her Troubles.")

June 2016

Through a former York Alternative High School colleague, I obtained the contact information of my former principal who had retired from York in 2007. I reached out and told her what had happened to me at York, including

Dr. Sims' claims that she (my former principal) had transferred me to another school division because I was "ostracizing," "demoralizing" and otherwise mistreating students. She was utterly shocked. "I *never* received any such complaints about you while I was principal. I can't believe this happened to you. You were always very cooperative," she said.

July 2016

On July 27, 2016, which was just a few months after I informed the ARDC about her contracts with the Board, the Board placed on its website following its monthly Board meeting, a new contract (16-0727-AR5), which stated "The General Counsel has continued the retention of the Law Offices of Sabrina L. Haake to represent the Board and its agents in various legal matters for Budget Classification Fiscal Year 2017." The amount, $175,000, was by far the most lucrative contract Haake either had received or the largest amount the Board had made public in relation to contracts she had received up to that point.

March 2017

According to its website, during the Board's monthly meeting, the Board approved yet another contract for Haake in 2017. Board Report Number 17-0322-AR5 shows Haake received a contract for $100,000 on March 22, 2017, which was only eight months after she received the $175,000 contract for Fiscal Year 2016. The report stipulated that $50,000 of the $100,000 was designated for Budget Classification Fiscal Year 2017. Added to the $175,000 she received for Fiscal Year 2017, Haake received $225,000 in contracts for Fiscal Year 2017. The additional $50,000 was designated for Budget Classification Fiscal Year 2018. The Board justified Haake's continued retention and the contract by naming specific cases on which Haake purportedly was working and "such other legal matters as determined by the General Counsel."

CHAPTER 18

The Final Chapter

Reflections

PEOPLE HAVE DESCRIBED WHAT HAPPENED to me as a "persecution" and a "tragedy." I call it a public lynching, employment apartheid, and the 21st Century Jim Crow. The United States Civil Rights Act of 1964, from which my Title VII victory was born became law because of the organized, sustained, relentless efforts of those involved in the civil rights movement. But I see little difference between what happened to black people during the Jim Crow era and what happened to me during my litigation against the Chicago Board of Education nearly five decades after the Civil Rights Act became law. Those who besmirched my good name and character, seized my livelihood, and conspired and maneuvered so conspicuously against me, obviously believed Jim Crow laws still existed, and they could, therefore, engage in employment apartheid at their very whim.

For far too long, the Chicago Board of Education's culture has been fueled by systemic and institutionalized racism, cronyism, disparate treatment of students and employees, misconduct, corruption (as evidenced by its annual inspector general's reports) and punitive behavior against its employees and former employees who have stood up for their civil rights after the Board blatantly violated those rights. My two lawsuits and *Thompson v. Chicago Board of Education*; *Meegan v. Chicago Board of Education*; *Monday v. Chicago Board of Education*; *Kelley v. Chicago Board of Education*; *Barnes v. Chicago Board of Education*; *Banks v. Chicago Board of Education*; *Eskridge v. Chicago Board of Education, et al.*; *Cooksey v. Chicago Board of Education*; *Milloy v. Chicago*

Board of Education; Bordelon v. Chicago Board of Education; Taylor v. Chicago Board of Education; Cunliffe v. Chicago Board of Educations; and *Newsome v. Chicago Board of Education,* do not represent even a fraction of the discrimination and/or retaliation-related lawsuits which black employees or former employees have filed against the Board since 2009.

In *Thompson v. Chicago Board of Education,* the plaintiff, former CPS teacher, Dr. Mark Thompson, specifically told me the Board retaliated against him so many times after he filed his initial lawsuit, and he amended his complaint to include charges of retaliation so frequently, the federal judge in his case threatened to dismiss his lawsuit because the complaint he filed became "too large." That illustrates the magnitude of the retaliation to which the Board subjected him. Dr. Thompson also told me, and court records corroborate it, that in one of his several lawsuits against the Board, he found documents about which he knew nothing in his personnel file. He also stated the Board solicited letters about him from students, but did not use those which were favorable to him, and the Board falsely accused him of inappropriate conduct with a female minor. Thompson ultimately won the related lawsuit.

Jackson v. Chicago Board of Education was another lawsuit which involved trumped up charges against a black teacher. The Board terminated tenured teacher, Victor Jackson, after he allegedly failed to immediately report his principal asked him to cheat on the Illinois Standard Achievement Test (ISAT). According to Cook County Circuit Court documents, after failing to prove that charge, the Board then accused Jackson of falsifying his employment application by omitting his previous employment and discharge with the Chicago Police Department, and persecuted him despite the facts and the law. J

Jackson filed a lawsuit against the Board, and after six long years of litigation, Chicago Teachers Union lawyers won his case when the Illinois Appellate Court ruled on March 29, 2016, the Board did not meet its burden of proving by a preponderance of the evidence Jackson had falsified his employment application. The Court also ruled Jackson must be made whole for six years of back pay with benefits and reinstated to his teaching position.

In a November 28, 2015 *Chicago Sun-Times* article entitled "CPS Lags in Hiring Black Teachers," current Chicago Teachers Union president, Karen

Lewis is quoted as saying "Black teachers are the first ones fired and the last ones hired." According to the article, interviews conducted and data released by CPS and/or the Illinois State Board of Education show the following:

- CPS hired more than 10,000 teachers during the past decade, but only 13 percent of them were black.
- The number of black educators at CPS has fallen to a modern-day record low.
- During the 2007-2008 school year, of the 22,773 CPS teachers, 31.4 percent, or 7,168, were black, according to Illinois State Board of Education data for traditional CPS schools.
- Although approximately 85 percent of CPS students are black or Latino, currently, only 4,910 or 22.6 percent of the 21,726 non-charter CPS teachers are black.
- In 2009, a federal court order was in effect requiring CPS to monitor the racial make-up of schools, students and teachers. According to a CPS principal, once the order was gone, CPS' central office stopped pressuring principals to hire a diverse staff. This corresponds with the fact that Amanda Rivera, the Hispanic former director in the Professional Development Unit, deliberately prevented me from being rehired to my position following my 2009 layoff, and instead, ensured a white woman was rehired. It also corresponds with what was happening to black employees throughout the school district at that time. Each of the aforementioned lawsuits by employees and/or former CPS employees were filed after the federal court order requiring CPS to monitor the racial make-up of schools was no longer in effect. Like me, some of the litigators were former CPS administrators.
- In 2013, Mayor Rahm Emanuel closed 50 schools which had predominantly black student populations and higher-than-average black teaching staffs.

The Board also has been accused by the US Department of Justice of violating the law by discriminating against its pregnant employees. On

December 16, 2015, CPS announced the school district had settled a lawsuit the Justice Department filed against it one year earlier on behalf of eight pregnant teachers whose principal allegedly subjected them to "disparate treatment with regard to performance evaluation ratings" and other matters, and "there existed a regular, purposeful, and less-favorable treatment of teachers because of their sex (pregnancies)."

According to a December 16, 2015 *Chicago Tribune* article entitled "Chicago Public Schools to pay damages over pregnancy discrimination lawsuits," A CPS spokesperson stated, "Chicago Public Schools is fully committed to promoting inclusive work environments free of discrimination or mistreatment. We are taking steps to bolster training and policy awareness to ensure every school and office in CPS is a welcoming environment." Also according to the article, CPS said it would conduct "training sessions" for district supervisors and review and update its nondiscrimination policy as part of the settlement agreement.

However, following the settlement of a February 20, 2009 pregnancy discrimination lawsuit the Justice Department filed against the Board on behalf of a former CPS teacher, in addition to a monetary settlement CPS paid to the teacher, the settlement agreement required the Board to (a) draft a fact sheet regarding certain maternity, child rearing and family leave practices; (b) distribute the fact sheet and related policies and procedures electronically to all teachers, principals, assistant principals and relevant human resources staff; (c) provide mandatory training on sex/pregnancy discrimination and equal employment opportunity; and (d) retain certain documents.

Five years later, (December 23, 2014), the Justice Department filed yet another pregnancy discrimination lawsuit against the Board because the school district again violated federal anti-discriminatory laws. In a December 16, 2015 press release, the Justice Department announced it had reached a settlement with the Board in the lawsuit which "establishes critical measures to provide a workplace environment free from sex-based discrimination."

I cannot stress enough the vital role of my CPS emails during my initial lawsuit which ended on appeal. I maintained them when I worked in the PDU, and they proved to be the difference-maker during my lawsuit as I used them repeatedly to refute the false allegations my three managers made about me.

Employees, never use your business email to send non-business-related messages. If you end up suing your employer, one of the first things they will do is determine how much time you spent using the company's email for non-work-related correspondence or on the Internet engaging in non-work-related matters. The Board was unable to find even one non-work-related email in my thousands of emails and there was nothing which showed I spent an inordinate amount of time using the Internet for anything other than work related to my job.

The quote "He who represents himself has a fool for a client" is frequently attributed to President Lincoln, an attorney, and purportedly is regarded as true by lawyers and judges everywhere. When considering that even most lawyers hire other lawyers to represent them in court, this statement makes sense. But my *pro se* victory on appeal proved that even without legal training, I was no fool when it came to representing myself, and I will always be grateful for my investigative journalism education and training at Columbia College Chicago and Roosevelt University which proved critical in my sweet appellate court victory.

Employment discrimination cases—particularly race discrimination cases, are very difficult to prove. In fact, while I sought counsel, a prominent attorney told me that because it is so difficult to win discrimination lawsuits in Illinois, his firm refuses to file them in Illinois, but files them in other states where their lawyers practice law.

I had no choice but to represent myself. Two lawyers abandoned me during my lawsuits, and I had no money to retain another lawyer. But I knew I had a constitutional right to justice and a constitutional right to represent myself *pro se*. I cannot begin to tell you how happy I am that I exercised those rights, and I thank those who made the ultimate sacrifice with their blood which afforded me a chance to do so.

I hope those of you who are reading my story will never have to file a discrimination lawsuit against your employer. You have a long, tough, lonely road ahead of you if you do. But regardless of how tough it might be, I believe you should stand up for your rights when a wrong has been perpetuated against you. If you choose to sue your employer and can afford a lawyer, please hire one because they have a better chance of winning your case than you. Please help your attorney as much as you can. I read several articles during my litigation which emphasized that litigants who are personally involved in their lawsuits end up winning their cases far more often than those who do not. I know from personal experience, and I have shown this is true.

I can say with certainty that if you file and litigate your employment discrimination case without a lawyer, you will be at a disadvantage from start to finish. Even if your case is strong, you easily can get lost in procedural rules, legal jargon, and opposing attorneys, who will take advantage of your ignorance of the law, which is what happened to me.

The Board would have been better off allowing me to work, because I had all the time in the world to research how to respond to the discriminatory and retaliatory practices their lawyers used against me and to create my summary judgment and appellate briefs which ultimately doomed them and their pseudo defenses. Preventing me from working—which I believe, unequivocally, is what the Board's Law Department did—backfired, and resulted in those holding law licenses defeated by someone with no legal training.

I also used Judge Chang's repeated continuances to my advantage. The more he continued my case, the more time I had to find evidence to help prove my complaints against the Board. There was no way I would or could have learned what I did, and there was no way I would have been able to self-educate myself about civil rights laws as thoroughly as I did, if he had ruled on my case in a timely fashion. The more time I had, the more evidence I dug up, and the more evidence I dug up, the stronger my case against the Board became.

When Judge Chang assumed jurisdiction over my first lawsuit, the matter before him was simple: I complained of race discrimination, and the Board denied Rivera had discriminated against me. I had thousands of documents which proved Rivera and nearly all of the Board's witnesses were lying under oath. Moreover, they produced nothing to support their allegations my work performance was poor. My evidence clearly proved my three managers and Sherfinski had repeatedly committed perjury during my first lawsuit, and it also proved certain third parties committed perjury during my second lawsuit. Despite the lies, despite my preponderance of evidence and despite the Board's complete lack thereof, Judge Chang ruled in the Board's favor and dismissed my initial lawsuit as if the United States' important civil rights laws did not exist and my beautiful black life did not matter. His numerous delays injured me severely—not only financially, but on so many other levels, personally and professionally.

Litigation is long, drawn-out, stressful, and painful, but there was no reason it should have taken six years for my lawsuit to be resolved. In fact, my two lawsuits were a six-year waste of time for which Chicago taxpayers ultimately had to pay. There absolutely is no reason I should have had to spend a second of my time and certainly not the waning years of my highly successful career involved in a single one of those legal proceedings. It is nothing less than a travesty I was forced to do so simply because other people believed they did not have to respect and comply with state and federal laws.

After learning about my case and following my appeal, many lawyers told me I *never* should have had to file a lawsuit in the first place, let alone endure six years of litigation. I was embroiled for a combined total of eight years in legal proceedings against a jail and the very school district I attended as an elementary and high school student, which eventually became my employer.

It's true that when times get tough, friends can't be found. I could not believe how people turned their backs on me during this extraordinarily difficult time in my life. But my *real* friends showed up every time I was down and stood with me consistently throughout my legal nightmare. Rarely did my blessings come from those I have known most of my life. Instead, they came from those who could ill-afford to share. But isn't that how it always happens?

Even when I had not a cent to my name, I never considered spending the ten-dollar bill I found in 2014, which to this day remains in the side compartment of my Flavor of the Day, Week, or Month purse. I call it my Lucky 10, and it goes wherever I go. It's worn, torn, yellowish, and raggedy now, but I will hang onto it forever.

My legal proceedings against the Board and Principal Glass began on October 29, 2007. My lawsuit against Captain Harrison and the Cook County Department of Corrections was filed on August 15, 2008 and ended in April 2010. My two lawsuits against Rivera and the Board began on December

22, 2009 and September 9, 2013. They both officially ended on October 27, 2015 when I settled both cases with the Board. Included in the settlement agreement was rescission of the Warning Resolution Glass had recommended I receive. Thus, both the "Unsatisfactory" performance evaluation Glass gave me and the Warning Resolution were rescinded over time. Although Glass won her initial battle, she ultimately lost her long-term war with me.

As I write this, Judge Chang still presides over cases in the Northern District of Illinois Court; the two attorneys who abandoned me during my litigation still practice law; and Deborah Glowacki, Tabita Sherfinski, and Lily McDonagh still work for the Board. Lisa Dreishmire remains a Board attorney and an ARDC hearing officer, and former Board attorney, Sabrina Haake, remains a Board vendor. The no-bid contracts she received between 2011-2016 include two for $90,000; one for $50,000; one for $64,186 (which does not appear to have followed the Board's authorization policy); and one for $175.000. To date, she has received a total of $569,186 in contracts she was awarded after her employment with the Board ended. She received the two $90,000 contracts while still under ARDC investigation.

Although Dreishmire represented the Board during my appeal, actually it was Haake who lost my lawsuit, for it was she who represented the Board during the entire four-year period prior to my appeal. She also was the attorney who represented the Board in *Bryant v Gardner, et al,* a high-profile case in which a popular black high school basketball coach won $500,000 in 2008 after a federal district court judge determined his principal used a falsified document to get him fired. Despite these two (at least) significant losses and despite apparently having to resign from the Board following my ARDC complaint against her, Haake still received nearly $600,000 in lucrative taxpayer-funded contracts between September 2011 and March 2017.

Although I never engaged in misconduct of *any* kind during my entire twelve-year employment history with CPS, my job was taken from me, and I was prevented from being re-hired before and after I filed my first lawsuit against the Board. Moreover, at every turn, the Board's Law Department retaliated against me by preventing me from working anywhere else because I engaged in protected activities.

Justice was delayed but it certainly was not denied. The thee-judge appellate panel's reversal of Judge Chang's ruling meant far more to me than any monetary settlement ever could have. Although the reversal did not and could not restore my life to what it was before my eight years of legal proceedings against the Board, or what I spent an entire lifetime planning and building for myself, it paved the way for me to begin the process of healing and fighting injustice against others.

Historically, American presidents have appointed federal judges who appear to have a similar political ideology to their own and who they believe will carry out their policy preferences on the bench. Judges Posner, Tinder, and Kanne were appointed to their judicial seats by Republican presidents who have poor track records for championing civil rights and affirmative action causes. Judge Chang was appointed by President Barack Obama, whose Democratic Party is known for fighting for equality and justice for all—especially minorities, those in protected classes, and other underrepresented populations. How things change.

When considering the York Alternative High School matter, in all, I endured nearly a decade-long legal nightmare against the Chicago Board of Education. It caused enormous trauma and upheaval in my life and changed it forever. Now that *Hutchens v. Chicago Board of Education,* 09 C 7931 and 13 C 6447 have been resolved, as long as I breathe, I will denounce racism, fight civil and constitutional rights injustice and do all I can to prevent what happened to me from happening to others. No human being deserves to be treated as I was. The emotional scars I endured have yet to heal, and I cannot imagine they ever will.

Without money, but with a lot of resolve and determination, I was forced to battle the "Establishment." In the end, good triumphed over evil and a *pro se* won justice.

WORKS CITED

Hunzicker, Jana. (2009). "National Board Certification: Too important to Ignore." IASB.com. Illinois Association of School Boards. Retrieved from https://www.iasb.com/journal/j010209_05.cfm

Karp, Sarah (2015, November 28) "CPS Lags in Hiring Black Teachers." The Chicago Sun-Times. Retrieved from http://chicago.suntimes.com/news/cps-lags-in-hiring-black-teachers/

Perez Jr., Juan (2016, December 16) "Chicago Public Schools to Pay Damages Over Pregnancy Discrimination Lawsuits." Retrieved from Http://www.chicagotribune.com/news/local/breaking/ct-chicago-public-schools-pregnant-teacheres-20151216-story.html

United States Department of Justice, Office of Public Affairs, (2009). "Justice Department Settles Pregnancy Discrimination Lawsuit against the Board of Education of the City of Chicago." [Press Release]. Retrieved from http://www.justice.gov/opa/pr/justice-department-settles-pregnancy-discrimination-lawsuit-against-board-education-city

Made in the USA
San Bernardino, CA
21 July 2018